Ideals and Illusions

Ideals and Illusions

On Reconstruction and
Deconstruction in
Contemporary Critical Theory

Thomas McCarthy

The MIT Press, Cambridge, Massachusetts, and London, England

This book was set in Baskerville by DEKR Corporation and printed and bound in the United States of America.

Library of Congress Cataloging-in-Publication Data

McCarthy, Thomas A.
  Ideals and illusions : on reconstruction and deconstruction in contemporary critical theory / Thomas McCarthy.
      p.   cm.
  Includes bibliographical references (p.   ) and index.
  ISBN 0-262-13268-0
  1. Critical theory. 2. Deconstruction. I. Title.
B809.3.M33   1991
142—dc20   90-47776
                                                                          CIP

For Pat

Contents

Acknowledgments

Some of these papers were written with the financial support of the John Simon Guggenheim Memorial Foundation, others with that of the American Council of Learned Societies. During both fellowship years I received supplementary support from Northwestern University. I would like to thank all three institutions for their generosity.

My debts to individuals from whose comments and criticisms these studies have benefitted are too numerous to list here, but I would like to acknowledge my general indebtedness to colleagues and students at Boston, Northwestern, and Frankfurt Universities who have taken the time to discuss these matters with me. I am grateful to Kristina Houston for the equanimity and patience she invariably brought to the preparation of the manuscript and to Larry Cohen of The MIT Press, with whom it has been a special pleasure to work over the years.

Finally, thanks are due to the following publishers for permission to use, in more and less revised forms, materials that first appeared under their imprints: "Private Irony and Public Decency: Richard Rorty's New Pragmatism," *Critical Inquiry* 16 (1990): 355–370; "Ironist Theory as a Vocation: A Response to Rorty," *Critical Inquiry* 16 (1990): 644–655; "The Critique of Impure Reason: Foucault and the Frankfurt School," *Political Theory* 18 (1990); 437–469; a review of William Connolly, *Politics and Ambiguity*, *Political Theory* 16 (1988): 339–346; "The Politics of the Ineffable: Derrida's Deconstructionism," *The Philosophical Forum* 21 (1989/1990): 146–168; "On the Margins of Politics: A Comment on Jacques Derrida," *Journal of Philosophy* 35 (1988): 645–648; "Rationality and Relativism: Habermas's 'Overcoming' of Hermeneutics," in *Habermas: Critical Debates*, J. B. Thompson and D. Held, eds. (Macmillan, 1982), 57–58; "Complexity and Democracy, or the Seducements of Systems Theory," *New German Critique* 35 (1985): 27–53; and "Philosophical Foundations of Political Theology," in *Civil Religion and Political Theology*, L. Rouner, ed. (Notre Dame, 1986), 23–40.

Introduction

Reason in the narrower sense was for Kant the faculty of
employing ideas. Ideas, he held, are necessary to thought, for
they supply the principles used in systematizing it. On the other
hand, nothing in experience can correspond to them. Thus
their only legitimate employment in the theoretical sphere is
regulative. If treated as constitutive, they give rise to the illusions of speculative metaphysics. As the sources of these illusions lie deep within the very nature of our thinking, their
detection does not mean their complete removal. They represent permanent possibilities of fallacious and deceptive reasoning. One might well view the metaphilosophical controversies
of today as disagreements about what to make of such ideas of
reason. Are they illusions of logocentric thinking that must
tirelessly be deconstructed, or are they unavoidable presuppositions of rational thought and action that must carefully be
reconstructed? The standpoint from which the studies in this
volume were written is that Kant was fundamentally right to
regard them as both.

Of course, the conception of reason at issue is considerably
changed now. Among the authors I shall be discussing, there
is general agreement that reason has to be understood as embodied, culturally mediated, and interwoven with social practice and that the embeddedness and variability of basic
categories, principles, procedures, and the like mean that the
critique of reason has to be carried out in conjunction with
social, cultural, and historical analysis. We can no longer hope

to fathom its "nature, scope, and limits" through an introspective survey of the contents of consciousness but have to study the acts and products, utterances and texts, practices and institutions in which it is embodied. There is, however, sharp disagreement as to just what form the critique of impure reason should take. On one side are those who, in the wakes of Niezsche and Heidegger, attack Kantian conceptions of reason and the rational subject at their very roots; on the other side are those who, in the wakes of Hegel and Marx, recast them in sociohistorical molds. From the point of view adopted here, this disagreement risks splitting Kant's bifocal vision of the ideas of reason.

Part I examines the problems encountered by critical theorists who take only the negative tack. Though their emphasis on the particular, changeable, and contingent is an understandable reaction to the traditional preoccupation with the universal, timeless, and necessary, it is no less one-sided for that, nor any less questionable in its practical implications. The discussions of Rorty's contextualism, Foucault's genealogy, and Derrida's deconstructionism try to make that one-sidedness palpable and to draw out its implications for critical social theory. In doing so, they inevitably recontextualize the thought of those virtuosos of recontextualization, but not, I hope, to the detriment of the internal criticisms that figure prominently in each study. The conclusion I try to reach along this path is that social-practical analogues of Kant's ideas of reason are so deeply embedded in our form of life as to make doing without them unimaginable, and undesirable. The proper response, then, to the illusions (and worse) that they repeatedly spawn is a social-practical analogue of Kant's critique of reason that combines both reconstruction (an "analytic") and deconstruction (a "dialectic").

Part II examines various aspects of Habermas's attempt to provide such a response in his theory of communicative action. Kant's ideas of reason reappear there as pragmatic presuppositions of communication. This has the effect of relocating the tension between the real and the ideal *within* the domain of social practice. The idealizing suppositions we cannot avoid making when attempting to arrive at mutual understanding—

suppositions, for instance, of the intersubjective availability of an objectively real world, of the rational accountability of interaction partners, and of the context transcendence of claims to truth and moral rightness—are actually effective in organizing communication *and* typically counterfactual in ways that open de facto agreements to future criticism. In reconstructing these *idealizing* presuppositions of communicative reason, however, Habermas pays insufficient attention to the sorts of *ontological* presuppositions that occupy deconstructionists under the rubrics of "language," "culture," "*Seinsgeschick,*" "*différance,*" "power," and the like. This, I think, is what lends his project the transcendental air that so exercises his critics. The papers collected in part II examine Habermas's conceptions of reason and rationalization, theory and discourse, and argue that they are stronger than his arguments warrant or his project requires. Because they are written from a point of view closer to that of their subject than the papers collected in part I, they are more detailed and more concerned to combine criticism with the suggestion of constructive alternatives. Those suggestions do not, however, add up to the delineation of an alternative, "weaker" program for critical theory, and so I shall use this preface to say a bit more about the vantage point from which they are made.[1]

There is a notable tendency for professedly postmetaphysical thinkers to engage in metaphysics of a negative sort. When this happens, one set of hypostatizations typically gets traded in for another: the one for the many, the universal for the particular, identity for difference, reason for the Other of reason, the structures of thought for the infrastructures of thought, the logical essence of language for the heterological essence of language, and so on. A common feature of these negative metaphysics is an abstract negation of the conceptual apparatus of rationalist individualism; the individual is represented as thoroughly submerged in some whole and the historical movement of the whole is viewed as governed by sub- or suprapersonal forces beyond the reach of reason. The idea of rationally influencing the shape of social life comes to appear as naive, dépassé, and in short, hopelessly modern. Trading in grand narratives of progress for equally one-sided *Verfallsgeschichten* of Nietzschean or Heideggerian prevenance only adds to the problem. The fixation on technocratization, informatization, bureaucratization, normalization, and so forth tends to make invisible hard-won gains in civil, political, social, and human rights—not to mention the positive fruits of science and technology, democratic politics and social-welfare arrangements.

Habermas is right, in my view, to want to get beyond these abstract negations by rethinking the *interdependence* of sociocultural grids and individual actions, of global shifts in horizons of meaning and innerworldly learning processes. He is also right, I think, to shift the level of the critique of reason to that of social practice and to look for ideas of reason among the pragmatic presuppositions of communicative interaction. Social cooperation requires the *ongoing accomplishment,* in ever changing circumstances, of stable meanings, an objective world known in common, a shared social world whose constitutive norms are recognized as legitimate, and individual identities capable of finding authentic expression. And it is the idealizing suppositions at work in these processes as normative orientations for reaching mutual understanding that lend them their coherence. Only disappointed metaphysicians could focus exclusively on the dissemination of supposedly fixed and stable meanings without simultaneously analyzing the constructive accomplishments, "for all practical purposes," in virtue of which social cooperation becomes possible.[2] If we take instead a pragmatic turn, we can appreciate both aspects of the social-practical ideas of reason: their irreplaceable function in cooperative social interaction *and* their potential for misuse. Under their regulative aegis, the claims we raise in communicating with consociates are intrinsically related to reasons that can be offered for and against them. The role of warranting and contesting reasons is in turn tied to the ability of accountable subjects to accept and reject them, to assess and revise them, to originate and crititize them. It is just this fact that fades from view in globalizing deconstructionist approaches. Rather than appearing as the simultaneously dependent and independent moments of this process that they are, responsible agents get transformed into cultural dopes, nodal points in grids of power, effects of the play of *différance,* and the like. Rational citicism and the learning processes that feed on it appear to be events of entirely local significance or incomprehensible shifts in horizons of meaning. The potential for arriving at un-coerced agreements on the basis of reasons open to intersub-jective assessment, that is, the potential for reason, gets downgraded to a capacity to serve as carriers of prevailing social and cultural forms.

It is important to see that the context transcendence of the ideas of reason harbors not only a dogmatic but also a subver-sive potential: claims to validity are permanently exposed to criticism from all sides. Poststructuralist critique is itself unin-telligible without the supposition that the views it criticizes claim a validity transcending the contexts in which they were put forward. Understood pragmatically, then, the uncondition-ality of validity claims *also* runs counter to what contextualist critics suppose: it invites an ongoing critique of dogmatism, prejudice, self-deception, and error in all their forms. The tension between the real and the ideal it builds into the con-struction of social facts represents an immanent potential for criticism that actors can draw upon in seeking to transcend and transform the limits of their situations. This "normative surplus" of meaning, which points beyond what we agree to here and now, is, as Habermas once put it, "a thorn in the flesh of social reality."[3]

In addition to relying tacitly on these same pragmatic pre-suppositions, "postmodernist" critics typically also rely on as-sumptions specific to the modern worldview they seek to undercut. To mention only a few of the more obvious, the radical critics of modern rationalism generally take for granted the disenchantment of the world it helped bring about, the possibility of reflectively questioning inherited beliefs and val-ues, the possibility of gaining critical distance from traditional roles and norms, and also the possibility of challenging ascribed individual and group identities. Moreover, the values that tac-itly underlie their criticism typically include a host of distinc-tively modern orientations toward pluralism, diversity, tolerance, equal respect, and the like. In a word, the radical critique of modernity has been pursued within a distinctively modern horizon. This should come as no surprise. There is no extramundane standpoint from which we can set the world as a whole at a distance. We are participants before, while, and after we are critics. Examining the performative contradictions that would-be total critics of modernity inevitably fall into has a constructive significance: it helps us to identify those presuppositions to which participants in the discourse of modernity have either no alternative at all or none they would care to defend.

Toward the end of his life, Foucault acknowledged the continuity of his work with the classical critique of reason: "I think the central issue of philosophy and critical thought since the eighteenth century has been, still is, and will, I hope, remain the question: What is this reason that we use? What are its historical effects? What are its limits and what are its dangers?"[4] But he continued to give this a one-sided emphasis: "Criticism is no longer to be practiced in the search for formal structures with universal value. . . . but will separate out from the contingency that has made us what we are the possibility of no longer being, doing, or thinking what we are, do, or think."[5] Habermas's pragmatics of communication tends to emphasize the other side, that is, the "search for formal structures with universal value." In the view I adopt here, a number of deconstructive motifs and techniques, stripped of their totalizing pretensions, could be integrated into a pragmatic approach to communication, where they might serve as antidotes to our deep-seated tendency to hypostatize ideas of reason into realized or realizeable states of affairs. If such ideas are ineluctable presuppositions of our participation in social life, and if participation cannot be wholly displaced by observation—not even by participant observation—we can at least try to become observant, reflective participants and allow the insights gained from distancing to inform our engagement. If deconstructionist concerns were made an abiding feature of social practice, we might carry out the socially necessary construction of concepts, theories, techniques, laws, institutions, identities, and so on with greater sensitivity to what doesn't fit neatly into our schemes.

In particular, the relentlessly negative thrust of poststructuralist social and political thought might be rechannelled into a constructive critique of "really existing democracy." The lessons it teaches us about the excluded Other that haunts any accomplishment of social order might figure in a rethinking of democratic ideals, principles, practices, and institutions. Of course, many post-Nietzscheans and post-Heideggerians will see this as one more insidious attempt to subdue the Other. But they have had rather too little to say about our obligations to *others*. Their efforts to situate their discourses beyond the reach of established forms have also distanced them from the matrix of rational dialogue and reasoned agreement. At this remove, the other whose repression gets the most attention is too often the other in the self. Thus it is that an aesthetics of self-invention has tended to dominate the "politics of postmodernism." There is clearly something inadequate about this in a world as awash in misery and injustice as ours. If neoromantic aspirations to "the elaboration of one's life as a personal work of art" (Foucault) are to be limited by considerations of justice, we have to ask what kinds of social orders will put such limits into effect and how these limits can be justified to those who are supposed to feel bound by them. The aesthetic individualism of much postmodern theory is even less able to deal with these questions than was the possessive individualism of early modern political theory, of which, indeed, it is in many ways the mirror image.

I

Deconstruction and Critical Theory

1

Philosophy and Social Practice: Richard Rorty's "New Pragmatism"

In 1967 Richard Rorty congratulated Anglo-American philosophers for having made it around "the linguistic turn"; fifteen years later he urged us to get on "the literary-historical-anthropological-political merry-go-around" subsequently set in motion.[1] These disparate images mark the rise and fall of the most recent attempt to set philosophy on the path of a science. The more or less neo-Kantian aspirations of analytic philosophy have been subverted from within by criticisms of the repeated attempts to establish and exploit some basic distinction between form and content: analytic/synthetic, conceptual/empirical, meaning/experience, scheme/content, and so on. And they have been challenged from without by the invasion of post-Kantian Continental philosophy, with its accounts of the historical variability of structures of thought and action and their embeddedness in lifeworlds and traditions, of the conventionality of criteria of rationality and their entanglement with power and interest, of rational subjects as embodied and practically engaged with the world—accounts, in short, of the impurity of "pure reason." All of this has served to produce a metaphilosophical tumult in which the leading parties have called for everything from the end of philosophy or its radical transformation to less radical, holistic and coherentist alterations of the analytic program.[2] My intention here is not to survey the contemporary philosophical scene but to examine a proposed path beyond it.

For better and for worse, philosophical thought has repeatedly been influenced by its close dealings with the specialized sciences. In the decades following World War II, the predominant influence on American philosophy came from the formal and physical sciences. There have since been more or less intimate relations with linguistics and, presently, a torrid love affair with neuroscience. Even the humanities and art criticism have recently managed, through the mediation of hermeneutics and literary theory, to establish relations with segments of the Anglophone philosophical community. My concern here is with history and the human sciences. Since their rapid development in the nineteenth century, these disciplines have had an enormous influence on Continental philosophy, an influence that carried into American Pragmatism but not much beyond it. Postwar Positivism could easily view Pierce as concerned chiefly with familiar problems of logic, language, and science; if it was not always possible to overlook James's and Dewey's appropriations of the human sciences, they themselves could be ignored; Mead was no problem, for he had very early on been put up for adoption by the social psychologists.

The end result of this (and other factors too complex to guess at) was the very peculiar spectacle of mainstream Anglo-American philosophy flowing along for years with virtually no influx from the human sciences. This was peculiar in both senses of the term. Not only was it distinctive of Logical Positivism that after a century of development of specialized modes of inquiry tailored to comprehending sociocultural phenomena, it all but ignored them except for persistent attempts to assimilate them to the natural sciences. It was also very queer. Since philosophy itself is a form of reflection on human thought and action, it might naturally be assumed to have an especially close relation to sciences that have developed other reflective approaches to the same domain. And in fact, in those limited areas in which sociohistorical research has seeped into the mainstream, its potential to alter the course of philosophical reflection has been evident. In philosophy of science, for instance, taking the history of science seriously spelled the end of Positivism, and current work in the sociology and ethnography of science is altering yet again our understanding of that paradigmatically rational practice.

Wittgenstein's later philosophy, with its suggestion of a quasi-ethnographic approach to "conceptual relations," seemed for a while to offer a promising point of entry for social research into the inner chambers of philosophy. Unfortunately, it was not much used in that way. Peter Winch did offer a thought-provoking Wittgensteinian account of "the idea of a social science and its relation to philosophy" in a book by that title (London, 1958) but he took scarce notice of the other side of the same coin, namely, "the idea of philosophy and its relation to social science." More recently, however, the view that the trajectory of linguistic philosophy leads to historical and anthropological studies of social practices has been gaining ground and is, in fact, one of the chief impulses behind the "new pragmatism" in Anglo-American philosophy. It is worth recalling that today is not the first time that philosophy has seen itself forced to renounce previously overinflated claims. This recurred with some regularity in the 150 years after Hegel—in the wakes of Marx and Darwin, Freud and Nietzsche, Historicism and Pragmatism—before its more recent occurrence in the wakes of Heidegger and Wittgenstein. If we keep that in mind, we are less likely to be overcome with vertigo at the rapid downfall of the latest regime of objectivism after its improbable restoration here in the decades following World War II. And we are less likely to suppose that the only alternative to objectivism is some form of relativism.[3] In what follows I want to examine an influential but mistaken way of taking seriously the turn to social practice, so as to bring into proper perspective some of the basic issues that turn raises.

1 After the Linguistic Turn

In *Philosophy and the Mirror of Nature* Rorty criticizes the idea of the mind as a special field for philosophical investigation and the associated quest for foundations in various forms of self-knowledge.[4] He is equally hard on the "successor subject" of traditional epistemology, the "impure" philosophy of language in which philosophical concerns are recast as questions to be dealt with through "the logical analysis of language." Invoking the names of Dewey, Wittgenstein, and Heidegger, he proposes instead a turn to social practice, which will bring us down from the clouds and back to earth, that is, back to the concrete, situated actions and interactions in which our working notions of reason, truth, objectivity, knowledge, and the like are embedded. He interprets this turn as leading to an "epistemological behaviorism" that uncompromisingly resists "the urge to see social practices of justifications as more than just such practices."[5] He means by this to emphasize the temporal rather than the atemporal, the contingent rather than the necessary, the local rather than the universal, the immanent rather than the transcendent features of such practices, or more precisely, to deny the latter in the name of the former.

The key to Rorty's epistemological behaviorism is viewing justification as a social phenomenon, so that understanding knowledge becomes a matter of understanding the social practices in which we justify beliefs. The traditional philosophical investigation of "the nature of human knowledge" becomes the study of certain modes of action and interaction, prominently among them those that "count as justification within the various disciplinary matrices constituting the culture of the day."[6] Studies of this sort do not require special philosophical methods but draw instead upon "the usual empirical-cum-hermeneutic methods" of cultural anthropology and intellectual history.[7] Explicating rationality and epistemic authority, then, is not a matter of coming up with transcendental arguments but of providing thick ethnographic accounts of knowledge-producing activities: "If we understand the rules of a language game, we understand all that there is to know about why the moves in that language game are made"—all, that is, except for a historical account of how the rules of the game came to have the shape they do, and other "non-epistemological" lines of inquiry.[8]

As an expression of opposition to the traditional quest for foundations, this is all to the good. But Rorty goes beyond that to a radically contextualist account—he denies that it is a theory—of reason, truth, objectivity, knowledge and related notions. This account is spiced with such formulas as "what our peers will let us say" and "conformity to the norms of the day."[9] Less epigrammatically, Rorty defends the currently widespread view that "truth and knowledge can only be judged by the standards of the inquirers of our own day. Nothing counts as justification except by reference to what we already accept. . . . There is no way to get outside our beliefs and our language so as to find some other test than coherence."[10] There is a way of understanding this on which it is unexceptionably but un-interestingly true: we can't get outside our own skins, we have to start from where we are, we have to judge things by our own lights—in short, we have to make do without a God's-eye view. Rorty's way is more interesting but also easier to take exception with. It amounts to flattening out our notions of reason and truth by removing any air of transcendence from them. He allows that Socrates and Plato introduced into our culture "specifically philosophical" uses of these terms, which, like Kant's ideas of reason, were "designed precisely to stand for the Unconditioned—that which escapes the context within which discourse is conducted and inquiry pursued."[11] But, he avers, these are nothing like the "ordinary" uses of these terms, the "homely and shopworn" uses with which we make do out-side of philosophy, where there is no divide between what can be justified by the resources of our culture and what is rational, true, real, objectively known, and so forth. It is the specifically philosophical uses that cause all the trouble, and the remedy is a familiar form of therapy: we are to get rid of the philo-sophical cramps caused by any such transcendent ideas by restricting ourselves to the commonsense notions immanent in our culture.

This move is not as unproblematic as it might seem and, with its widespread acceptance, apparently does seem. To begin with, it runs counter to the general thrust of epistemological behaviorism by seeking not to describe but to reform at least some of our practices. Rorty acknowledges this but thinks that we have little to lose from dropping ideas that were invented by philosophers and have never been of much use outside philosophy. It would be possible, I think, to show that other, "non-Platonic" cultures also have context-transcending senses of truth and reality, but I won't attempt to argue that here. It would also be possible to open the Bible and show that its authors regularly assumed senses of truth and reality (and, of

course, justice) beyond conformity to the norms of their culture
and to trace the routes by which these senses entered into the
pores of our culture together with the religions of the Bible,
but I won't attempt that either. What I would like to point out
is that, whatever the sources, our ordinary, nonphilosophical
truth talk and reality talk is shot through with just the sorts of
idealizations that Rorty wants to purge. In everyday talk we
normally mean by "true" nothing like "what our society lets us
say" but rather something closer to "telling it like it is, like it
really is." And by "real" we normally mean nothing like "referred to in conformity with the norms of our culture" but
rather something closer to "there anyway, whether we think so
or not."

When Rorty describes truth talk in *Philosophy and the Mirror
of Nature,* he singles out, in addition to the disquotational uses
of "true," its use as a term of praise to commend to others
beliefs we approve of. Similarly, in "Solidarity or Objectivity"
he asserts that the word "true" is "merely an expression of
commendation" for beliefs we hold to be justified, so that
"there is nothing to be said about truth save that each of us
will commend as true those beliefs which he or she finds good
to believe."[12] It is only more recently that he pays attention to
what he calls the "cautionary" uses through which we remind
ourselves that things may turn out not to be the way that the
beliefs we accept as justified say they are.[13] But this acknowledgment comes too late, for his epistemological behaviorism
has already been built on a site from which the situation-
transcending, idealizing elements of culture have been cleared.

The ironic result is that a project designed to promote a
frank self-acceptance of our culture through curing its philosophical ills is metamorphized into a deflationary revisionism
supported primarily by philosophical arguments. Part of the
problem is Rorty's tendency to give the same treatment to
Plato's and Kant's very different attempts to articulate aspects
of context transcendence in philosophical terms. On his account, both attempts issue in "transcendentalia" that, unlike
their "commonsense counterparts," float free of actual practices of justification.[14] He doesn't take seriously enough the fact
that Kant introduced his regulative ideas precisely by way of

contrast to the constitutive ideas of the Platonic tradition. Nothing in experience can correspond to them; they are representable not in and of themselves but only in relation to the practices they regulate. Thus Rorty's constant worries about our not being able to conceive of an ideal limit point of inquiry, ideal conditions of acceptability, or an ideal sppech situation are beside the point. What he should be concerned with is the role that such idealizations actually play in structuring our practices in the various departments of life—with, for instance, how the idea of an objective world structures the way we deal with factual disagreements in everyday life and in science or how the idea of a common humanity structures the way we deal with justifications of injustice and oppression based on class, racial, or gender differences. Rorty would say, These just are *our* practices. But that response only lands him in another, equally formidable tangle. "Our" culture is shot through with transcultural notions of validity. If to be ethnocentric is to use the forms of justification prevalent in one's own culture, for us it will involve constructing arguments that claim to be universally valid, for that is what we have long been up to in philosophy, ethics, science, technology, and elsewhere—whether rightly or wrongly is not the issue at this juncture. In short, Rorty's frank ethnocentrism seems to enjoin just the sorts of context-transcending claims he is trying to avoid.

This is obviously not what he intends. He has in mind the ways in which historical, social, and cultural studies have gradually but inexorably eroded our cultural self-confidence, shaken to the roots our universalist self-understanding, and made us ever more aware of our own particularities and limitations. The real issue is what to make of the historicist self-awareness that has been developing in the West for more than 150 years now. One of the ways in which Rorty tries to deal with it is by adapting to his purpose the Kantian notion of two standpoints. "To be a behaviorist in epistemology," he tells us, is to look at inquiry in our culture "bifocally" both as "the achievement of objective truth" and as "patterns adopted for various historical reasons." From the former standpoint the results of inquiry are "the best idea we currently have about how to explain what is going on." From the latter standpoint they are "just the facts about what a given society, or profession, or other group takes to be good grounds for an assertion of a certain sort."[15] These are incompatible standpoints in the sense that we cannot occupy both simultaneously. But there is no need to; we may shift from one point of view to the other.[16] It is important to keep in mind that the standpoint of the observer of cultural practices is the viewpoint not of God but of, say, the historian of ideas or the anthropologist, and that, as we now realize, is not a view from nowhere. Interpreters inevitably bring with themselves the perspectives and concerns of their own cultures; they cannot avoid relying upon the taken-for-granted assumptions built into the languages and practices that comprise their own forms of life. In the case at hand, this means that we can distance ourselves from certain of our cultural practices only by taking others for granted. We can never be observers without at the same time being participants.

This point is worth considering with some care, for misunderstanding it gives rise to a type of fallacious reasoning that has been enormously influential: the fallacy of treating ontological conditions as normative principles. The natural home of this fallacy is philosophical hermeneutics, and the paradigm case of it is Gadamer's critique of enlightenment criticism. He points out quite correctly that the traditional enlightenment consciousness of being beyond prejudice, tradition, and convention is a false consciousness. We are always and inevitably *mehr Sein als Bewusstsein,* more (historical) being than consciousness.[17] What we take for granted in any act of reflective critique is immeasurably vaster than what we call into question. From this ontological insight Gadamer tries to draw normative conclusions against enlightenment criticism and in favor of traditionalism, and that, of course, is a non sequitur. If we grant that we are always "more being than consciousness," as he says, this is no less true of the revolutionary critic than of the traditional conservative. Both will inevitably take much more for granted than they will consciously question, accept, or reject. But this does not tell us which to be or with respect to what we are to be either. Its value is as a *corrective to false consciousness*—the sense of being outside of or above history and tradition—and not as a prescription for belief or action. As a reflective participant, I can critically interrogate and reject this or that element of my culture, and ontology as such will not determine whether I am right to do so. Similarly, to acknowledge that we cannot help but debate with people with whom we share enough to make debate possible is not to say that we cannot criticize and revise features of our common background, nor does it preclude making claims that are meant to be valid beyond our ethnos.

The fact that we can only make a topic of our culture by simultaneously drawing upon it as a resource has implications that actually run counter to Rorty's intentions. For instance, the very practice of describing "the facts about what a given group takes to be good grounds" is itself a normatively structured activity that involves appealing to good grounds. Rorty sometimes writes as if it were only when we are engaged in such dubious enterprises as epistemology that we endorse the established patterns of normal inquiry rather than simply treating them as "pattern[s] adopted for historical reasons," but of course we endorse them whenever we are engaged in the types of inquiry in question. And while he does characterize the two standpoints as complementary, he has a marked tendency to ignore the participant's standpoint when he is promoting his own brand of historicism. In general, it is not *because* we agree that we hold a claim to be valid; rather, we agree because we have grounds for granting its validity. Particularly in practices of reflective inquiry, it is the reasons or grounds offered for a claim that comprise its warrant and, when conditions are right, lead to agreement in the relevant community. In such cases my description of my community's agreement represents my fellow community members as accepting validity claims on grounds that I, as a party to the agreement, also regard as good grounds. The detached third-person description, then, does not *replace* the engaged first-person endorsement but *reports* it. And it is not the reported agreement that warrants the claim, but the warrant for the claim that grounds the agreement.

Rorty's ethnos is heir to centuries of distinguishing between appearance and reality, doxa and episteme, prejudice and reason, and so on. To justify his beliefs to us, he has to provide just the sorts of reasons we are accustomed to receiving for claims such as he makes, reasons meant to support not their "truth for us" but their truth, period. Thus it is that he does not try to convince us to accept his claims about language, mind, knowledge, morality, politics, and the rest by adducing community agreement, cultural approval, or anything of the sort. Participating in recognizable forms of rational justification, he attempts to get us to agree with his views by presenting, in his own voice, a variety of supporting reasons, including philosophical arguments against received forms of foundationalism. We are clearly meant to respond to these as participants, to accept them as good reasons, reasons that warrant the positions he espouses.

Ours is and has been for some time a broadly reflective culture. The round of reflexivity set going with the rise of the cultural, historical, and social sciences in the last century is proving to be as profound in its effects on our self-understanding as were the rounds launched in ancient Greece and early modern Europe. Though we still have a long way to go, we have at least begun to see the importance of considering alternative possibilities existing in other times and places when trying to determine what is true and what is false, right and wrong, good and bad in ours. But throwing historical and comparative considerations into the balance does not magically absolve us from weighing claims to validity on our own. That we now understand our capacities for reasoning to be tied to culturally variable and historically changeable forms of social practice can mean the end of the Enlightenment only for thinkers who remain so captivated by absolutist conceptions of reason, truth, and right that their passing means there is nothing left that really makes a difference—the "God is dead, everything is permitted" fallacy of disappointed expectations.

2 Sublimity and Decency

Whereas Rorty's epistemological behaviorism is a variant of the contextualism common to most postmodernist thinkers, his views on politics and society are by no means typical. But they are nonetheless of general significance, for he defines his own standpoint by reference to other positions in the contemporary postmodernism debates. To put it somewhat crudely, Rorty finds himself in broad agreement with the philosophical views of French post-Nietzscheans and post-Heideggerians, while he disagrees rather sharply with the social and political implications they draw from those views. On the other hand, he is in broad agreement with what he takes to be the social and political views of Jürgen Habermas, while he disagrees emphatically with the philosophical ideas Habermas sees as undergirding them. The question behind this section could be put as follows: Are Habermas and the French poststructuralists wrong about the connections they think exist between their views on philosophy and politics, or is Rorty wrong to think that he can have it both ways?

Rorty credits Michel Foucault with showing that what counts as rationality at a given time is wholly contingent, the outcome not of universal-historical tendencies but of rather suddenly formed "grids," ways of ordering things, whose genealogies reveal the multiple forms of power invested in them. On the other hand, Foucault's resentment of bourgeois society was so deep that he was blind to its undeniable social and political achievements and represented it one-dimensionally as merely a disciplinary society. There is, says Rorty, no "we" to be found in Foucault's writings: "He forbids himself the tone of the liberal sort of thinker who says to his fellow citizens: *We* know that there must be a better way of doing things than this; let us look for it together!"[18] In a similar vein, Rorty endorses Jean-François Lyotard's incredulity toward philosophical metanarratives about the progress of reason and freedom, the emancipation of humanity, and the like. Lyotard is right, in his view, to resist the nostalgia for unity, totality, and foundations that haunts Western logocentrism and to seek to bring an end to the philosophical tradition that is its expression. But Lyotard's politics also suffer from a deficient sense of community, as is reflected in his attempt to extend the ideology of innovation and experimentation from the aesthetic into the social domain. Like other post-Nietzschean thinkers, he tends to confuse legitimate personal needs with social purposes. But, Rorty objects, "social purposes are served, just as Habermas says, by finding beautiful ways of harmonizing interests rather than sublime ways of detaching oneself from others' interests. The attempt of leftist intellectuals to pretend that the avant-garde is serving the wretched of the earth by fighting free of the merely beautiful is a hopeless attempt to make the special needs of the intellectual and the social needs of the community coincide."[19]

If the great temptation of left-Nietzscheans is the inflation of philosophical antifoundationalism into a politics of the sublime, the temptation of post-Heideggerians is to repeat the errors of philosophical fundamentalism by inflating the overcoming of metaphysics into a substitute for politics. The problem started with Heidegger himself, who used his "ontological difference" between Being and beings as a springboard to a "history of Being" in which "the scientific, cultural, and political life of society" was viewed as the "working out of a set of [philosophical] ideas." In line with this, Rorty continues, Heidegger "carried over into philosophy the attitude characteristic of religious prophets: that their own voice is the voice of some greater power . . . that is about to bring in a new age of the world."[20] A cogent critique of the philosophical tradition was translated into a questionable politics, this time because philosophy was taken too seriously.

According to Rorty, the same temptation lay along the path traveled by Jacques Derrida, but he managed in the end to resist it and give us "Heidegger without the *Seinsfrage*."[21] In fact, of all the postmodernist "overcomers" on the contemporary scene, Derrida is obviously Rorty's favorite. He has been sufficently vague on the subject of poltics to avoid giving offense to Rorty's liberal sensibility, while he does to philosophy what Rorty himself wants to do, namely, treat it as a genre of "literature." In this view, philosophy seeks constantly, and without argument, to displace accepted vocabularies, problems, critiera, etc., by inventing new and more interesting ones.

According to Rorty, it was Hegel's great accomplishment to have transformed our conception of philosophy by shifting our attention from the truth and falsity of propositions to the advantages and disadvantages of vocabularies. In doing so, he created a new literary genre "which exhibited the relativity of significance to choice of vocabulary, the bewildering variety of vocabularies from which we can choose, and the intrinsic instability of each."[22] To be sure, Hegel presented this as a new kind of *Wissenschaft* that brought us, step by step, to the philosophical truth finally achieved in his own system. But Nietzsche and James and others have since taught us how to live without such "metaphysical comfort." This is what lies behind Rorty's characterization of the postphilosophical philosopher as a kind of literary intellectual who reads and writes for purposes of playing vocabularies off against one another, trying to see how they all hang together, and attempting to invent new ones.[23] But that cannot be the whole story for someone who conceives of himself as renewing the Pragmatist tradition, for it leaves out one of its main concerns, the social-political concern with improving the lot of humankind.

Rorty's recent essays are, in fact, preoccupied with the tension he feels between the aestheticist and elitist tendencies of the literary culture on the one hand and the civic-minded and egalitarian ethos of social-democratic liberalism on the other. Are philosophers, as literary intellectuals, to identify with the human struggle for happiness or ironically to distance themselves from it? Should criticism respect and enrich the common moral consciousness or playfully mock it? Rorty wants somehow to combine both: the literary intellectual's self-centered aestheticism with the pragmatist's sense of common humanity, the search for self-creation and private fulfillment with a concern for public morality and justice. How can the poet and the liberal reformer, the ironist and the social engineer be brought together under one roof? Or if not to cohabit, at least to cooperate? Or failing this, at least to coexist peacefully?

Rorty's answer is, in essence, a separation of powers and a corresponding demarcation of spheres of influence. Poetry and philosophy are to be private matters. The big mistake of universalist intellectuals from Socrates to Sartre was to take philosophy seriously, to think that they could somehow contribute to the public good by getting clear about the nature of reason and truth, morality and justice. Poststructuralist thinkers have helped us to see that any such effort is condemned to failure, that philosophy, as a kind of writing, can aspire to no more than other genres of literature, namely to private edification. Once we accept this fact, we can leave the public sphere to piecemeal reform that is free of philosophical pretensions, to social engineering that does not claim to be based on grand theoretical constructions of any sort.

This way of resisting the post-Nietzschean temptation to project an aesthetics of the sublime onto the social-political reality generates its own problems. To begin with, Rorty conveniently forgets that he is talking about "a kind of writing" when he consigns philosophy as literature to the sphere of the intellectual's private pleasure. Writing belongs, of course, to the public sphere, and so the claim that Rorty has to defend is that the public political sphere can and should be insulated from the public cultural sphere, or at least from all aspects of the latter inspired by quests for the sublime. It is difficult to see how he could make such an arrangement fit comfortably with his professed liberalism. I shall not pursue this question, however, but shall turn directly to his account of the political sphere itself. For this purpose he has come to rely increasingly on a peculiar adaptation of Rawls notion of reflective equilibrium.

Politics, he urges, can and should be separated from matters of ultimate importance. Just as the establishment of the democratic constitutional state involved privatizing religion, treating it as "irrelevant to social order, but relevant to individual perfection," so its continued health depends on privatizing philosophy.[24] His strategy is to follow Rawls in "staying on the surface, philosophically speaking" by restricting political theory to the method of "reflective equilibrium."[25] We must confine ourselves to collecting the settled convictions of our political tradition and organizing "the basic intuitive ideas and principles implicit in these convictions into a coherent concept of justice."[26] Rorty thinks that this is all we need to rid our political culture of its bad philosophical residues, for it restricts the scope of justification to a particular community, and the basis of justification to that community's shared beliefs. In his view, the question of whether justifiability to the community with which we identify entails validity is simply irrrelevant.[27] But to whom is it supposed to be irrelevant? Certainly not to a community nurtured on the Bible, on Socrates and Plato, on the Enlightenment. In short, we are back to the problems of the first part of this paper. "Our" settled convictions include things like basic human rights, human dignity, distinctions between mores and morals, justice and prudence, and most of the other things Rorty wants to get rid of. On the other hand, he would not find among our settled convictions the belief that what is settled among us is *ipso facto* right. That is, he will not find his detached observer's view to be the *content* of our engaged participants' view. So if he wants to deuniversalize our political culture, he will have to do this too not as an ethnographer or "equilibrator" but as a deflationary critic. And this is, in fact, what we find him doing. He hopes to preserve liberal institutions while getting rid of such universalist props as the ideas of the community of all human beings and their intrinsic dignity and inalienable rights, of the "illusory contrast between loyalty to a person or a historical community and to something 'higher' than either."[28] He admits that the self-image of liberal democracies is indeed bound up with such notions but thinks that we would be better off without them—better off, that is, "defending on the basis of solidarity alone a society that has traditionally asked to be based on something more."[29] One would expect a self-professed pragmatist to consider carefully the possibility that this could weaken the glue holding our institutions together and thus might not be "good in the way of belief" after all. But he does not back up his sanguine prognosis with any large-scale analysis of contemporary society, its history, its problems, and its prospects, for he emphatically denies the usefulness of this genre. Politics is an "experimental" discipline and not a "theoretical" one.[30]

And so Rorty is left with his poets on the one side and his engineers on the other. There are no mediating links between them, no socially minded philosophers or philosophically minded social theorists. Philosopher-poets are permitted to indulge in radical and total critiques of the Enlightenment concept of reason and of the humanistic ideals rooted in it, but only in private. They must not push this too far, as Nietzsche and Heidegger and many of their followers have done. Philosophically inspired cultural and political criticism of liberal practices and institutions is ruled out of court. The theorist simply comes to a halt at the boundaries of the public sphere. On the other side of these boundaries are the civic-minded social reformers who, when considering questions of social policy, are required to "stay on the surface" by appealing only to the settled convictions of the "rich North Atlantic democracies" to which they belong. They are forbidden to delve into philosophy for purposes of criticizing their culture and institutions. At most, they can draw quietly upon it to cleanse the public sphere of the dross of Enlightenment universalism. There must be no illusory public appeals to ideas of reason or truth or justice that transcend the prevailing consensus or to large-scale analyses of contemporary society that call into question its basic structures.

It is no small irony that this split between a depoliticized theory and a detheoretized politics should be the final outcome of a project that understands itself as a neopragmatic attempt to overcome the dichotomy between theory and practice. A contributing factor is clearly Rorty's attempt to neutralize the political implications of radical theorizing of any sort, whether postmodernist or neo-Marxist. Critical thought is aesthetisized and privatized, stripped of any social-political implications. There can be no politically relevant critical theory and hence no theoretically informed critical practice. No place is allowed to those large-scale theoretical accounts of social-structural change basic to any politics that aims at restructuring social institutions. We are prevented from even thinking, in any theoretically informed manner, the thought that the basic structures of society might be inherently unjust in some way, that they might work to the systematic disadvantage of certain social groups.[31]

3 Avoiding the Ethnocentric Predicament

Philosophy is widely perceived to be at a major turning point, one marked by an intensified historical and cultural self-consciousness. The question is where we go from here. Rorty adds his voice to the chorus of those who see this as signaling a wholesale critique of received notions of reason, truth, and freedom—the end of the Enlightenment. But he parts ways with them in wanting to retain the political and social fruits of the Enlightenment heritage, albeit without the traditional conceptual garnishings. The snares and pitfalls he encounters on both legs of his journey suggest that we try another route. If the subject of knowledge and action can no longer be viewed as solitary, disengaged, and disembodied and if structures of reason can no longer be viewed as timeless, necessary, and unconditioned, then a redirection of philosophy toward sociohistorical inquiry is indeed the order of the day. But this by no means warrants a pendulum swing to the antirationalist extremes promoted by post-Nietzscheans and post-Heideggerians. We need rather to reconstruct our conception of reason so that while no longer pretending to a God's-eye view, it retains something of its transcendent, regulative, critical force.

A first step in this direction is suggested by Habermas's theory of communicative action. It offers an alternative to radical contextualism not by denying the situatedness of reason but by illuminating features of our situation that are invisible from the contextualist perspective, features that might be characterized as social-practical analogues to Kant's "ideas of reason." The basic move here is to relocate the tension between the real and the ideal *within* the domain of social practice by showing how communication is organized around idealizing, context-transcending presuppositions.[32] As suppositions that we cannot avoid making when seeking to arrive at mutual understanding, they are actually effective in structuring communication, but at the same time they are typically counterfactual in ways that point beyond the limits of actual situations. In this final section I would like to indicate, very briefly and very roughly, how this line of thought goes by considering the social-practical embodiments of three reconstituted ideas of reason that run directly counter to Rorty's epistemological behaviorism: the accountability of subjects, the objectivity of the world, and the truth of statements.

The Accountability of Subjects

The stress by Rorty and other contemporary philosophers on conformity and agreement and the consequent marginalization of questions of agency are reminiscent in certain ways of the emphasis on conformity and consensus in sociological action theory after World War II.[33] In the then dominant Parsonian paradigm, social order was explained through the internalization and institutionalization of cultural values and norms. Correspondingly, social actors were depicted as by and large committed, in consequence of socialization, to prescribed or expected courses of action, while social action was conceptualized as normatively regulated behavior such that deviation from established patterns would, regularly enough, be sanctioned. This model was effectively criticized in the 1960s by approaches to social action developed in the symbolic interactionist tradition stemming from George Herbert Mead and in the phenomenological tradition of sociology stemming from Alfred Schutz. Particularly in the sociologies of everyday life constructed by Erving Goffman and Harold Garfinkel and their followers, the picture of social actors as unreflective rule followers was rendered implausible beyond repair. Here I want only to note certain features of the ethnomethodological critique.[34] This will serve two purposes simultaneously: first, it will indicate more precisely just why consensus and conformity models of rationality are mistaken, even at the descriptive level, and second, it will itself illustrate how philosophical lines of questioning can move fruitfully be pursued in the medium of social research by avoiding the usual neohistoricist shortcuts.

In his "Studies of the Routine Grounds of Everyday Activities," Garfinkel inveighs against models of the social actor that portray him or her as a "judgmental dope" who acts "in compliance with preestablished and legitimate alternatives of action that the common culture provides."[35] Such models treat as epiphenomenal the actor's own knowledge of social structure and his or her reflexive use of the resources for making sense that the culture makes available. It is primarily to counter this portrayal that ethnomethodology focuses on practical reasoning in everyday settings and treats the "rational properties of practical activities" as the "ongoing accomplishment" of actors themselves.[36] What emerges from this is an account of social practice that gives subjects an active role in creating and sustaining the shared meanings that structure and define situations of interaction. It is not possible to go into all the details of that account here, nor to assess its general strengths and weaknesses. I want only to highlight a few of its features that are ignored in the oversimplified conformity models of social practice that, philosophically transfigured, are now enjoying a renaissance.

Garfinkel's "breaching experiments" bring out very nicely the ways in which we use our commonsense understanding of social structure to make situations of interaction both intelligible and accountable. This shared understanding informs the normative expectations we bring to social situations, and thus it serves simultaneously as a cognitive and a normative background to interaction. We orient our behavior to shared schemes of interpretation and expectation, mutually attributing knowledge of them to one another and holding each other accountable in terms of them. Unwarranted deviations from background expectations are sanctionable by everything from negative affective responses and breakdowns of cooperation to explicit reprimands and punishments. Our awareness of this differential accountability for behavior that departs from, versus that which conforms to, socially standardized expectations is a primary source of the motivated compliance that characterizes routine interaction.

Up to this point Garfinkel's account might seem to support conformity models. But he goes on to stress the reflexivity that characterizes the ways in which we use our knowledge of what is required in situations to analyze, manage, and transform those very situations. We are usually aware of what's going on and what's expected of us, we have an idea of what we can and cannot get away with, and we realize that our actions can reconstitute the very situations of which they are a part. We know how to play off established definitions of a situation to get our point across, to put our partners at ease, to make them feel uncomfortable, or whatever. The intersubjectivity of mutual understanding is something that we ourselves accomplish, and we do so in ever changing situations and "for all practical purposes."

This account highlights the irreducible activity of agents in sustaining the mutual intelligibility of their interactions. They do not simply say "what society lets them say" or act "in conformity with the norms of the day." They are competent actors who have mastered the necessary cultural knowledge and the required social skills to deal with situations as they arise. This is not a matter of following set rules in predefined situations, for social rules are neither fully spelled out nor algorithmically applicable, and social situations are not predefined but are actively constituted by the participants' own activities. What is normally called for is not mere conformity, but competent practical reasoning to deal with the contingencies that arise. There is always an element of the discretionary, elaborative, and ad hoc about how we apply rules and schemes, for they do not define their own applications. Each new application requires judgment in the light of the specifics of the situation. Moreover, there are always unstated conditions and qualifications—what Garfinkel calls "et cetera clauses"—to balance the unavoidable simplification of social complexity that attaches to any general rule. Thus if we want to make sense of social situations, we cannot help but to relate reflexively to background schemes of interpretation and expectation and to draw actively on our capacities for practical reasoning in concrete situations. In any case, as competent actors we shall be held accountable for doing so. That is to say, we believe ourselves to be, and take others as being, knowledgeable subjects, confronted by real choices, for which we and they will be held accountable.[37] In normal social interaction we reciprocally impute practical rationality to interaction partners, credit them with knowing what they are doing and why they are doing it, view their conduct as under their control and done for some purpose or reason known to them, and thus hold them responsible for it. Although this pervasive supposition of rational accountability is frequently—strictly speaking, perhaps even always—counterfactual, it is of fundamental significance for the structure of human relations that we normally deal with one another as if it were the case.

The accent certainly falls differently here than in models that focus only on "agreement in responses," "conformity to the norms of the day," "community approval," and the like. What these models give us are pictures of social practice without a subject, where the determining factors are language, tradition, society, rules, criteria, norms, and the like. Garfinkel's thicker description of making sense in everyday settings, with its emphasis on the agents' own practical reasoning, brings the subject back into social practice. But how does that help us with the questions of cultural relativism raised above? It seems to leave us with essentially the same picture of mutually exclusive, self-contained lifeworlds even if we grant that under the ethnomethodological microscope there is more going on in placid scenes of "community agreement" than appears to the naked philosophical eye. The hinge on which my critique of epistemological behaviorism turned was the idea that social practice is structured by context-transcending notions of truth and reality. I want to return to that point now and examine it more closely. For this purpose, Melvin Pollner's study of "mundane reasoning" offers a convenient point of departure.[38]

The Objectivity of the World

The phenomena that attract Pollner's interest are the practices by which we maintain the supposition of an objective world known in common in the face of discrepant reports about just what belongs to that world. He finds in studying them that conflicts of experience and testimony are typically dealt with in ways that themselves presuppose, and thus reconfirm, the intersubjective availability of an objectively real world. For example, discrepancies are attributed to errors in perception owing to poor visibility, physical obstacles, deficient eyesight, lack of proper equipment, optical illusions, hallucinations, and so forth; to errors in interpretation due to the fact that the observer is a novice, doesn't have the whole story, is telling the story from a particular, restricted vantage point, and the like; or to errors in reporting, ranging from unclarity and imprecision to outright lying. It is an interesting feature of such "error accounts" that we are held sanctionably accountable for producing them in the appropriate circumstances. That is to say, the maintenance of an intersubjectively available, objective world is normatively required by the network of expectations structuring everyday interaction. We are held accountable, and in turn hold our interaction partners accountable, for treating the transcendent objectivity of the world as invariant to discrepant reports. We do this by drawing on a repertoire of procedures for resolving conflicts of experience and testimony that are themselves based upon the very presupposition they maintain. Thus the objectivity of real-world events—their validity for "consciousness in general," as Kant would say, or as we can say in a more sociological mode, their intersubjective validity—is the *presupposition and product* of social practices for which we are held accountable. We are expected to employ only explanations of discrepancies that are predicated upon that presupposition, and we are sanctioned for failure to do so—and with good reason: it is the basis of our cooperative activities.[39]

This provides us with at least a starting point for empirically fleshing out Habermas's view of the objective world as an "idea of reason" or idealizing supposition of social interaction. Pollner's work gives us a feel for how that idea regulates our everyday practices of resolving conflicts about what is really the case so as to leave the world's objectivity intact. If there were space, we might go on to examine how it regulates scientific practice as well. The recent flow of ethnographic studies of science provides ample material for that purpose. To be sure, their authors are frequently caught up in the same flush of antirationalism that motivates contextualist reactions in other fields. And so they present their thick descriptions of laboratory life in radically antiobjectivitist terms, stressing above all the contingent, local, contextual, ad hoc features of scientific practice in opposition to the overly rationalized images that dominated our imaginations for all too long. Scientists too, it turns out, are practical reasoners, in Garfinkel's sense, and not judgmental dopes following rules and applying criteria in predefined situations. They too operate with schemes of interpretation and expectation that are irremediably vague and loose fitting, and as in everyday life, this vagueness and loose fit are not a defect but a functional necessity if general schemes are to be applied to an unpredictable variety of particular situations. All of this is a valuable antidote to the received view of scientific rationality, but it need not push us to embrace the simple antithesis of that view. As ethnographers of science are coming to realize, there is a very wide middleground to be staked out between the extremes of straightforward scientific realism and pure social constructivism.

The Truth of Statements

As the repeated attempts to define truth in terms of idealized rational acceptability, warranted assertability under ideal conditions, and the like indicate, idealizing presuppositions of rational accountability and intersubjective validity figure in our conception of truth as well. There is no need to insist on *defining* truth in this way (thus to court a naturalistic fallacy); what is important for our purposes is the internal relation between truth and idealized rational acceptability embedded in our practices of truth telling in such a way that, for instance, it makes perfectly good sense to say things like, We have good reason to believe that *p,* and we are all agreed that it is so, but of course, we may be wrong; it may turn out to be false after all. Any adequate account of our practices of truth will have to attend not only to the situated, socially conditioned character of concrete truth claims and of the warrants offered for them but to their situation-transcending import as well. While we have no idea of standards of truth wholly independent of particular languages and practices, "truth" nevertheless functions as an "idea of reason" with respect to which we can criticize not only particular claims within our language but also the very standards of truth that we have inherited. Though never divorced from social practices of justification, from the rules and warrants of this or that culture, it cannot be reduced to any particular set thereof. We can and typically do make contextually conditioned and fallible claims to unconditional truth (as I have just done). It is this moment of unconditionality that opens us up to criticism from other points of view. Without that idealizing moment there would be no foothold in our accepted beliefs and practices for the critical shocks to consensus that force us to expand our horizons and learn to see things in different ways. It is precisely this context-transcendent—in Kantian terms, this "regulative"—surplus of meaning in our notion of truth that keeps us from being locked into what we happen to agree on at any particular time and place, that opens us up to the alternative possibilities lodged in otherness and difference that have been so effectively invoked by postmodernist thinkers.

Rorty's emphasis on the particular, changeable, and contingent is an understandable reaction to the traditional preoccupation with the universal, timeless, and necessary. But it is no less one-sided for that, nor any less questionable in its practical implications. To dispense with the ideal in the name of the real is to throw out the baby with the bathwater. Idealized notions of accountability, objectivity, and truth are pragmatic presuppositions of communicative interaction in everyday and scientific settings. They form the basis of our shared world and are the motor force behind expanding its horizons through learning, criticism, and self-criticism. In the encounter with other worlds they represent a major alternative to resolving differences through coercion, the alternative of reasonable dialogue. Replacing rational accountability with conformity to established patterns, ideal acceptability with de facto acceptance, and objectivity with solidarity, as Rorty does, undercuts that alternative. It entraps us in an ethnocentric predicament that, while somewhat roomier than its egocentric prototype, is no more liveable.[40] An alternative is to recognize the idealizing elements intrinsic to social practice and build upon them.

Postscript

Ironist Theory as a Vocation

In a reply to my critique of his "epistemological behaviorism" and "postmodern liberalism," Rorty has urged that "when we look for regulative ideals, we stick to freedom and forget about truth and rationality. We can safely do this because, whatever else truth may be, it is something we are more likely to get as a result of free and open encounters than anything else. Whatever else rationality may be, it is something that obtains when persuasion is substituted for force. . . . If we take care of political and cultural freedom, truth and rationality will take care of themselves."[1] But his own discussion of freedom is seriously deficient as measured by these aspirations, for he nowhere provides a satisfactory analysis of free *encounters* or of *political* freedom. Instead, his treatment moves almost exclusively at the level of the isolated individual; it scarcely thematizes structures of intersubjectivity or institutional arrangements. Thus in his reply, freedom is characterized negatively as "leaving people alone to dream and think and live as they please, so long as they do not hurt other people."[2] In *Contingency, Irony, and Solidarity*, it is given positive content through such neoromantic notions as "self-creation" and "human life as a poem" (p. 35).[3] The "strong poet" is seen as one who is struck with horror at the thought of "finding oneself to be a copy or replica" and inspired by the hope of "giving birth to oneself" (p. 29). Rorty notes that this conception of "private perfection" as a "self-created autonomous human life" is in tension with "the effort to make our institutions more just and less cruel"

(p. xiv). There is, he says, no way of bringing the two together in a single theory, for "the vocabulary of self-creation is necessarily private, unshared, unsuited to argument," whereas "the vocabulary of justice is necessarily public and shared, a medium of argumentative exchange" (p. xiv). The overriding concern of his political-theoretical musings is whether it is possible to bring them together at all. In the end, I shall argue below, he does so merely by fiat. Since "autonomy" has been reduced to what Kant called *Willkür*, with no trace of the rational *Wille*, it is compatible with morality and justice only if the autonomous individual happens to include them among his "ungroundable desires" (p. xv).

Rorty manoeuvres us into his every-man-is-an-island picture with a series of highly dubious moves. To begin with, he consistently equates the *contingency* of individual existence—the "sheer" contingency, as he puts it (p. 26)—with the absence of universal conditions or features of human life. But contingency is opposed to necessity, not universality, and so one might well ask whether there are any contingent universals relevant to thinking about morality and politics.[4] With scarcely a glance at the human sciences, Rorty assures us that the only species universal is "the ability to feel pain" (p. 177), to which he sometimes adds the "susceptibility to humiliation" as a distinctively human form of pain. Why not the ability to speak, act, think, work, learn, interact, play roles, be guided by norms, have desires, and feel feelings other than humiliation? Rorty's answer seems to be, Because there is no universally shared language, system of actions, and so forth. That may be, but the empirical evidence suggests that there are common features in all of these areas and that they are at least as extensive as the shared features of humiliation. Rorty seems to be uninterested in any of the research concerned with social, cultural, linguistic, or psychological universals. At times he suggest that any attempt to "get at something universal" is ipso facto an attempt to "grasp real essences" (p. 76). But unless metaphysics is the only science, that is evidently not the case. At other times he implies that whichever universals we may find, they will not be sufficient to determine the shape of individual existence (p. 26).[5] This is certainly true, but insuffience is not irrelevance.

Commonalities would be relevant if they began to spin a web of shared humanity across Rorty's unbridgeable divide between the ineffable singularity of personal identity and the discursive publicity of social life. This becomes apparent in his discussions of morality and politics.

Rorty's treatment of morality revolves around two sets of binary oppositions. The first includes such items as private versus public (p. 120), becoming who we are versus improving relations with others, what helps autonomy versus what helps fellow feeling (p. 141), idiosyncratic poetic imagination versus common moral consciousness, private perfection versus social responsibility (p. 30). Each of these attests to his failure to take seriously the fact that processes of inviduation are interwoven with processes of socialization. This is not to say that the tensions he points to are not real; it is to reject the way in which he frames them, a way in which becoming who we are points in the opposite direction from improving our relations with others. Familiar and difficult problems of modern life are here being transformed into ontological dilemmas.

The other set of binary oppositions includes items like community versus humanity (p. 59), fellow *x*s (e.g., Americans) versus fellow human beings (p. 190), being "one of us" versus being human (p. 191), benevolence, pity, and solidarity versus specifically moral obligation (p. 192). The point of these seems to be that *if* we happen to be *liberal* ironists and include a regard for others in our definition of ourselves, it can be realized only on the basis of actually or imaginatively shared life situations and not on the basis of a purportedly common humanity. "We are," Rorty assures us, "under no other obligations than the 'we intentions' of the community with which we identify"; "no one *can*" identify with humanity (p. 198, his emphasis). The consequences he draws from this are disquieting: what is objectionable about the hopelessness and misery of so many Americans, for example, is that they are "fellow Americans" and "it is outrageous that an *American* should live without hope" (p. 191, his emphasis). It is "impossible to ask the question 'Is ours a moral society?'" for an immoral action, on this account, is "the sort of thing *we* don't do" (p. 59, his emphasis). This effect is softened somewhat by his assurance that his kind of liberals seek to extend the range of the "we" as far as journalists, novelists, and ethnographers can carry their imaginative identification with the sufferings of others (p. 192). This is a step in the direction of the common humanity to which religion and morality long sought to transport us with a single leap, as it were. But Rorty will have none of that. He wants us to approach universality laboriously detailed description by detailed description. Something conceptually very strange is going to here. He *presupposes* the idea of universal human solidarity as a regulative ideal—or rather, as a *focus imaginarius*—to urge us on, with a whole series of *should*'s (p. 196), to expand our capacities for imaginative identification to include previously marginalized groups. As no one would deny the motivational significance of such an expanded sympathy, the *only* issue seems to be Rorty's insistence that the process be understood as one of *creating* human solidarity rather than of *recognizing* our common humanity. But this is the either/or issue he makes it out to be only if "creation" here means *creatio ex nihilo,* i.e., creation of solidarity in the absence of any commonalities. It is clear from his urging us to identify with the details of other people's lives, however, that he supposes that we have far more in common than pain. We have to start from where we are, says Rorty, but it is much too late in the game to suppose that a sense of human solidarity has now to be created for the first time.

The same tensions between Rorty's philosophical romanticism and his moral universalism shows up in his discussion of the liberal polity. As we saw, he defines freedom as leaving people alone so long as they don't harm others. But the history of liberalism, in practice and in theory, has taught us that there is more to the idea of freedom than merely negative liberties. Rorty acknowledges that "more" by adding another proviso: so long as they "use no resources needed by those less advantaged" (p. xiv). Government must seek to "optimize the balance between leaving people's private lives alone and preventing suffering" (p. 63). Against the "background of an increasing sense of the radical diversity of private purposes, of the radically poetic character of individual lives, and of the merely poetic foundations of the 'we-consciousness' which lies behind our social institutions," it must seek to promote "freely arrived at agreement" regarding such "common purposes" as "equalizing life-chances" and "decreasing cruelty" (p. 67 f.). But why should post-Nietzschen self inventors or post-Heideggerian strong poets freely agree to equalizing life chances for the slow-witted masses? For that matter, why should anyone agree to equalizing opportunities for others to pursue purposes different from or even opposed to his or her own? One problem here is what we take to be basic. Post-Kantian thinkers like Rawls and Habermas make the framework of justice basic and leave individuals and groups to pursue their particular purposes within it. Rorty, for whom freedom is the only regulative idea, makes the radical diversity of individual lives and private purposes the (philosophically privileged) basis and justice the hoped-for outcome of what we all individually want: "if we take care of political freedom, truth and goodness will take care of themselves" (p. 84). In a political culture in which reason is no longer regarded as a reconciling force (p. 68) and social institutions are no more a matter for justification than the choice of friends or heroes (p. 54), this is a rather desperate hope. Since reason and justification presuppose but do not produce consensus (p. 83), the whole scheme hangs on whether there happens to be sufficient overlap in radically diverse final vocabularies, especially around ideas of justice, equality, and the like.

Even Rorty doubts that this would be the spontaneous result of the romantic individualism he espouses, and so he creates two classes in his "ideal liberal society": "intellectuals," who are not only nominalists and historicists but also ironists, and "non-intellectuals," who are the first two but not the last: "I cannot imagine a culture which socialized its youth in such a way as to make them continually dubious about their own process of socialization" (p. 87). The alienating thrust of ironist intellectual life requires that it be kept private. Will Rorty then prevent his ironist intellectuals from publishing? Will he somehow erect a barrier between the cultural and political public spheres? What will the youth read? Who will teach them? As there is no discernible way of resolving these quandaries in the culture and institutions of a *liberal* society, Rorty projects a solution into the heads of his ironist intellectuals. In the ideal liberal society they would be *liberal* ironists; they would, so to speak, police themselves by accepting a "public-private split in their final vocabularies" (p. 120). In public they would use the edifying part, containing such terms as "decency," "dignity," "kindness," and the like; for private purposes, however, they might redescribe their fellow citizens in ways that had nothing to do with their attitudes toward suffering (p. 91). "Private purposes" refers here to purposes of self-creation, for while ironist theory is "at best useless and at worst dangerous" to public life (p. 68), it is "invaluable in our attempt to form a private self-image" (p. 83). So once again, the solution is to "privatize" ironist theory and thus "prevent it from being a threat to political liberalism," only now it is apparently self-imposed. It is pointless to speculate on how this might be done, for that would only be to work out the details of an intellectual suicide. It is more fruitful to ask, once more, how Rorty got himself into this situation.

Rorty thinks there is no way to answer Nietzsche, Heidegger, and Derrida—and not, as his official line goes, because there is no way of answering any consistent theorist. Deny it as he will, his writings teem with refutations of virtually every "straight" theorist from Plato to Habermas. Nietzsche et al. are different: they are basically right. To be sure, they do have to be cleaned up a bit, purged of a metaphysics of power here or political self-delusions there, but on metaphilosophical issues they are the last word. On the other hand, he also favors the political liberalism those deconstructionists tend to despise, and not just in general but specifically: he thinks that we have the right ideas and the right institutions already in place (p. 63). Theoretically informed criticism of basic cultural practices or basic institutional structures is, then, out of place.[6]

For whatever reasons Rorty has never been very impressed by social theory. Recently the only genres of social inquiry that receive favorable mention from him are, so far as I am aware, narrative history and descriptive ethnography. The common feature seems to be the absence of theory in any strong sense, and that, I'm sure, is the saving grace. Rorty allows that "philosophers and social theorists have, in the past, done a lot of good by giving us ways to put in words our vague sense that something has gone terribly wrong. Notions like 'the rights of man,' 'surplus value,' 'the new class,' and the like have been indispensable for moral progress." But he suspects that "we already have as much theory as we need."[7] Does this mean that there is nothing "terribly wrong" with the world today? Or that there is no longer any need for "moral progress"? That is certainly not Rorty's view, but he does believe that there is nothing *fundamentally* wrong with the culture and institutions of contemporary liberalism.[8] And so, to understand the wrongs that do exist "we need no fancier theoretical notions than 'greed,' 'selfishness,' 'racial prejudice,'" and the like, that is to say, the sorts of notions that journalists and novelists could come up with on their own. The improbable assertion that we have nothing important to learn about how the world works from social and political theorists is supported, so far as I can see, only by the even less probable assertion that there is nothing *basically* wrong with the way culture, economy, politics, and society are structured today—nothing, that is, that couldn't be set right by changing the attitudes of the white middle class. But how did Rorty arrive at *this* diagnosis of the present situation? How would he defend it against the competing diagnoses of Marx and Weber, Habermas and Foucault? Should such matters be left solely to the intuitive judgments of people who read lots of novels and newspapers, or should they be an object of large-scale social analysis? Rorty does not provide convincing answers to any of these questions. One either shares his views or doesn't, either succumbs to the rhetoric of his redescriptions or doesn't. I cannot see that this approach will enhance the quality of our analyses or assessments of the complex world we live in.

In his famous essays "Politics as a Vocation" and "Science as a Vocation," Max Weber urged that intellectuals keep out of politics, where passionate commitment and "sterile excitation" were out of place, and that scientists and scholars do the same, for only then could they maintain the integrity of their calling. His aim was to keep politics in the hands of charismatic leaders and trained officials. In retrospect, that recipe did not work very well in Germany. Rorty wants intellectuals and theorists to stay away from political and social questions and to pursue their own private perfection. His aim is to keep the liberal public sphere free of radical criticism. This does not seem to me to be a very good recipe for politics in America. Under this recipe there would be no public place for sentiments like the following:

Liberalism must now become radical, meaning by "radical" perception of the necessity of thorough-going changes in the set-up of institutions and corresponding activity to bring the changes to pass. For the gulf between what the actual situation makes possible and the actual state itself is so great that it cannot be bridged by piecemeal processes undertaken *ad hoc*. The process of producing the changes will be, in any case, a gradual one. But "reforms" that deal now with this abuse and now with that without having a social goal based on an inclusive plan, differ entirely from efforts at reforming, in its literal sense, the institutional scheme of things. The liberals of more than a century ago were denounced in their time as subversive radicals, and only when the new economic order was established did they become apologists for the *status quo,* or else content with social patchwork. If radicalism be defined as perception of the need for radical change, then today any liberalism which is not also radicalism is irrelevant and doomed.[9]

2

The Critique of
Impure Reason:
Foucault and the
Frankfurt School

1

Following Michel Foucault's own example, commentators have generally paid much more attention to his break with earlier forms of critical social theory than to his continuities with them. It is not surprising that a thinker of his originality, having come intellectually of age in postwar France, would eventually assert his intellectual identity in opposition to the varieties of Marxism prevalent there. But for purposes of developing a critical theory adequate to the complexities of our situation, focusing only on discontinuities can become counterproductive. In fact, viewed at some remove from the current debates, what unites Foucault with neo-Marxist thinkers is as significant as what divides them. This is particularly true of the group of theorists loosely referred to as the Frankfurt School, to whom he did not address himself in any detail. Let me begin by noting certain broad similarities between Foucault's genealogy of power/knowledge and the program of critical social theory advanced by Max Horkheimer and his colleagues in the early 1930s and recently renewed by Jürgen Habermas.[1]

• Both Foucault and the Frankfurt School call for a transformation cum radicalization of the Kantian approach to critique. The intrinsic impurity of what we call reason—its embeddedness in culture and society, its entanglement with power and interest, the historical variability of its categories and criteria, the embodied, sensuous and practically engaged character of its bearers—makes its structures inaccessible to the sorts of introspective survey of the contents of consciousness favored by early modern philosophers and some twentieth-century phenomenologists. Nor is the turn to language or sign systems an adequate response to this altered view of reason; all forms of linguistic or discursive idealism rest on an indefensible abstraction from social practices. To explore the "nature, scope and limits of human reason," we have to get at those practices, and this calls for modes of sociohistorical inquiry that go beyond the traditional bounds of philosophical analysis. The critique of reason as a nonfoundationalist enterprise is concerned with structures and rules that transcend the individual consciousness. But what is supraindividual in this way is no longer understood as transcendental; it is sociocultural in origin.

• Correspondingly, both Foucault and the Frankfurt School reject the Cartesian picture of an autonomous rational subject set over against a world of objects that it seeks to represent and, through representing, to master. Knowing and acting subjects are social and embodied beings, and the products of their thought and action bear ineradicable traces of their situations and interests. The atomistic and disengaged Cartesian subject has to be dislodged from its position at the center of the epistemic and moral universes, and not only for theoretical reasons: it undergirds the egocentric, domineering, and possessive individualism that has so disfigured modern Western rationalism and driven it to exclude, dominate, or assimilate whatever is different. Thus the desublimation of reason goes hand in hand with the decentering of the rational subject.

• More distinctive, perhaps, than either of these now widely held views is that of the primacy of the practical over the theoretical, which Foucault shares with the Frankfurt School. A reversal of the traditional hierarchy was already proposed by Kant, only to be retracted by Hegel; it was then reinstated by the young Marx but soon faded into the background of scientific socialism. Once we have turned our attention from consciousness to culture and society, however, there is no good reason why knowledge and representation should enjoy the privilege over values and norms that Western philosophy has accorded them. Moreover, if knowledge is itself understood as a social product, the traditional oppositions between theory and practice, fact and value, and the like begin to break down, for there are practical, normative presuppositions to any social activity, theorizing included. Like other practices, epistemic practices have to be comprehended in their sociocultural contexts. In this sense, the theory of knowledge is part of the theory of society, which is *itself* embedded in practical contexts, and in rather distinctive ways. It is his recognition of the peculiarly reflexive relation of thinking about society to what is being thought about that leads Foucault to characterize his genealogy as "history of the present." Situated in the very reality it seeks to comprehend and relating the past from the practically interested standpoint of an anticipated future, it is anything but a view from nowhere. And though Western Marxism has repeatedly succumbed to the siren calls of a scientific theory of history or a speculative philosophy of history, it has usually found its way back to a similar notion of practical reflexivity.[2] In this version of critical social theory, there is an essentially prospective dimension to writing the history of the present in which one is situated. And the projected future, which gives shape to the past, is not a product of disinterested contemplation or of scientific prediction but of practical engagement; it is a future that we can seek to bring about.

• With suitable changes in terminology, much of the above could also be said of philosophical hermeneutics. It too takes seriously the fact that reason, in its cognitive employment as well, is embedded in sociocultural contexts, mediated by natural languages, and intrinsically related to action. It too maintains that speech and action occur against immeasurable, taken-for-granted backgrounds, which are historically and culturally variable and which can never be brought fully to conscious awareness. And yet genealogy is as distinct from hermeneutics as is critical social theory. Despite some very real differences on this point, neither genealogy nor critical theory wishes to leave to the participants and their traditions the final say about the significance of the practices they engage in. Both approaches see the need for an objectivating "outsider's" perspective to get beyond shared, unproblematic meanings and their hermeneutic retrival. Foucault's way of creating distance from the practices we live by is to display their "lowly origins" in contingent historical circumstances, to dispel their appearance of self-evident givenness by treating them as the outcome of multiple relations of force. From the start, critical social theory was also based on a rejection of what Marx viewed as the specifically "German ideology," and Horkheimer called "the idealist madness," of understanding ideas solely in terms of other ideas. It has insisted that the full significance of ideas can be grasped only by viewing them in the context of the social practices in which they figure, and that this typically requires using sociohistorical analysis to gain some distance from the insider's view of the participants. Genetic and functional accounts of how and why purportedly rational practices came to be taken for granted play an important role in both forms of the critique of impure reason.

• In neither perspective, however, does this mean simply adopting the methods of the established human sciences. Both Foucault and the Frankfurt School see these sciences as particularly in need of critical analysis, as complicit in special ways with the ills of the present age. There are, to be sure, some important differences here, for instance, as to which particular sciences are most in need of critique and as to how total that critique should be.[3] But there are also a number of important commonalities in their critiques of the epistemological and methodolical ideas in terms of which we have constituted ourselves as subjects and objects of knowledge. Furthermore, both schools are critical of the role that the social sciences and social-scientifically trained "experts" have played in the process of "rationalization." They see the rationality that came to prevail in modern society as an instrumental potential for extending our mastery over the physical and social worlds, a rationality of technique and calculation, of regulation and administration, in search of ever more effective forms of domination. Inasmuch as the human sciences have assisted mightily in forging and maintaining the bars of this "iron cage," to use Max Weber's phrase, they are a prime target for genealogical and dialectical critique.

• As ongoing practical endeavors rather than closed theoretical systems, both forms of critique aim at transforming our self-understanding in ways that have implications for practice. It is true that Foucault persistently rejected the notions of ideology and ideology critique and denied that genealogy could be understood in those terms. But the conceptions of ideology he criticized were rather crude, and the criticisms he offered were far from devastating to the more sophisticated versions propounded by members of the Frankfurt School. It is, in fact, difficult to see why Foucault's efforts to analyze "how we govern ourselves and others by the production of truth" so as to "contribute to changing people's ways of perceiving and doing things" do not belong to the same genre.[4] On this reading, in both genealogy and critical social theory the objectivating techniques employed to gain distance from the rational practices we have been trained in afford us a critical perspective on those practices. Making problematic what is taken for granted—for instance, by demonstrating that the genesis of what has heretofore seemed to be natural and necessary involves contingent relations of force and an arbitrary closing off of alternatives, or that what parades as objective actually rests on prescriptions that function in maintaining imbalances of power—can weaken their hold upon us. Categories, principles, rules, standards, criteria, procedures, techniques, beliefs, and practices formerly accepted as purely and simply rational may come to be seen as in the service of particular interests and constellations of power that have to be disguised to be advanced or as performing particular functions in maintaining power relations that would not be subscribed to if generally recognized. Because things are not always what they seem to be and because awareness of this can create critical distance—because, in particular, such awareness can undermine the authority that derives from presumed rationality, universality, or necessity— it can be a social force for change. Whether or not this is so, as well as the extent to which it is so, is, in the eyes of both Foucault and the Frankfurt School, not a question of metaphysical necessity or theoretical deduction but of contingent historical conditions. That is, the practical significance of critical insight varies with the historical circumstances.

If the foregoing comparisons are not wide of the mark, Foucault and the Frankfurt School should be located rather close to one another on the map of contemporary theoretical options. They hold in common that the heart of the philosophical enterprise, the critique of reason, finds its continuation in certain forms of sociohistorical analysis carried out with the practical intent of gaining critical distance from the presumably rational beliefs and practices that inform our lives. This would certainly place them much nearer to one another than to other varieties of contemporary theory, including the more influential varieties of textualism. Why, then, have the oppositions and differences loomed so large? Part of the explanation (but only part) is that the disagreements between them are no less real than the agreements. Though genealogy and critical social theory do occupy neighboring territories in our theoretical world, their relations to one another are combative rather than peaceable. Foucault's Nietzschean heritage and the Hegelian-Marxist heritage of the Frankfurt School lead them to lay competing claims to the very same areas.

• While both approaches seek to transform the critique of reason through shifting the level of analysis to social practice, Foucault, like Nietzsche, sees this as leading to a critique that is radical in the etymological sense of that term, one that attacks rationalism at its very roots, whereas critical social theorists, following Hegel and Marx, understand critique rather in the sense of a determinate negation that aims at a more adequate conception of reason.

• While both approaches seek to get beyond the subject-centeredness of modern Western thought, Foucault understands this as the "end of man" and of the retinue of humanist conceptions following upon it, whereas critical social theorists attempt to reconstruct notions of subjectivity and autonomy that are consistent with both the social dimensions of individual identity and the situated character of social action.

• While both approaches assert the primacy of practical reason and acknowledge the unavoidable reflexivity of social inquiry, Foucault takes this to be incompatible with the context transcendence of truth claims and the pretensions of general social

theories, whereas the Frankfurt theorists seek to combine contextualism with universalism and to construct general accounts
of the origins, structures, and tendencies of existing social
orders.

• While both approaches refuse to take participants' views of
their practices as the last word in understanding them, critical
social theorists do take them as the first word and seek to
engage them in the process of trying to gain critical distance
from those views, whereas the genealogist resolutely displaces
the participants' perspective with an externalist perspective in
which the validity claims of participants are not engaged but
bracketed.

• While both approaches are critical of established human sciences and see them as implicated in weaving tighter the web
of discipline and domination, Foucault understands this to be
a general indictment—genealogy is not a science but an "anti-
science"—whereas critical social theorists direct their critique
against particular forms of social research while seeking to
identify and develop others that are not simply extensions of
instrumental rationality.

• Finally, while both approaches see the critique of apparently
rational practices as having the practical purpose of breaking
their hold upon us, Foucault does not regard genealogy as
being in the service of reason, truth, freedom, and justice—
there is no escaping the relations and effects of power altogether, for they are coextensive with, indeed constitutive of,
social life generally—whereas Frankfurt School theorists understand the critique of ideology as working to reduce such
relations and effects and to replace them with social arrangements that are rational in other than an instrumentalist sense.

2

With this broad comparison as a background, I would like now
to take a closer and more critical look a the radical critique
of reason and the rational subject that Foucault developed in
the 1970s in the context of his power/knowledge studies. For
purposes of defining what is at issue between him and the

Frankfurt School, I shall use Habermas's attempt to renew Horkheimer's original program as my principal point
of reference.

As remarked above, Foucault's genealogical project can be
viewed as a form of the critique of reason. Inasmuch as modern
philosophy has understood itself to be the most radical reflection on reason, its conditions, limits, and effects, the continuation through transformation of that project today requires
a sociohistorical turn. What have to be analyzed are paradigmatically rational *practices,* and they cannot be adequately
understood in isolation from the sociohistorical contexts in
which they emerge and function. Foucault is, of course, interested in the relations of power that traverse such practices and
their contexts. He reminds us repeatedly that "truth is not the
reward of free spirits" but "a thing of this world" that is "produced only by virtue of multiple forms of constraint."[5] Analytical attention is redirected to the rules, prescriptions,
procedures, and the like that are constitutive of rational practices, to the relations of asymmetry, nonreciprocity, and hierarchy they encode, and to the ways in which they include and
exclude, make central and marginal, assimilate and differentiate. This shift in focus makes us aware that there is something
like a politics of truth and knowledge already at this level of
analysis.[6] Irrationality, incompetence, deviance, error, nonsense, and the like get marked off in various ways from their
opposites; people and practices get valorized or stigmatized,
rewarded or penalized, dismissed or vested with authority on
this basis. But genealogical analysis does not confine itself to
the political aspects of rules and regulations "internal" to discursive practices. It also examines the "external" relations of
theoretical discourses, especially the discourses of the "sciences
of man," to the practical discourses in which they are "applied"—the discourses of psychologists, physicians, judges, ad-
ministrators, social workers, educators, and the like—and to
the institutional practices with which they are interwoven in
asylums, hospitals, prisons, schools, administrative bureaucracies, welfare agencies, and the like. As soon as one tries to
comprehend why a particular constellation of rules and procedures should define rational practice in a given domain,

consideration of the larger sociohistorical context becomes unavoidable.

"Each society," as Foucault puts it, "has its regime of truth."[7] And genealogy is interested precisely in how we govern ourselves and others through its production. Focusing especially on the human sciences—the sciences of which humankind is the object—he examines the myriad ways in which power relations are both conditions and effects of the production of truth about human beings. In areas of inquiry ranging from psychiatry and medicine to penology and population studies, he uncovers the feedback relations that obtain between the power exercised over people to extract data from and about them—by a variety of means, from observing, examining, and interrogating individuals to surveying and administering populations—and the effects of power that attach to the qualified experts and licensed professionals who possess and apply the knowledge thus gained. According to Foucault, the sciences of man not only arose in institutional settings structured by hierarchical relations of power; they continue to function mainly in such settings. Indeed, what is distinctive of the modern disciplinary regime, in his view, is just the way in which coercion by violence has been largely replaced by the gentler force of administration by scientifically trained experts, public displays of power by the imperceptible deployment of techniques based on a detailed knowledge of their targets. From Foucault's perspective, then, the human sciences are a major force in the disastrous triumph of Enlightenment thinking, and the panoptical scientific observer is a salient expression of the subject-centered, putatively universal reason that that thinking promotes. By tracing the lowly origins of these sciences in struggle and conflict, in particularity and contingency, in a will to truth that is implicated with domination and control, genealogy reveals their constitutive interconnections with historically changing constellations of power: "Power and knowledge directly imply one another. . . . The subject who knows, the objects to be known, and the modalities of knowledge must be regarded as so many effects of these fundamental implications of power-knowledge and their historical transformations."[8]

Although Habermas agrees with Foucault in regarding truth

as "a thing of this world," he distinguishes between fundamentally different cognitive approaches marked by different configurations of action, experience, and language.[9] He does this with the aim of resisting the identification of instrumental and strategic rationality with rationality *tout court*. To construe sociocultural rationalization as the growing hegemony of techniques of power and control, of domination and administration, is not so much erroneous as partial. That reading does not grasp the selectivity of capitalist modernization, its failure to develop in a balanced way the different dimensions of rationality opened up by the modern understanding of the world. Because we are as fundamentally language-using as tool-using animals, the representation of reason as essentially instrumental and strategic is fatally one-sided. On the other hand, it is indeed the case that those types of rationality have achieved a certain dominance in our culture. The subsystems in which they are centrally institutionalized, the economy and government administration, have increasingly come to pervade other areas of life and make them over in their own image and likeness. The resultant "monetarization" and "bureaucratization" of life is what Habermas refers to as the "colonization of the life world."

This picture of a society colonized by market and administrative forces differs from Foucault's picture of a disciplinary society in, among other ways, targeting for critique not the Enlightenment idea of a life informed by reason as such but rather the failure to pursue it by developing and institutionalizing modalities of reason other than the subject-centered, instrumental ones that have come increasingly to shape our lives. The two pictures do overlap in a number of areas. For instance, both focus on the intrication of knowledge with power that is characteristic of the sciences of man. But Foucault regards this analysis as valid for all the human sciences, whereas Habermas wants to distinguish objectivating (e.g., behavioral) approaches from interpretive (e.g., hermeneutical) and critical (e.g., genealogical or dialectical) approaches. The interests that inform them are, he argues, fundamentally different, as are consequently their general orientations to their object domains and their characteristic logics of inquiry. From this perspective, only purely objectivating approaches are *intrinsically* geared to expanding control over human beings, whereas other approaches may be suited to extending the intersubjectivity of mutual understanding or to gaining reflective distance from taken-for-granted beliefs and practices.

There is broad agreement between Foucault and Habermas that the expansion of the welfare state is increasingly dependent on the generation and application of expert knowledge of various sorts. In this regard, Foucault's account of the interrelation between social institutions geared to normalization and the growth of knowledge suited to that purpose parallels Habermas's account of the interconnection between the administrative colonization of the life world and the rise of objectivating social science. Here too the differences have chiefly to do with how all-inclusive this critical perspective can claim to be. Foucault extrapolates the results of his analyses of knowledge generated in the more or less repressive contexts he singles out for attention to the human sciences in general. One consequence of this is his clearly inadequate account of hermeneutic approaches.[10] Another is his inability to account for his own genealogical practice in other than actionistic terms— genealogical analysis ends up being simply another power move in a thoroughly power-ridden network of social relations, an intervention meant to alter the existing balance of forces. In the remainder of section 2, I want to look more closely at two key elements of his metatheory of genealogical practice: the ontology of *power* and the representation of the *subject* as an effect of power.

Power: Ontology versus Social Theory

The differences between Foucault and Habermas are misrepresented by the usual opposition between the nominalistic particularism of the former and the abstract universalism of the latter. In his Nietzschean moments, Foucault can be as universalistic as one might like, or dislike. While he insists that he wants to do without the claims to necessity typical of foundationalist enterprises, he often invokes an ontology of the social that treats exclusion, subjugation, and homogenization as inescapable presuppositions and consequences of any social practice. And while he targets for genealogical analysis social institutions that are clearly marked by hierarchies of power, his own conception of power as a network of relations in which we are all always and everywhere enmeshed devalues questions of who possesses power and with what right, of who profits or suffers from it, and the like. (These are questions typical of the liberal and Marxist approaches that he rejects.) What we gain from adopting this conception is a greater sensitivity to the constraints and impositions that figure in any social order, in any rational practice, in any socialization process. In this expanded sense of the term, *power* is indeed a "productive network that runs through the whole social body."[11] Giving this insight an ontological twist, one could then say with Foucault, "Power produces reality, it produces domains of objects and rituals of truth,"[12] or alternatively, "Truth is not the product of free spirits" but is "produced by virtue of multiple forms of constraint."[13] It is clear, for instance, that any "regime of truth" involves privileging certain types of discourse, sanctioning certain ways of distinguishing true from false statements, underwriting certain techniques for arriving at the truth, according a certain status to those who competently employ them, and so forth. In this sense, there is indeed a "political economy" of truth, as there is of any organized social activity. That insight is the principal gain of Foucault's ontologizing of the concept of power.

There are also losses incurred: having become more or less coextensive with constraint, power becomes all too like the night in which all cows are black. Welcoming or denouncing someone, putting someone at ease or into prison, cooperating or competing with someone—these are all equally exercises of power in Foucault's conceptualization. If his aim is to draw attention to the basic fact that patterned social interaction always involves normative expectations and thus possible sanctions, this is a rhetorically effective way of doing so. But the costs for social theory of such dedifferentiation are considerable. Distinctions between just and unjust social arrangements, legitimate and illegitimate uses of political power, strategic and cooperative interpersonal relations, coercive and consensual measures—distinctions that have been at the heart of critical social analysis—become marginal. If there were no possibility of retaining the advantages of Foucault's Nietzschean move without taking these disadvantages into the bargain, we would be faced with a fundamental choice between different types of social analysis. But there is no need to construe this as an either/or situation. We can agree with Foucault that social action is everywhere structured by background expectations in terms of which we hold one another accountable, that deviations from these are sanctionable by everything from negative affective responses and breakdowns of cooperation to explicit reprimands and punishments, and that our awareness of this accountability is a primary source of the motivated compliance that characterizes "normal" interaction.[14] And we can agree with him that the modern period has witnessed a vast expansion of the areas of life structured by instrumental, strategic, and bureaucratic forms of social interrelation. None of this prevents us from then going on to mark the sociologically and politically crucial distinctions that have figured so centrally in the tradition of critical social theory. Nancy Fraser has stated the issue here with all the desirable clarity: "The problem is that Foucault calls too many different sorts of things power and simply leaves it at that. Granted, all cultural practices involve constraints. But these constraints are of a variety of different kinds and thus demand a variety of different normative responses. . . . Foucault writes as if oblivious to the existence of the whole body of Weberian social theory with its careful distinctions between such notions as authority, force, violence, domination and legitimation. Phenomena which are capable of being distinguished via such concepts are simply lumped together. . . . As a consequence, the potential for a broad range of normative nuances is surrendered, and the result is a certain normative one-dimensionality."[15]

The Subject: Deconstruction versus Reconstruction

Foucault has related on various occasions how "people of [his] generation were brought up on two forms of analysis, one in terms of the constituent subject, the other in terms of the economic-in-the-last-instance."[16] As we have seen, he worked himself free of the latter by, among other things, drawing upon Nietzsche to develop a "capillary" conception of power as co-extensive with the social. In working free of the former, he was able to call upon the assistance of structuralist semiotics to argue for the priority of systems of signification over individual acts thereof. Even after he distanced himself from structuralism by taking as his point of reference "not the great model of language and signs, but that of war and battle," he retained this order of priority in the form of the "regimes," the inter-connected systems of discourses, practices, and institutions that structure and give sense to individual actions.[17] From the perspective of the genealogist, the subject privileged by phenomenology is in reality not the *constituens* but the *constitutum* of history and society, and phenomenology itself is only a recent chapter in the long tradition of subjectivism. At the core of that tradition is a hypostatization of the contingent outcome of historical processes into their foundational origin—not in the sense, typically, of a conscious creation but in that of an alienated objectification of subjective powers, which has then to be consciously reappropriated. This latter figure of thought is, for Foucault, the philosophical heart of the humanist project (including Marxist humanism) of mastering those forces, without and within that compromise "man's" autonomy and thus block his true self-realization. Like Horkheimer and Adorno in the *Dialectic of Enlightenment,* Foucault sees this as inherently a project of domination, a project that defines modern Western man's domineering relation to otherness and difference in all forms.

Foucault's reaction to this perceived state of affairs is, I want to argue, an overreaction. Owing in part to the continued influence of structuralist motifs in his genealogical phase, he swings to the opposite extreme of hypostatizing wholes—regimes, networks, *dispositifs,* and the like—over against parts, thus proposing to replace an abstract individualism with an equally abstract holism. To argue that "the individual is not to be conceived as a sort of elementary nucleus, a primitive atom," it is not necessary to maintain that the individual is merely "one of the prime effects of power."[18] One might instead defend the less radical thesis that individuation is inherently linked to socialization: we become individuals in and through being socialized into shared forms of life, growing into preexisting networks of social relations. From this perspective, Foucault's claim that the individual, who is an effect of power, is at the same time "the element of its articulation" or "its vehicle,"[19] might be construed as advancing the common sociological view that social structures are produced and maintained, renewed and transformed only through the situated actions of individual agents. But this view entails that agency and structure are *equally* basic to our understanding of social practices and that is decidedly not Foucault's approach. He wants to develop a form of analysis that treats the subject as an effect by "accounting for its constitution within a historical framework." If this were only a matter of "dispensing with the constituent subject," of avoiding all "reference to a subject which is transcendental in relation to the field of events," the disagreement would be merely terminological.[20] But it is not only the constituent, transcendental subject that Foucault wants to do without; he proposes a mode of inquiry that makes *no explanatory reference* to individual beliefs, intentions, or actions. Genealogy, he advises us, "should not concern itself with power at the level of conscious intention or decision": it should refrain from posing questions of the sort, Who has power and what has he in mind? The focus should instead by on "how things work at the level of ongoing subjugation, at the level of those continuous and uninterrupted processes," through which "subjects are gradually, progressively, really and materially constituted."[21] Again, if this were merely an argument for the need of *supplementing* an internalist view of social practices with an externalist one, of *balancing* an account of agency with an account of structure, of *integrating* a microanalysis of social practices with a structural analysis of persistent patterns of interaction or with a functional analysis of their unintended consequences or with an institutional analysis of the normative contexts of individual action, there would be no incompatibility in principle between genealogy and approaches operating with some concept of agency. But Foucault does not want to supplement or balance or integrate, he wants to replace. And the results of this either/ or thinking are no happier here than in the traditional theories he criticizes.

There is no hope of arriving at an adequate account of social integration if the only model of social interaction is one of asymmetrical power relations and the only model of socialization is that of an intrusion of disciplinary forces into bodies. Nor can we gain an adequate understanding of most varieties of social interaction by treating agents simply as acting in compliance with preestablished and publicly sanctioned patterns— as what Foucault calls "docile bodies" or Garfinkel calls "cultural dopes." We have to take account of their own understandings of social structures and their own reflexive use of cultural resources for making sense. This is no less true of the types of setting that most interest Foucault. As Goffman and others have made so abundantly clear, interpreting social situations, understanding what is expected in them, anticipating reactions to conformity and deviance, and using this knowledge for one's own strategic purposes are basic elements of interaction in disciplinary settings too.[22] These elements open up space for differential responses to situations, the possibility of analyzing, managing, and transforming them. Furthermore, the same competence and activity of agents is required for an adequate analysis of the rule-following practices central to Foucault's notion of power/knowledge regimes. Since rules do not define their own application, rule following is always to some degree discretionary, elaborative, ad hoc. Each new application requires the agent's judgment in the light of the specifics of the situation.[23]

One could go on at length in this vein. The point is simply to indicate how deeply the conceptual framework of agency and accountability is ingrained in our understanding of social practices. Foucault cannot simply drop it and treat social practices as anonymous, impersonal processes. To be sure, he does insist on the interdependence of the notions of power and resistance.[24] Yet he refuses to link the latter to the capacity of competent subjects to say, with reason, yes or no to claims made upon them by others. As a result, he is hard put to identify just what it is that resists. Often he alludes to something like "the body and its pleasures."[25] But that only plunges us deeper into just the sorts of conceptual tangles he wants to avoid. For it is Foucault, after all, who so forcefully brought home to us just how historical and social the body and its pleasures are. But when the need arises, he seems to conjure up the idea of a presocial "body" that cannot be fitted without remainder into any social mold. This begins to sound suspiciously like Freud's instinct theory and to suggest a refurbished model of the "repressive hypothesis" that Foucault so emphatically rejected.[26]

If treating the subject merely as "an effect of power," which must itself then be conceptualized as a subjectless network, undercuts the very notions of discipline, regime, resistance, and the like that are central to genealogical "theory," it raises no less havoc with genealogical "practice." Who practices genealogical analysis? What does it require of them? What promise does it hold out to them? If the self-reflecting subject is nothing but the effect of power relations under the pressure of observation, judgment, control, and discipline, how are we to understand the reflection that takes the form of genealogy? Whence the free play in our reflective capacities that is a condition of possibility for constructing these subversive histories? Foucault certainly writes as if his genealogies advanced our self-understanding, and in reading them we repeatedly have the experience of their doing just that. Can we make any sense of this without some, perhaps significantly revised, notion of subjects who can achieve gains in self-understanding with a liberating effect on their lives? Charles Taylor captures this point nicely when he writes, "'Power' belongs in a semantic field from which 'truth' and 'freedom' cannot be excluded. Because it is linked with the notion of imposition on our significant desires and purposes, it cannot be separated from the notion of some relative lifting of this restraint. . . . So 'power' requires 'liberty,' but it also requires 'truth'—if we want to allow, as Foucault does, that we can collaborate in our own subjugation. . . . Because the imposition proceeds here by foisting illusion upon us, it proceeds by disguises and masks. . . . The truth here is subversive of power."[27] This metatheory, deriving from our Enlightenment heritage and shared by the Frankfurt School, seems to make better sense of Foucault's practice than his own metatheory. If that is so, we may learn more from inquiring, as Foucault himself finally did in the 1980s, how his work develops and enriches the critical tradition extending

from Kant through the Frankfurt School than from insisting
that it has brought that tradition to an end.

3

In his first lecture of 1983 at the Collège de France, Foucault
credited Kant with founding "the two great critical traditions
between which modern philosophy is divided." One, the "analytic philosophy of truth in general," had been a target of
Foucault's criticism from the start. The other, a constantly
renewed effort to grasp "the ontology of the present," he acknowledged as his own: "It is this form of philosophy that,
from Hegel, through Nietzsche and Max Weber, to the Frankfurt School, has formed a tradition of reflection in which I
have tried to work."[28] This belated affirmation of what he calls
the "philosophical ethos" of the Enlightenment signals important changes in Foucault's understanding of his critical project.
In this final section I want briefly to characterize those changes
in respects relevant to the discussion and then critically to
examine their consequences for Foucault's treatments of the
subject and power.[29]

Perhaps the clearest indication of Foucault's altered perception of the Enlightenment tradition can be found in his reflections on Kant's 1784 essay "Was ist Aufklärung?"[30] He regards
that essay as introducing a new dimension into philosophical
thought, namely the critical analysis of our historical present
and our present selves. When Kant asked "What is Enlightenment?" writes Foucault, "he meant, What's going on just
now? What's happening to us? What is this period, this precise
moment in which we are living? Or in other words, What are
we? As *Aufklärer,* as part of the Enlightenment? Compare this
with the Cartesian question, Who am I? as a unique but universal and unhistorical subject? For Descartes, it is everyone,
anywhere, at any moment. But Kant asks something else: What
are we? in a very precise moment of history?"[31] From Hegel
to Habermas, Foucault continues, this question has defined a
way of philosophizing that he, Foucault, has adopted as his
own. What separates this way from a universally oriented "analytic of truth" is an awareness of being constituted by our

own history, a resolve to submit that history to critical reflection, and a desire thereby to free ourselves from its pseudonecessities.

As I argued above, Foucault could and should have said the same of the genealogy he practiced in the 1970s, but it became clear to him only in the 1980s that his form of critique also belongs to what Taylor called the "semantic field" of Enlightenment discourse. "Thought," he now tells us, "is what allows one to step back from [a] way of acting or reacting, to present it to oneself as an object of thought and question it as to its meaning, its conditions, and its goals. Thought is freedom in relation to what one does, the motion by which one detaches oneself from it, establishes it as an object, and reflects on it as a problem."[32] Freedom, in turn, is said to be the condition and content of morality: "What is morality if not the practice of liberty, the deliberate practice of liberty? . . . Liberty is the ontological condition of ethics. But ethics is the deliberate form assumed by liberty."[33] By releasing us from a state of "immaturity," critical thinking makes possible a "practice of freedom" oriented toward a "mature adulthood" in which we assume responsibility for shaping our own lives.[34]

To be sure, behind all these Kantian formulas there lies a considerably altered critical project. Foucault stresses that faithfulness to the Enlightenment means not trying to preserve this or that element of it but attempting to renew, in our present circumstances, the type of philosophical interrogation it inaugurated—not "faithfulness to doctrinal elements, but rather the permanent reactivation of an attitude, that is, of a philosophical ethos which could be described as a permanent critique of our historical era."[35] Since the Enlightenment, this type of reflective relation to the present has taken the form of a history of reason, and that is the form in which Foucault pursues it: "I think that the central issue of philosophy and critical thought since the eighteenth century has always been, still is, and will, I hope, remain the question: *What* is this Reason that we use? What are its historical effects? What are its limits, and what are its dangers? How can we exist as rational beings, fortunately committed to practicing a rationality that is unfortunately crisscrossed by intrinsic dangers?"[36] As noted in section 2, Foucault's genealogical histories stress the local and contingent aspects of prevailing forms of rationality rather than their universality. In one way this is continuous with Kant's linking of enlightenment and critique: when we dare to use our reason, a critical assessment of its conditions and limits is necessary if we are to avoid dogmatism and illusion. On the other hand, genealogy is a very different way of thinking about conditions and limits:

If the Kantian question was that of knowing what limits knowledge has to renounce transgressing, it seems to me that the critical question today has to be turned back into a positive one: in what is given to us as universal, necessary, obligatory, what place is occupied by whatever is singular, contingent, and the product of arbitrary constraints? The point, in brief, is to transform the critique conducted in the form of necessary limitation into a practical critique that takes the form of a possible transgression. . . . Criticism is no longer going to be practiced in the search for formal structures with universal value, but rather as an historical investigation into the events that have led us to constitute ourselves and to recognize ourselves as subjects of what we are doing, thinking, saying. . . . It will not deduce from the form of what we are what it is impossible for us to do and to know; but it will separate out, from the contingency that has made us what we are, the possibility of no longer being, doing, or thinking what we are, do, or think. It is not seeking to make possible a metaphysics that has finally become a science, it is seeking to give new impetus, as far and as wide as possible, to the undefined work of freedom.[37]

As this passage suggests, Foucault's critical histories of the "practical systems" of rationality that "organize our ways of doing things" are at the same time genealogies of the subjects of these rational practices, investigations into the ways in which we have constituted ourselves as rational agents.[38] And their point is not to reinforce established patterns but to challenge them. Genealogy is "practical critique": it is guided by an interest in the "possible transgression" and transformation of allegedly universal and necessary constraints. Adopting an experimental attitude, it repeatedly probes the "contemporary limits of the necessary" to determine "what is not or no longer indispensable for the constitution of ourselves as autonomous subjects."[39]

Let us turn now to the two topics on which I criticized

Foucault's earlier self-understanding: the subject and power. That will serve to focus my account of the theoretical shifts in his later work and to determine more precisely where they leave him in relation to Habermas.

Power Again: Strategic and Communicative Action

My criticisms of Foucault in section 2 turned on his one-dimensional ontology: in the world he described, truth and subjectivity were reduced in the end to effects of power. He escapes this reductionism in the 1980s by adopting a multi-dimensional ontology in which power is displaced onto a single axis. Referring to Habermas in his first Howison Lecture at Berkeley in the fall of 1980, he distinguishes three broad types of "techniques": techniques of production, of signification, and of domination.[40] To this he adds a fourth, namely techniques of the self, which subsequently becomes the principal axis of analysis in the second and third volumes of his *History of Sexuality*. These same four dimensions are distinguished (as "technologies") in the seminar he conducted at the University of Vermont in the fall of 1982.[41] And the first three of them are elaborated (as "relations") in the afterword (1982) to Dreyfus and Rabinow, *Michel Foucault: Beyond Structuralism and Hermeneutics*, where, referring once again to Habermas, he notes that they are not "separate domains" but analytically distinguishable aspects of social action that "always overlap" in reality.[42] By 1983 Foucault seems to have settled on a three-dimensional ontology vaguely reminiscent of Habermas's tripartite model of relations to the objective world, to the social world, and to ourselves.

In volume 2 of the *History of Sexuality*, for example, he works with a distinction between fields of knowledge, types of normativity, and forms of subjectivity, with three correlated axes of analysis: discursive practices, relations of power, and forms in which individuals recognize themselves as subjects.[43] What immediately strikes one in comparing this scheme with Habermas's is that normatively structured social relations are, as a matter of course, construed as relations of power. Earlier, when rules and norms constitutive of rational practices were re-

garded simply as technologies for "governing" and "normalizing" individuals, this is what one would have expected. But
now we have to ask what has been accomplished by distinguishing the three ontological dimensions if we are still left with a
reduction of social relations to power relations. Part of the
answer, I think, is a shift of attention from relations of domination to strategic relations. I want to suggest, in fact, that
Foucault's final ontology tends to equate social interaction with
strategic interaction, precisely the equation Habermas seeks to
block with his concept of communicative action.

The most elaborate explication of his later notion of power
appears in Foucault's afterword to the first edition of the Dreyfus and Rabinow study. There he construes the exercise of
power as "a way in which certain actions modify others," a
"mode of action upon the action of others," which "structures[s] the possible field of [their] action."[44] The relationship
proper to power is neither violence nor consensus but "government," in the very broad sense of "guiding the possibility
of conduct and putting in order the possible outcome."[45]
Viewed in this way, says Foucault, power is "coextensive with
every social relationship,"[46] for "to live in society is to live in
such a way that action upon other actions is possible and in
fact ongoing."[47]

Foucault's matter-of-course treatment of social relations as
power relations is less startling once we realize that he now
defines power relations in terms not unlike those that the sociological tradition has used to define social relations. What
makes actions social is precisely the possibility of their influencing and being influenced by the actions and expectations
of others. On Foucault's definition, only actions that had no
possible effects on the actions of others, that is, which were not
social, would be free of the exercise of power. What is at stake
here? Is this merely a rhetorical twist meant to sharpen our
awareness of the ways in which our possibilities of action are
structured and circumscribed by the actions of others? In part,
perhaps, but there is also a metatheoretical issue involved. His
conceptualization of social interaction privileges strategic over
consensual modes of "guiding the possibility of conduct and
putting in order the possible outcomes."

To see how this is so, we must first take a brief look at his distinction between power and domination. Whereas earlier, situations of domination—asylums, clinics, prisons, bureaucracies, and the like—were treated as paradigms of power relations generally in the panoptical society, now they are clearly marked off as a particular type of power situation.

When one speaks of "power", people think immediately of a political structure, a government, a dominant social class, the master facing the slave, and so on. That is not at all what I think when I speak of "relationships of power." I mean that in human relations, whatever they are—whether it be a question of communicating verbally . . . or a question of a love relationship, an institutional or economic relationship—power is always present: I mean the relationships in which one wants to direct the behavior of another. . . . These relations of power are changeable, reversible, and understandable. . . . Now there are effectively states of domination. In many cases, the relations of power are fixed in such a way that they are perpetually asymmetrical and the margin of liberty is extremely limited.[48]

Thus Foucault now distinguishes "relationships of power as strategic games between liberties" in which "some people try to determine the conduct of others" from "the states of domination . . . we ordinarily call power."[49] The idea of a society without power relations is nonsense, whereas the reduction to a minimum of states of domination—that is, fixed, asymmetrical, irreversible relations of power—is a meaningful political goal. "Power is not an evil. Power is strategic games. . . . To exercise power over another in a sort of open strategic game, where things could be reversed, that is not evil. . . . The problem is rather to know how to avoid . . . the effects of domination."[50] In short, whereas "games of power" are coextensive with social relations, "states of domination" are legitimate targets of political struggle aimed at freeing up space for open strategic games. "The more open the game, the more attractive and fascinating it is."[51]

It is difficult to judge just how far Foucault would have been willing to take this line of thought. It leads in the end to conceptualizing social relations as strategic relations and social interaction as strategic interaction. It would be ironic indeed if his wholesale critique of modern social theory should finally end in an embrace of one of its hoarier forms.[52] But rather than rehearsing the familiar debates concerning game-theoretical approaches to the general theory of action, I shall remark only on one key issue that separates Foucault from Habermas.

There are, at least on the face of it, ways of influencing the conduct of others that do not fit very neatly into the model of strategic games. Habermas's notion of communicative action singles out for attention the openly intended illocutionary effects that speech acts may have on the actions of others.[53] Establishing relations through the exchange of illocutionary acts make it possible for speakers and hearers to achieve mutual understanding about their courses of action, that is, to cooperate rather than compete in important areas of life. Foucault, however, views even the consensus that results from raising and accepting validity claims—claims to truth, rightness, sincerity, and so forth—as an instrument or result of the exercise of power.[54] Though he avoids any direct reduction of validity to power in his later work, his definition of power ensures that every communication produces it: "Relationships of communication," he writes, "produce effects of power" by "modifying the field of information between parties."[55] Of course, if producing effects of power amounts to no more than influencing the conduct of others, we have here a sheep in wolf's clothing. Habermas's notion of noncoercive discourse was never intended to refer to communication that is without effect on the behavior of others! Foucault comes closer to what is at issue between them when, in an apparent allusion to Habermas, he criticizes the idea of dissolving relations of power in a "utopia of a perfectly transparent communication."[56] He elaborates on this as follows: "The thought that there could be a state of communication which would be such that the games of truth could circulate freely, without obstacles, without constraint, and without coercive effects, seems to me to be Utopia."[57] This takes us back to the discussion of rational practices in section 2 and particularly to the idea that "truth is produced by virtue of multiple forms of constraint." As we saw there, the issue cannot be whether there are "games of truth" without the constraints of rules, procedures, criteria, and the like. And it does not seem to be whether constitutive constraints could *possibly* obligate participants in a symmetrical and reciprocal manner.[58] So the question appears to be whether what Habermas calls communication free from domination, in which claims to validity are decided on the basis of the reasons offered for and against them, can actually be realized in practice. And that seems to be a matter of more or less rather than all or nothing. If so, Habermas's idea of rational discourse would make as much sense as a *normative ideal* as Foucault's notion of a level playing field. It would be utopian only in the sense that the full realization of any regulative idea is utopian.

The Subject Again: Autonomy and Care of the Self

Foucault's growing emphasis on the "strategic side" of the "practical systems" that organize our ways of doing things—the freedom we have to act within, upon, or against them—is not the only way the individual comes to the fore in his later thought.[59] His balancing of the "technological" with the "strategic" in conceptualizing power is accompanied by a shift of attention from "subjectification" via "individualizing power" to "self-formation" via "care of the self." This shift occurred between the publication of volume 1 of the *History of Sexuality* in 1976 and the publication of volumes 2 and 3 in 1984. As Foucault explains it, earlier in *Discipline and Punish* and similar writings he had been concerned with "techniques for 'governing' individuals" in different areas of life. When he turned his attention to the genealogy of the modern subject in the *History of Sexuality,* there was a danger of "reproducing, with regard to sexuality, forms of analysis focused on the organization of a domain of learning or on the techniques of control and coercion, as in [his] previous work on sickness and criminality."[60] And this is indeed what we find happening prior to his work in volumes 2 and 3. In volume 1 he could still describe the aim of his study as follows: "The object, in short, is to define the regime of power-knowledge-pleasure that sustains the discourse on human sexuality in our part of the world. . . . My main concern will be to locate the forms of power, the channels it takes, and the discourses it permeates in order to reach the most tenuous and individual mode of behavior."[61] In the Tanner Lectures delivered at Stanford three years later (1979), one still finds a treatment of individuality in relation to "individualizing power", that is, to "power techniques oriented toward individuals and intended to rule them in a continuous and permanent way."[62] What Foucault calls "pastoral techniques," from Christian examination of conscience and cure of the soul to contemporary methods of mental health, are analyzed there as instruments for "governing individuals by their own verity."[63] And "governmentality" apparently continued to serve as the general perspective on individualization in the years immediately following.[64]

By 1983, however, the perspective had clearly shifted. In an interview conducted by Dreyfus and Rabinow in April of that year, Foucault, hard at work on the later volumes of his *History of Sexuality*, announces that "sex is boring" and that he is interested rather in techniques of the self.[65] Clarifying that remark, he goes on to draw a clear distinction between technologies of the self geared to normalization and ethical techniques aimed at living a beautiful life.[66] What the Greeks were after, he says, is an aesthetics of existence: "The problem for them was 'the *techne* of life,' . . . how to live . . . as well as [one] ought to live," and that, he tells us, is his interest as well: "The idea of the bios as material for an aesthetic piece of art is something which fascinates me."[67] Accordingly, he now characterizes the third axis of genealogical-archeological analysis as directed not toward modes of normalizing subjectification but toward "the kind of relationship you ought to have with yourself, *rapport à soi*, which I call ethics, and which determines how the individual is supposed to conduct himself as a moral subject of his own action."[68] Elsewhere this is described as a shift from the investigation of "coercive practices" to the study of "practices of freedom," "exercises of self upon self by which one tries . . . to transform one's self and to attain a certain mode of being."[69] And this "care of the self," which establishes a form of self-mastery, is now said to be a sine qua non of properly caring for others, that is, of the art of governing.[70]

According to Foucault, the search for an ethic of existence that was stressed in antiquity differed fundamentally from the obedience to a system of rules that came to prevail in Christianity. "The elaboration of one's own life as a personal work of art, even if it obeyed certain collective canons, was at the center, it seems to me, of moral experience, of the will to morality in Antiquity; whereas in Christianity, with the religion of the text, the idea of the Will of God, and the principle of obedience, morality took on increasingly the form of a code of rules."[71] To be sure, there are "code elements" and "elements of ascesis" in every morality, prescriptive ensembles of rules and values as well as ways in which individuals are to form themselves as ethical subjects in relation to those rules and values.[72]

Nevertheless, some moralities are more "code oriented," and others more "ethics oriented." In the former the accent is on code, authority, and punishment, and "subjectivation occurs basically in a quasi-juridical form, where the ethical subject refers his conduct to a law, or set of laws, to which he must submit."[73] In the latter the main emphasis is on self-formative processes that enable individuals to escape enslavement to their appetites and passions and to achieve a desired mode of being, and "the system of code and rules of behavior may be rather rudimentary [and] their exact observance may be relatively unimportant, at least compared with what is required of the individual in the relationship he has with himself."[74] Whereas histories of morality have usually focused on the different systems of rules and values operative in different societies or groups or on the extent to which the actual behavior of different individuals or groups were in conformity with such prescriptive ensembles, Foucault's *History of Sexuality* focuses on the different ways in which "individuals have been urged to constitute themselves as subjects of moral conduct," on the different "forms of moral subjectivation and the practices of the self that are meant to ensure it."[75] This choice is motivated in part by his diagnosis of the present state of morality: "If I was interested in Antiquity it was because, for a whole series of reasons, the idea of morality as disobedience to a code of rules is now disappearing, has already disappeared. And to this absence of morality corresponds, must correspond, the search for an aesthetics of existence."[76] Thus the problem of our present and of our present selves to which Foucault's later work is oriented is the "ethopoetic" one of how to revive and renew "the arts of individual existence."

This certainly constitutes a major shift from his earlier emphasis on networks or fields of power, in which individuals were only nodal points, and his methodological injunction to do without the subject and modes of analysis that rely on it. Both the ethical subject and the strategic subject are now represented as acting intentionally and voluntarily—within, to be sure, cultural and institutional systems that organize their ways of doing things.[77] But they are not simply points of application of these practical systems; they can critically-reflectively detach themselves from these systems; they can, within limits, modify these systems; they can, in any case, make creative use of whatever space for formation of the self that these systems permit or provide. This model now enables us to make sense of the possibilities of resistance and revolt that, Foucault always insisted, are inherent in systems of power. It corrects the holistic bias we found in his work of the 1970s. The question now is whether he hasn't gone too far in the opposite direction and replaced it with an individualistic bias.

Though the later Foucault refers appreciatively to Kant's ideas of maturity and autonomy, he gives them a very different twist. For example, in "What is Enlightenment?" his analysis of Kant's notion of *Mündigkeit* is immediately followed by a discussion of Baudelaire's attitude toward modernity: "Modern man, for Baudelaire, is not the man who goes off to discover himself, his secrets, his hidden truth; he is the man who tries to invent himself. This modernity does not 'liberate man in his own being': it compels him to face the task of producing himself."[78] In this respect, Baudelaire's attitude is Foucault's own, but it is not Kant's.[79] The representation of autonomy as aesthetic self-invention eliminates the universality at the heart of his notion, the rational *Wille* expressed in norms binding on all agents alike. This is, of course, no oversight on Foucault's part. As we saw, he distinguishes code-oriented moralities, in which a quasi-juridical subject refers his or her conduct to a set of laws, from ethics-oriented moralities, in which general rules of behavior are less developed and less important than individual self-formation. There can be no doubt as to how he ranks them: "The search for styles of existence as different from each other as possible seems to me to be one of the points on which particular groups in the past may have inaugurated searches we are engaged in today. The search for a form of morality acceptable to everybody, in the sense that everybody should submit to it, strikes me as catastrophic."[80] In the context of his history of sexuality, it is Christianity that serves as the paradigm of a code-oriented morality: "The Church and the pastoral ministry shared the principle of a morality whose precepts were compulsory and whose code was universal."[81] And this, it seems to me, is what motivates the either/or approach expressed in the lines quoted above: universal morality is construed not formally but materially, that is, in a pre-Kantian manner.

Contemporary neo-Kantians treat justice and the good life as complementary and not opposed concerns. Thus Habermas differentiates the type of practical reasoning proper to questions of what is morally right from that concerned with what is ethically prudent.[82] If questions of justice are involved, fair and impartial consideration of conflicting interests is called for; when questions of value arise, deliberation on who one is and who one wants to be is central. Like Kant, Habermas regards matters of justice, rather than matters specifically of the good life or of individual self-realization, to be the proper domain of universal morality. This is not to say that ethical deliberation exhibits no general structures of its own, but the disappearance of value-imbued cosmologies and the disintegration of sacred canopies have opened the question of how should I (or we or one) live to the irreducible pluralism and individualism of modern life. To suppose that it could be answered once and for all, that moral theory could single out one form of life right for everyone, is no longer plausible. On that point Habermas agrees with Foucault. For Habermas, however, this does not eliminate the need for a general theory of a more restricted sort: a theory of justice that reconstructs the moral point of view from which competing interest- and value-based claims can be fairly adjudicated. Like Kant, Habermas understands this type of reasoning to be universal in import; however, he replaces the categorical imperative with the idea that for general norms to be valid they have to be acceptable to all those affected by them as participants in practical discourse.

I cannot go into the details of that approach here, but enough has been said, perhaps, to indicate that Foucault's representation of universal morality, geared as it is to substantive codes, misses the point of formal, procedural models, namely to establish a general framework of justice within which individuals and groups may pursue differing conceptions of the good or beautiful life. Although Foucault does not address himself to this most general level of morality, he too cannot do without it. When asked on one occasion if the Greek arts of existence present a viable alternative to contemporary conceptions of the moral life, he responded, "The Greek ethics were linked to a purely virile society with slaves, in which the women were underdogs whose pleasure had no importance"[83] That is to say, Greek ethics were tied to unjust practices and institutions. And when asked on another occasion whether consensus might not serve as a regulative principle in structuring social relations, he replied, "I would say, rather, that it is perhaps a critical idea to maintain at all times: to ask oneself what proportion of non-consensuality is implied in such a power relation, and whether that degree of non-consensuality is necessary or not, and then one may question every power relation to that extent. The farthest I would go is to say that perhaps one must not be for consensuality, but one must be against non-consensuality."[84] And as we have seen, Foucault proposes as a goal for political practice the transformation of states of domination into open and symmetric (fair?) strategic games. In these and other contexts it is clear that Foucault conceives the "elaboration of one's life as a personal work of art" to be limited by considerations of justice. That is the unmistakable orientation of his studies, and it is an orientation that calls for *its own* reflective elaboration: universal morality is not opposed but complementary to the search for a personal ethics, it that search is to be open to everyone.

The problems with Foucault's account of the practice of liberty stem from his antithetical conceptualization of individual freedom and social interaction. As any operation of the other upon the self is conceived to be an exercise of power in which the other governs my conduct, gets me to do what he or she wants, liberty can consist only in operations of the self upon the self in which one governs or shapes one's own conduct. The one-dimensional view of social interaction as strategic interaction displaces autonomy outside of the social network. There are, of course, post-Kantian alternatives to this in which individual freedom includes reasoned agreement to the norms of common life, individual identity is formed and maintained in reciprocal relations with others, and group memberships contribute to self-fulfillment. Foucault's aesthetic individualism is no more adequate to this social dimension of autonomy than was the possessive individualism of early modern political theory. The same problem turns up in a different form in his views on the relation of ethics to politics and society: "The idea that ethics can be a very strong structure of existence, without any relation to the juridical per se, to an authoritarian system, a disciplinary structure, is very interesting," he tells us.[85] "For centuries," he continues, "we have been convinced that between our ethos, our personal ethics, our everyday life, and the great political and social and economic structures there were analytic relations, and that we couldn't change anything, for instance, in our sex life or in our family life, without ruining our economy, our democracy and so on. I think we have to get rid of this idea of an analytical or necessary link between this and other social or economic or political structures."[86] And a bit further on he asks rhetorically, "But couldn't everyone's life become a work of art?"[87] In his earlier work Foucault himself gave us ample grounds for answering that question in the negative under existing social, economic, and political conditions. The problem is not with "analytic and necessary links" but with de facto empirical interdependencies between structures and events at the personal and societal levels. The existence of such interconnections does not, of course, mean that we cannot change anything in our individual lives without changing society as a whole. But it does mean that the conditions of individual existence, and thus the chances of making one's life into a work of art, are different at different locations in the social system. As Hans-Herbert

Kögler puts it, "The sociocultural resources and opportunities for developing an autonomous personality are inequitably distributed, and this cannot be evened out by an ethical choice of self. . . . That approach leaves fully unanswered the question of how we might criticize contexts that themselves render impossible [autonomous] modes of subjectivation."[88]

Viewed from the perspective of critical social theory, Foucault's later framework of interpretation lies at the opposite extreme from his earlier social ontology of power. Then everything was a function of context, of impersonal forces and fields, from which there was no escape—the end of man. Now the focus is on "those intentional and voluntary actions by which men not only set themselves rules of conduct but also seek to transform themselves . . . and to make their life into an œuvre"—with too little regard for social, political, and economic context.[89] Neither scheme provides an adequate framework for critical social inquiry. The ontology of power was too reductive and one-dimensional for that purpose; the later, multidimensional ontology still depicts social relations as strategic and thus forces the search for autonomy, so central to the critical tradition, onto the private path of a *rapport à soi*. This is not at all to deny the power and insight of Foucault's historical-critical studies; it is to question his own accounts of their presuppositions and implications. I have been arguing that his work is better understood as a continuation and enrichment of the critical-theoretical tradition. His strengths are often weaknesses of mainstream critical social theory; his nominalism, descriptivism, and historicism a counterweight to the usual emphasis on the general, the normative, and the theoretical. However universal critical theory may be at the level of concepts and principles, in pursuing its practical interests, it must finally reach the variable, contingent, "transformable singularities" that so occupied Foucault and made his work so powerful a factor in the contemporary politics of identity. In this regard, his investigations into the historical contexts in which specific "practical systems" arise and function and his studies of the formation of the moral-rational subject are a valuable complement to more global discourses about rationalization. Moreover, his relentless scrutinizing of the impositions, constraints, and hierarchies that figure in rational practices challenges critical theorists to go further than they have in detranscendentalizing their guiding conceptions of reason, truth, and freedom.

In shaping his approach, Foucault devoted himself single-mindedly to matters about which he cared a great deal. Too often his single-mindedness found expression in an either/or stance toward existing frameworks and modes of critical inquiry. I have tried to suggest that the strengths of genealogy are better viewed as complementary to those of classical critical theory. The point is not to choose between them but to combine them in constructing theoretically informed and practically interested histories of the present.

Postscript
Politics and Ambiguity

In his *Politics and Ambiguity* William Connolly attempts to draw constructive lessons for democratic theory and practice from Foucault's genealogical studies.[1] He makes a strong case for the need to incorporate deconstructive elements in a reconstruction of democratic ideas, principles, procedures, and institutions. "Any authoritative set of norms and standards," he writes, "is at best an ambiguous achievement: it excludes and denigrates that which does not fit into its confines" (p. 138). But in our political theory and practice we are seldom able to resist "the powerful human urge to suppress disharmonies within our most cherished achievements" (p. 138). This intolerance of ambiguity is closely linked with the tolerance of discipline imposed on "the other." The theoretical antidote to this, he argues, is to replace the reigning "ontology of concord" with an "ontology of discordance or necessary dissonance within concord," an ontology that recognizes what doesn't fit, the excluded and subjugated other that is the "unavoidable effect of socially engendered harmonies" (p. 11). This could help us to resist the impulse to project in theory ever "more inclusive forms of selfhood and community" and could encourage us to establish in practice "more space for otherness to be" (p. 11). With this in view, Foucault's work can be used as a vehicle for rethinking the liberal ideas of tolerance for difference, freedom from the constraints of the state, individual rights, and the like. But first, his own largely critical reflections on democracy have to be supplemented with a frank acknowledgment of its positive achievements and untapped potentials.

Under the right conditions, democratic practices and institutions need not repress but can express the essential tensions in self and society; they hold out the permanent possibility of unsettling the settled, encouraging the expression of difference, defining the limits of our common life. What are the right conditions? Abstractly stated, they obtain when the order required for social life "can sustain itself without drawing so much of the self into the orbit of social control" (p. 14) and when the authoritative coordination indispensable to modern societies allows sufficient space for politics to give effective expression to ambiguity. And it is just the degeneration of these conditions—the ever deeper penetration of private life by bureaucracies, therapies, incentives, and the like, and the ever greater displacement of democratic politics by administrative and economic rationality—that draws the web of discipline ever tighter and squeezes what space is left for giving difference its due.

In this situation Foucault's focus on the mircostructures of power, rather than the macrostructures traditionally targeted by critical social theory, and his promotion of "local, specific struggles," rather than national political movements aimed at changing the priorities of the state, are valuable counterweights to mainstream approaches. Taken in isolation, however, they remain politically ineffectual: "We have here the beautiful soul in radical disguise. . . . Localism and radical resistance cannot suffice in a world where the state is intertwined in the details of life and [is] the focal point of imperatives facing the political economy as a whole" (p. 50). Connolly's more or less Habermasian macroanalysis runs roughly as follows. The liberal conjunction of two fundamental sets of priorities, prosperity in an economy of growth and accountability in a constitutional democracy, has proved to be inherently unstable. The first set of priorities, with its corresponding institutions and practices (which Connolly refers to collectively as the civilization of productivity), has "solidified into an interdependent structure" with its own dynamic, a dynamic that inexorably increases the burdens placed on the welfare state and erodes its capacity for democratic accountability. The motivation and legitimation problems that ensue—growing disaffection from the civilization of productivity, scepticism regarding its promise to make the good life universally available, declining allegiance to the welfare state—make necessary an ever expanding web of discipline, an ever denser network of conscious and unconscious "contrivances of social control," and an ever contracting space for democratic politics. Far from easing this tension between democracy and productivity, reindustrialization, with its heightened need for coordination and regulation, discipline and control, can only exacerbate it beyond endurance.

Rather, "the future of democracy requires a reconstitution of the ends and imperatives governing the system of productivity" (pp. 82–83). The aim here is to "tame" or "relax" the growth imperatives of the economic system so as to allow sufficient "slack" for ambiguity to be acknowledged and expressed. These metaphors get translated into a program for altering the "social infrastructure of consumption," which presently drives economic growth by incessantly converting luxuries and privileges into necessities. The core of the program is a shift away from "exclusive goods" (roughly, those that can't be universalized without decreasing their value and increasing their social costs, e.g., the automobile), around which the American dream has been built, toward "inclusive goods" (roughly the opposite, e.g., public transportation), which ease pressure for growth while making the good life more widely available. Connolly acknowledges that we can't change the structure of consumption in this way without changing everything with which it is systematically interconnected—modes of investment, profit, work, state expenditures, etc. (p. 95)—but he does not furnish an account of the system and its workings that would make it plausible to start with the mode of consumption rather than, say, the mode of production. He is concerned here to convince us only that certain *ends* are worth pursuing, and indeed must be pursued, if we are to open and maintain space for democratic politics.

It is in his conception of these ends that Connolly's differences with the Habermasian approach to democratic theory emerge most clearly. In his view, the ideal of a collectivity in which people freely identify with the ends and norms of their way of life and the correlated project of expanding the scope for democratic participation to foster this identification obscure the normalizing tendencies built into democratic practice itself. Deconstruction offers a counterperspective: the ideals of rationality and reflexivity, participation and consensus, self-consciousness and self-determination are the subtlest of means for making discipline and control appear to be rational and fulfilling. They foster a "countertyranny of insidious leniency" that "practices denial in the name of free discourse" (p. 92). But "critical legitimists," among whom Connolly numbers himself, grab hold of neither end of this stick. Rather, they seek to reconstruct a collectivist idea of legitimacy that "accepts Foucault as a double," that interrogates itself "from the vantage point of conceptualizations it finds alien, questions it tends to ignore, and answers it tends to exclude," that persistently poses the questions, "What is to be done to, with, or 'for' the other which does not fit into the actual or ideal order? And what is the justification for it?" (p. 92). This kind of reflexivity does not assume that we can assimilate the other into our categories but confronts us instead with the limits of our ability to do so and thus encourages us to leave sufficient slack in the order. It requires the theorist to adopt an ironic stance toward the very democratic ideals he or she espouses, a conscious effort to maintain the tension between "affirming the legitimacy of limits and conventions essential to democratic politics, while otherwise exposing and opposing the modern drift toward rationalization, normalization and dependency" (p. 107). But the search for the "limits most deserving of our allegiance" is by no means simply a theoretical matter. It is only in and through democratic politics that ambiguities can be effectively expressed and limits effectively probed. And for this, as we have seen, we need the space that can only come from relaxing the growth imperatives of the system of productivity.

Connolly's approach to democratic theory offers some valuable suggestions for incorporating deconstructive concerns into critical social theory. But he stays too close to the Nietzschean side of Foucault to arrive at an adequate integration, as the following brief points are meant to indicate.

• Connolly wants to break with the claims to universality and necessity characteristic of foundationalist aspirations. Yet he proposes an "ontology" of discordance or of "necessary" dissonance within concord, an ontology that sees otherness as the "unavoidable" effect of social harmonies, that asserts that "any" human construct "must" spawn what doesn't fit (all on p. 11). The appeal to Nietzsche and Foucault does not help much here, as their power ontologies are arguably the least plausible elements of their thought.[2] Why not leave it an open, empirical-theoretical question as to whether, how far, and in what ways cultural and social constructs have such effects?

• The ontology of discordance states that the organization of the self necessary to the good life with others also destroys, excludes, and subjugates elements in the self that do not fit. In elaborating this thesis, Connolly gives little play to the psychoanalytic tradition. Relying instead on Foucault's account of the subject as an effect of modern disciplinary and confessional technologies of power, he doesn't always resist the temptation to romanticize the excluded other. It is of course true that criminality, deviance, abnormality, irrationality, and the like are also effects of the very orders established to contain them and that they must be seen as such to be fully comprehended. And it does follow from this that any social criticism that lacks a developed sensitivity for difference and its suppression will lack credibility. But as we know from the Freudian tradition of social thought, the implications of this for social organization are more complex than is suggested by the formula of enlarging the social space in which otherness can find expression. (When and where and in what forms? All otherness, even the violent and aggressive types? Etc.) A theorist who so emphatically rejects any social ontology of concord will have to deal with the sorts of issues Freud posed in his *Civilization and Its Discontents*.

• There is a further problem caused by Connolly's reliance on Foucault and Nietzsche. In many ways these two great antagonists of the subject-centeredness of modern thought never completely broke free of its constraints.[3] The same problem is visible in Connolly's essays when violations of the private sphere are consistently characterized as multiform violations of the self. Deformations in *structures of intersubjectivity*, in patterns of communication and interaction, strangely fade from the sight of an approach, whose express aim is to get beyond the subjectivism of modern social and political thought.

• The focus on the self and its subjugation also makes it difficult for Connolly to give us a clear idea of how the desired public space, once gained, might be better filled. His stress on acknowledging and expressing otherness could, at this abstract level, just as plausibly be fleshed out in terms of the traditional liberal public sphere. What does he have in mind beyond the protection of individual rights and liberties and the like? If the point of "slack" is to permit effective expression of otherness, and if this is conceived largely in counterpoint to the disciplining and normalizing of selves, do we have the conceptual means to think beyond, to put it crudely, a radicalized version of Mill's *On Liberty?*

• Despite the preponderance of the rhetoric of rejection directed against "ideals of collectivity in which people freely identify with the ends and norms of their way of life," Connolly's own position would collapse without them. For he does not simply drop the notions of consensus and legitimation but reconstitutes them in terms of reflective allegiance to "ends and principles worthy of admiration even when the ambiguities within them have been acknowledged" (p. 160). What he objects to, then, is overidentification, easy identification—in a word, unselfconscious indentification. He wants us as theorists and practitioners of democracy not only to keep alert to the essential ambiguity of all achievements of order but also to acknowledge that the ideals of pure self-transparency and self-determination, of perfectly rational discourse and consensus are unrealizable and therefore dangerous. They cause us to underestimate the immense and irreplaceable role of unconscious commitments and orientations in political life, the unfathomable sea of presuppositions upon which any consensus floats, the openness of many practical questions to more than one reasoned response, the fundamental role of rhetoric in producing noncoercive agreements about nondemonstrable issues—and thus, for all these reasons, to underplay *the creative role of politics* in a democratic society. These are important warnings, and we are in Connolly's debt for having formulated them so perspicuously *within,* rather than against, a theory of democratic accountability. On the other hand, it is not entirely clear whether he recognizes this as a continuation of the self-critique of reason that has, as Habermas puts it, accompanied every step of enlightenment like a shadow. Softening and ambiguating our ideals of collective harmony and legitimacy, rendering our aspirations to self-consciousness and reasoned agreement more modest, injecting a dose of irony into our identification with the norms, roles, and institutions in which our lives are played out—this is self-critical reason at its best, reason criticizing itself, for good reasons. But what we come back to after this most recent turn of the critical screw is a more reflective notion of reasoned agreement. Reposing the central question as, Which standards are worthy of endorsement once the ambiguity within them is recognized? does not change that.

Heidegger and Critical Theory:
The First Encounter

The "first encounter" in my title refers to the Heideggerian Marxism developed by, Herbert Marcuse during his years in Freiburg. Admittedly, this is a restricted focus. Even if we leave aside the variants of phenomenological Marxism developed by Jean-Paul Sartre, Maurice Merleau-Ponty, Karel Kosík, Gajo Petrović, Enzo Paci, and others and concentrate on the critical theory of what has come to be known as the Frankfurt School, there is more to the story of its relation to Heidegger's thought than can be gotten from studying the early Marcuse. And yet this focus has its rationale. Only two of the major figures in the Frankfurt School tradition, Marcuse at one end and Jürgen Habermas at the other, were avowed Heideggerians for a period of their careers: Marcuse from about 1928, when he joined Heidegger in Freiburg, until the end of 1932, when he left Freiburg shortly before Hitler came to power; Habermas from about 1949, when he began his university studies, until 1953, when Heidegger published his 1935 lectures, *Introduction to Metaphysics,* with no explanations and no apologies. Heidegger's influence on the other philosophically minded members of the school was either negligible or, in the case of Theodor Adorno, conjectural.

During the year he spent at Freiburg with Husserl (1920/ 1921), Max Horkheimer seems to have been more impressed with Husserl's assistant, Martin Heidegger. Shortly after returning to the neo-Kantian philosophical atmosphere of Frankfurt, he wrote in a letter to a friend, "The more I am taken with philosophy, the further I distance myself from what is understood by that at this university. We have to look not for formal laws of knowledge, which are in the end quite unimportant, but for substantive propositions concerning life and its meaning. I know today that Heidegger was one of the most significant persons that spoke to me."[1] But he immediately went on to confess that he knew next to nothing about Heidegger's work: "Do I agree with him? How could I, as I know only one thing for certain about him—for him the motive of philosophizing springs not from intellectual ambition and some prefabricated theory, but every day, from his own experience."[2] And though in his inaugural address upon assumption of the directorship of the Institute for Social Research in 1931, Horkheimer singled out *Being and Time* as "the only modern philosophical work" that "radically refuses" to be an ideological form of social philosophy, he never discussed it in any detail.[3]

Walter Benjamin, on the other hand, was hostile to Heidegger's thought from the start, as we can read in a letter to Gershom Scholem from 1930: "There was a plan afoot here to establish a very small reading circle this summer, led by Brecht and myself, to destroy Heidegger. But unfortunately Brecht, who is not doing well at all, will have to go out of town soon, and I won't be able to take it on by myself."[4]

Adorno's relation to Heidegger is much more complicated. Despite his critical remarks on Heidegger in *Zur Metakritik der Erkenntnistheorie* (1956) and his frontal attacks in *Jargon der Eigentlichkeit* (1964) and *Negative Dialektik* (1966), his own thought exhibits certain affinities to Heidegger's. The first volume of his *Gesammelte Schriften,* in particular his 1931 inaugural address as a *Privatdozent* at Frankfurt University, "Die Aktualität der Philosophie," and his 1932 lecture on "Die Idee der Naturgeschichte," suggest that from very early on Heidegger was an important, albeit unacknowledged, interlocuter in the development of Adorno's thought.[5] But those same papers make clear that Adorno's version of critical theory was never the version propounded by Horkheimer in the 1930s and indeed that he was at that very time sketching an alternative approach that came to full expression only in the 1960s.[6] For both of these reasons—the distinctiveness of his approach to critical theory and the conjectural nature of Heidegger's influence upon it—the question of Adorno's relation to Heidegger is best left to a separate inquiry.[7]

By contrast, Habermas has acknowledged on a number of occasions the importance of Heidegger in his philosophical development.[8] But he was still a student when the publication of *Introduction to Metaphysics* provoked an open break and an effort to enter upon a different path.[9] Though Heidegger's influence certainly did not disappear with that break,[10] Habermas's discussions of his thought are overwhelmingly critical from that point on.[11] A number of his basic criticisms had already been formulated by Marcuse. In fact, Habermas several times remarks on the fascination with which he read the work of the young Marcuse, for he found there someone who had previously trodden his own path "from Heidegger to Horkheimer."[12] Of course, their paths diverged widely in other respects, and even in this respect, the differences are as noteworthy as the similarities. Of the two, only Marcuse expressly attempted to combine Marx and Heidegger in a version of critical social theory, and even after he abandoned the project, the distance he traveled from Heidegger was never as great as it was for Habermas.[13]

In this paper I shall confine my remarks to Marcuse's early and explicit Heideggerian Marxism. The rationale behind this choice, which I hope to render plausible in what follows, is that many of the basic affinities, tensions, and oppositions between existential ontology and critical social theory already came to light, and to a particularly revealing light, in that early encounter. More specifically, Marcuse already formulated the basic issues that still separate critical theory from Heidegger today.

1

Marcuse's four years with Heidegger, though early in his philosophical career, came later in his political-intellectual development.[14] He joined the Social Democrats in 1917 in protest against the war, participated in a solders' council during the November Revolution in 1918, quit the Social Democratic Party in the same year because of what he saw to be its increasingly reactionary and repressive policies, and turned bitterly against it after the murder of Rosa Luxemburg and Karl Liebknecht. From that point on, Marcuse was attracted to revolutionary politics and began to read Marx seriously. In 1919 he returned to his studies, which had been interrupted by the war, spending two years in Berlin and another two in Freiburg, where he received his doctorate in German literature with his dissertation "Der Deutsche Künstlerroman" in 1922. For the next several years he worked with an antiquarian bookdealer and publishing firm in Berlin, all the while continuing his reading of Marx and Marxism. It seemed to him that official Marxism had crushed the life out of Marx's thought. His reading of Lukács and later Korsch convinced him that what was needed was a retrieval of the philosophical dimension that the "Marxism of the parties" had buried under.

It was into this pregnant atmosphere that *Sein und Zeit* flashed in 1927. As Marcuse tells us in a later interview, he saw in Heidegger "a new beginning, the first radical attempt to put philosophy on really concrete foundations—philosophy concerned with human existence, the human condition, and not merely with abstract ideas and principles."[15] He was convinced that "there could be some combination between [Heidegger's] existentialism and Marxism, precisely because of their [common] insistence on concrete analysis of actual human existence, of human beings and their world."[16] This retrospective account does, in fact, echo the views Marcuse expounded in two programmatic essays published in 1928 and 1929: "Beiträge zu einer Phänomenologie des historischen Materialismus" and "Über konkrete Philosophie."[17] In the former, an immensely suggestive interweaving of Marxian and Heideggerian motis, he characterizes *Sein und Zeit* as a "turning point in the history of philosophy: the point at which bourgeois philosophy disintegrates from within and opens the way to a new 'concrete' science" (B, p. 358). And he begins the second essay by acknowledging that it is written from a perspective opened up by *Sein und Zeit* and seeks to illuminate not only "the possibility of a concrete philosophy" but "its necessity in the present circumstances" (K, p. 385).

In the interview mentioned above, Marcuse goes on to say that he "soon realized that Heidegger's concreteness was to a great extent a phony, a false concreteness, and that in fact his philosophy was just as abstract and just as removed from reality, even avoiding reality, as the philosophies which at that time dominated German universities."[18] His principal concepts "are 'bad' abstracts in the sense that they are not conceptual vehicles to comprehend the real concreteness in the apparent one. They lead away."[19] Again, this account does, in fact, echo a criticism of Heidegger's work that is already present in Marcuse's essays from the Freiburg period, though it did not receive so sharp an expression until his first publications from exile in 1933 and 1934.

What did Marcuse, who was then engaged in a systematic reading of the works of Karl Marx, see in *Sein und Zeit* that excited him so? Recall that Marx's *Economic and Philosophical Manuscripts* were not published until 1932 (when Marcuse wrote one of the first and most brilliant reviews of it, a review that had a lasting impact on the reception of the young Marx by Western Marxists).[20] Prior to its publication the hegemony of naturalistic and scientistic versions of official Marxism had all but made invisible the debt that Marx owned to Hegel, more precisely the philosophical anthopology that he had contructed by reading Hegel's phenomenology through a Feurbachian lens. What Marcuse attempted in 1928 was to use Heidegger to close the gap between the sketch of historical materialism he found in *The German Ideology* and the philosophical-anthropological foundations he felt it required.[21] He could do this, he believed, because notwithstanding Heidegger's declared interest in the question of the meaning of Being, the "part of *Being and Time* that has appeared to date deals with the interpretation of a preeminent Being, Dasein, by which is always understood human Dasein" (B, p. 358).

From this philosophical-anthropological perspective Marcuse wove together existential-ontological and historical-materialist ideas in fashioning an approach he characterized as "concrete philosophy." The result was neither simply an appropriation of Heidegger from a Marxian perspective nor simply the converse. There was genuine interpenetration, reciprocal influence. What especially inspired Marcuse about *Being and Time* was the way in which the analytic of Dasein culminated in an existential resolve to transform inauthentic into authentic existence, for it was just this concrete relation to human life that he found missing from both the Marxism of the parties and the neo-Kantianism of the schools: "In the consciousness of its acute necessity, the basic question of all living philosophy is raised: what is authentic existence and how is authentic existence possible in general? . . . Philosophy has again found its original necessity; it is concerned only with existence, with its truth and fulfillment" (B, p. 362).

Marcuse did, of course, connect these notions of concrete Dasein, acute necessity, and authentic existence to similar-sounding but more sociopolitically oriented notions in Marx. The connecting lines were drawn through a series of points on which historical materialism and existential ontology are in general, if not specific, agreement in opposition to mainstream post-Cartesian philosophy. To begin with, both approaches seek to overturn the traditional primacy of theory over practice. Not only is philosophy guided by a practical orientation toward authentic existence, theory in general, both Marx and Heidegger hold, is founded upon, and in some sense derivative from, practice. As Marcuse puts it, "The theoretical mode of behavior . . . is a modification of that original view of the world as significance. Our encounter with the world in practical, needy concern comes first, and all theoretical, cognitive approaches are founded upon it" (B, pp. 359–360). In both Marx and Heidegger this approach entails a rejection of the subject-object paradigm that dominated philosophy after Descartes: human Dasein is from the start a practically engaged Being-in-the-world. It also entails a rejection of that paradigm's ego-centrism: Dasein is always already *Mitsein,* and its world a *Mitwelt.* Further conjunctions of Heidegger and Marx are clustered around the concept of historicity. Showing that this is a basic determination of Dasein is for Marcuse "the decisive point of Heidegger's phenomenology" (B, p. 361). Correspondingly, historical materialism is for him "the whole domain of knowledge relating to historicity: to the Being, structure, and movement of historizing" (B, p. 347). As this juxtaposition might suggest, Marcuse moves rather freely along the ontic-ontological spectrum of significations of "history" and "historicity." For Marx, he tells us, human existence is essentially historical: "The determination of existence is historical. It is circumscribed by the historical situation, for the possibilities of concrete human beings are marked out by that situation, as are their reality and their future" (B, p. 352). Similarly, for Heidegger, "In the throwness of Being-in-the-world, everyday Dasein takes its possibilities from the inherited interpretation of the they. . . . Even in the resoluteness in which the authentic Being of Dasein is constituted, Dasein remains thrown," for authenticity can be won only "through a countering [rejoinder] to what factically exists" (B, p. 361). Marcuse also points out that for Heidegger, "fateful Dasein" always already exists in "Being-with-others" and thus that its "historizing is always a co-historizing," the "density of a community of people" (B, p. 361). Dasein's world is caught up in this historical process as well, "inasmuch as it is not hardened into a rigid world of things purely present at hand but, as a world of signification, has its roots in a particular Dasein" (B, p. 373).

2

By enabling us to see the "historical throwness" of Dasein and to grasp resoluteness as "taking historical fate upon oneself," Heidegger has, says Marcuse, brought philosophy as far as it can go, namely face to face with our historical situation, its concrete determinations and possibilities for action (B, p. 363). As thought practically concerned with authentic existence, radical philosophizing can now remain true to itself only by transcending itself. The key points in Marcuse's argument are the following:

1. To begin with, questions concerning authentic existence and its possibility, if posed only with regard to "Dasein überhaupt," remain empty (B, p. 364). If they are to become genuine existential questions, they must be posed with regard to specific human beings in specific historical circumstances. The first step required in the "process of philosophy's becoming concrete"

(K, p. 397), then, *is an analysis of the contemporary historical situation*—"the basic structures of contemporary existence, the general circumstances that have led to it, and the historical consequences flowing from it" (K, p. 395). For only when concrete philosophy has grasped the sociohistorical situation of "contemporary Dasein," when it understands "how this determinate Dasein suffers and acts, what its real needs are, what modes of existence and paths to change the situation marks out," can it provide substantive suggestions about possibilities of authentic existence (K, p. 398).

2. This means that concrete philosophy will require *a change in method*. In particular, it will have to break through "the long-practiced fencing-off" of such "really historical sciences" as history, sociology, and economics and incorporate their results in its own reflections. For the "fullness of existence" with which concrete philosophy is concerned, encompasses all "the factical modes of existing" that these types of inquiry are designed to study.

3. These ontic inquires provide access to *the material circumstances of historical existence,* which Heidegger tends to ignore. In this respect, Marcuse believes, Dilthey went further than Heidegger (B, p. 365). But Marx went further than both in understanding that Dasein is "in its very essence always concrete Dasein in a definite historical situation, and as such is in its very essence determined by concretely ascertainable material circumstances" (B, p. 374). Pushing forward to the material constitution of historicity makes it possible to understand the existential crisis of contemporary Dasein also as an institutional crisis of contemporary society.

4. Once this perspective has been adopted, another abstraction of existential ontology become problematic: "We are not dealing here with a unitary world of significance tied to a unitary Dasein. . . . As thrown Being-in-the-world, Dasein is always determined by its world, not only in the mode of fallenness to some 'they'—itself again of the character of Dasein—but as defined by its concrete historical *Mit-* and *Umwelt*" (B, p. 374). This means that the worlds of signification of different cultures will be different and that within a given culture "there will be

large divergences of meaning between worlds," between, for instance, the worlds of the bourgeois, the peasant, and the worker (B, p. 365). In short, concepts like "Dasein" and "das Man" direct our attention away from *socially, economically, and culturally constituted group differences.*

5. And this, writes Marcuse, has practical consequences for the notions of resoluteness and authenticity based upon them. Despite the attention given to Being-with, destiny, and the like, it is, for Heidegger, "the isolated Dasein" that has to decide for authentic existence (B, p. 364). But the individual is not the proper unit of sociohistorical analysis and political practice (B, p. 376). Practically oriented reflection on the determinations and possibilities of concrete historical existence will have to consider larger units, for example, classes, communities, and societies in their shared conditions of living (K, p. 393). This does not mean, Marcuse hastens to add, that the "seriousness of deciding" can be lifted from the individual and transferred to society as whole (K, p. 404). It does mean, however, that the project of authentic existence cannot be pursued in isolation from one's fellow human beings. It is *a public and not a private project*: "Concrete philosophy becomes public in becoming historical" (K, p. 400). Since "contemporaneity" signifies not just temporally living alongside one another but a commonality of fate, taking the real fate of Dasein upon oneself means that one has to concern oneself with real struggles and needs (K, p. 400). Concrete philosophy "exists in public," then, because "it is only in public that it can really get at existence" (K, p. 401); it is only "in and through the historical situations in which they live that individuals can be spoken to and reached" (K, p. 404).

6. Accordingly, the type of practice for which concrete philosophy calls is a *political practice of social transformation,* which Marcuse characterizes as follows: the aim of this practice is to clear the way for a "new reality as the realization of the whole human being," in a situation in which that realization "appears to be factically impossible" (K, p. 350). With this in view, it must be guided by a careful analysis of the contemporary situation, its origins, its tendencies, its structures, and its pos-

sibilities. Heidegger's analysis, however, comes to an end before it gets to "the decisive fact of today" in respect to which the question, How is authentic existence concretely possible? would have to be posed: "Taking into account the present situation would make clear that authentic existence . . . can today come about only as concrete transformative action, that it is the fate of today to have to go through the overthrow of factically established existence" (B, p. 364). The domination of the past, which Heidegger analyzed abstractly in terms of fallenness, today has the concrete form of reification that Marx and Lukács analyzed. Its "disavowal" requires a transformation of the socioeconomic conditions of existence.

3

When he wrote the essays I have been discussing (1928–1929), there was no doubt in Marcuse's mind that Heidegger had gone further than any previous philosopher in elucidating the basic structures of historicity and that the limits of his thought were the limits of philosophy as such. Developing an adequate theory of historicity was, then, a matter of transcending (sublating) Heidegger in the direction of historical concreteness rather than of refuting him. In the years immediately following (1930–1932), when he was still working with Heidegger at Freiburg, there was a subtle but perceptible shift in this estimation. As we saw, in 1928 Marcuse had credited Dilthey, whom he had previously encountered in his dissertation, with having done better than Heidegger in one respect, namely in grasping the materiality of historicity (B, p. 365). In his 1930 essay "Zum Problem der Dialektik, I," however, Dilthey is given equal billing with Heidegger in the development of an adequate theory of historicity.[22] The appearance of *Vom Wesen des Grundes* and Heidegger's book on Kant (both in 1929) had in the meantime led Marcuse to doubt "that the inner meaning of Heidegger's philosophizing really takes us in the direction of history and historicity."[23] And in a lengthy 1931 review of Korsch's *Marxismus und Philosophie* entitled "Das Problem der geschichtlichen Wirklichkeit," Marcuse goes so far as to replace Heidegger with Dilthey as the "turning point" from philosophy to social theory: "In Dilthey's work, philosophy is driven beyond itself . . . to encounter the dimension of historical-social reality opened up by Hegel and Marx."[24]

The mention of Hegel and Marx in this connection points ahead to Marcuse's two major publications of 1932: his review of Marx's *Economic and Philosophical Manuscripts* and his *Habilitationsschrift*, "Hegels Ontologie und die Grundlegung einer Theorie der Geschichtlichkeit."[25] It is likely that the latter was completed before the former, as Marcuse refers in a footnote of the review to his "book" on Hegel's ontology.[26] In any case and for whatever reasons, Marx is absent from the pages of his *Habilitationsschrift*. Heidegger, with whom he planned to habilitate,[27] is credited at the start and rarely mentioned thereafter: "Any contribution this work may make to the development and clarification of problems is indebted to the philosophical work of Martin Heidegger. This is emphasized at the beginning instead of being indicated throughout with special references."[28] As the very title of the book suggests, Heidegger's influence is indeed evident throughout.[29] Nevertheless, in his heterodox reading of Hegel's *Logic* as a fundamental ontology of historicity, it is a Diltheyan concept that occupies center stage, i.e., *Leben*. In fact, in the 1931 review of Korsch mentioned above, Marcuse had credited Dilthey with having reopened the question of the *Seinscharakter* of historical-social reality, which had been closed off since Hegel, and with having shown that "the character of this being is defined by the concept of life."[30] This approach enables Marcuse to interpret Hegel's "objective spirit" in terms of Dilthey's objectivations of life. And it is precisely this concept that will also figure centrally in his influential reinterpretation of the young Marx.

Without going into detail, one might characterize the evolution of Marcuse's thought during this period as follows: feeling the need for philosophical foundations of historical materialism, which might help rescue it from official Marxism and relate it to the concrete concerns of human existence, Marcuse turned first to Heidegger's analytic of Dasein, and then after 1929, when it became clear that Heidegger was moving in another direction, he returned to Dilthey, in whom he found a sustained focus on "historical-social reality."[31] Dilthey, with his neo-Hegelian roots, provided a path back from Heidegger to Marx's own roots in Hegel. This journey was essentially completed when the *Paris Manuscripts* appeared in 1932, and Marcuse thus found himself in an unusually favorable position to appropriate them for what later came to be called "Western Marxism."

Though Heidegger is nowhere mentioned in Marcuse's discussion of the *Manuscripts,* the continuing influence of his thought is evident in the reading offered. Marx's 1844 *Manuscripts* are said to supply the long missing philosophical foundations of his critique of political economy. At their core is a philosophical interpretation of human essence and its historical realization, the key to which is Marx's critical appropriation of the Hegelian concept of *Vergegenständlichung* for his own account of labor as an externalization of essential human powers. Throughout, the languages of Marx and Heidegger are freely translated into one another, *Wesenskräfte* into *Grundbestimmungen* and back again. For there is no doubt in Marcuse's mind that the young Marx was interested in elucidating "the ontological character of the concept [of labor]."[32] At the same time, however, Marcuse's discussion reflects the distance he had already traveled from existential ontology: "To play off essence and facticity against one another . . . is wholly to misconstrue the new standpoint that Marx already adopted at the start of his investigations. For Marx essence and facticity . . . are not independent regions or levels separate from one another."[33]

The same intertranslation *and* distancing can be found in his 1933 essay "Über die philosophischen Grundlagen des wirtschaftswissenschaftlichen Arbeitsbegriffs."[34] There he tells us that "labor is an ontological concept, that is, a concept which grasps the Being of human Dasein itself and as such."[35] Hegel and Marx, he goes on, were the last philosophers to comprehend this,[36] though Dilthey subsequently made an important contribution by explicating the "historicity of the objective world" in terms of the "objectivations of life."[37] Heidegger is again a silent partner in Marcuse's interpretation of the young Marx. As he later explained, the discovery of the *Manuscripts* resolved the tension he had been experiencing between his philosophical convictions, which were strongly Heideggerian, and his social-theoretical outlook, which was decidedly Marx-ian, for they captured Marx in the very act of transforming Hegelian philosophy into the conceptual foundations of his critique of political economy. This Marx could be appropriated in terms of the *lebensphilosophisch* oriented interpretation of Hegel he had worked out in his *Habilitationsschrift*. The existential-ontological motifs that still pervaded that study could now be partly replaced by Hegelian-Marxist correlates and partly retained, but without decisive systematic import. As yet there was no explicit break with Heideggerian ontology. But that was not long in coming.

In the 1933 review "Philosophie des Scheiterns: Karl Jaspers' Werk," written in exile in Switzerland, Marcuse favorably contrasted Jaspers' version of existentialism with Heidegger's.[38] For the latter, he wrote, the "existential analytic" is only preparatory to what is basically a "transcendental-ontological problematic." As a result, "the categories of existence are with Heidegger meant purely ontologically, whereas they receive an 'ethical' sense in Jaspers."[39] Nevertheless, Jaspers too failed in the end to address the concrete problems of contemporary existence: "Existence philosophy halts its concretizing of the concept of historicity exactly where really dangerous problems begin. . . . All talk of historicity remains abstract and unbinding as long as it fails to accentuate the concrete 'material' situation in which the philosophizing existence actually lives, and as long as it fails to consider actual possibilities and realities from the standpoint of the factical structures [of that situation]."[40] The next year as Marcuse arrived in the United States (on the fourth of July 1934), his first contribution to the *Zeitschrift für Sozialforschung* appeared under the title "Der Kampf gegen den Liberalismus in der totalitären Staatsauffassung."[41] With Heidegger's *Rektoratsrede* and his contributions to the *Freiburger Studentenzeitung* in hand, Marcuse expanded his critique of the existential-ontological approach for cutting itself off from sociohistorical inquiry.[42] Its attempt to recapture the "full concretion of the historical subject in opposition to the abstract 'logical' subject of rationalism" had foundered on its failure to analyze the historical situation of the subjects it addressed.[43] The notions of historicity, authenticity, and resoluteness were so many empty sails waiting to be filled, and the devaluation of ontic and ethical inquiry left this filling at the mercy of the prevailing winds. Heidegger, Marcuse wrote, "remained content to talk of the nation's link with destiny, of the 'heritage' that each individual has to take over, and of the community of the 'generation,' while other dimensions of facticity were treated under such categories as 'they' and 'idle talk' and relegated in this way to inauthentic existence. [He] did not go on to ask about the nature of this heritage, about the people's mode of being, about the real processes and forces that *are* history. Philosophy thus renounced all possibility of comprehending the facticity of historical situations and distinguishing between them."[44] It is indicative of things to come, though only some time later, that in the same essay Marcuse refers favorably to Kant's conception of the critical mission of philosophy and to his ideas of reason, autonomy, and responsibility. "A theory of society is *rationalist,*" he wrote, "when the practice it enjoins is subject to the idea of autonomous reason. . . . Within society, every action and every determination of goals, as well as the social organization as a whole, has to legitimate itself before the decisive judgment of reason. . . . The rationalist theory of society is therefore essentially *critical.*"[45] This emphasis on critical reason persisted in Marcuse's writings of the 1930s and into his altered interpretation of Hegel in *Reason and Revolution* (1941). It waned again in the 1950s and thereafter, even as it was waxing in the work of Jürgen Habermas, whose early intellectual development also trod the path from Heidegger to Horkheimer. But that is another story.[46]

Here I have wanted only to show that the basic issues separating critical theory from Heideggerian ontology were not raised post hoc in reaction to Heidegger's political misdeeds but were there from the start. Marcuse formulated them in all clarity during his time in Freiburg, when he was still inspired by the idea of a materialist analytic of Dasein.

4

The Politics of the Ineffable:
Derrida's Deconstructionism

In an interview conducted in 1981, Jacques Derrida acknowledged that he had "never succeeded in directly relating deconstruction to existing political codes and programs" and complained that "the available codes for taking a political stance are not at all adequate to the radicality of deconstruction." He went on to note that this "absence of an adequate political code to translate or incorporate the radical implications of deconstruction has given many the impression that deconstruction is opposed to politics or is at best apolitical." "But this impression only prevails," he explained, "because all our political codes and terminologies still remain fundamentally metaphysical, regardless of whether they originate from the right or the left."[1] This is an admirably concise statement of the much discussed problem of the politics of deconstruction. On the one hand, Derrida has repeatedly insisted on the political character of deconstructionist practice: "It is not neutral," he assures us; "it intervenes."[2] One the other hand, he has been rather evasive about just which politics, or approach to politics, it involves. His politically "codable" stands—on neocolonialism, women's liberation, and apartheid, for instance—

This is a revised and expanded version of comments on Jacques Derrida's paper "The Politics of Friendship," read at the 85th annual meeting of the American Philosophical Association, Eastern Division, in December 1988. An abbreviated version of Derrida's paper appeared under the same title in the *Journal of Philosophy* 85 (1988): 632–645, together with my initial comments, "On the Margins of Politics," pp. 645–648. As the full text on which Derrida based his APA talk has not yet been published, I refer at times to his oral presentation.

have shown him to be generally on the "progressive" side, but they have been backed by little historical or institutional analysis and not much more explicit normative critique. As a result, his readers can and do disagree widely about just which general political standpoint the particular stands reflect. They cannot turn to Derrida's political "theory" to settle the issue, for he hasn't offered one, and indeed, he regards the whole genre as eminently deconstructible. As to other means of conveying his general point of view, he has bemoaned, as we just heard, the absence of any adequate political code.

Thus the debate concerning deconstructionist politics stems in no small measure from Derrida's unwillingness or inability to "decide" it by word or example. "The Politics of Friendship" is important in this context because it addresses itself specifically to political philosophy. Unfortunately, after reading it, we are left with much the same questions and doubts as before. I want to argue that this is no accident, that the "radicality of deconstruction," as Derrida conceives it, inexorably carries it in the direction of the ineffable, and that while this may have its point when dealing with metaphysics, it is seriously disabling where morals and politics are concerned. To make this argument, it will first be necessary (in section 1) to review, very broadly, Derrida's conception of deconstruction and its political implications. This is no routine exercise, as he has self-consciously built into his own texts the undecidability he attributes to meaning in general. One can, in short, find passages on the other side(s) of any interpretation. Thus it is no surprise that the standard response to Derrida's critics has been that they have misunderstood him. I cannot hope to avoid this, but I will rely heavily on citations to indicate just which texts I am misreading. In section 2, I will turn to criticisms of Derrida's approach to politics, both in general and in his paper on the politics of friendship.

1

Derrida has written of the politics of deconstruction in a number of different tones. Toward the end of the 1960s the tone was at times apocalyptic, if not revolutionary. In "The Ends of

Man," a paper first read in 1968, he spoke of the "total trembling" (or shaking: *ébranlement*) of the Man-Being coappurtenance that "inhabits and is inhabited by the language of the West." This "radical trembling," he told us, is being "played out in the violent relationship of the whole of the West to its other, whether a 'linguistic relationship' . . . or ethnological, economic, political, military relationships, etc."[3] During the same period and subsequently, the tone was often one of patient resistance to the ultimately unslayable Hydra of Western logocentrism. Thus in an interview with Julia Kristeva, Derrida professed his disbelief in "decisive ruptures": "Breaks are always, and fatally, reinscribed in an old cloth that must continually, interminably be undone."[4] Deconstruction, then, cannot aim to rid us, once and for all, of the concepts fundamental to Western rationalism, but only, again and again, "to transform [them], to displace them, to turn them against their presuppositions, to reinscribe them in other chains, and little by little to modify the terrain of our work and thereby to produce new configurations."[5] By these means it "organizes a structure of resistance" to the dominant conceptuality.[6]

In the 1980s the tone becomes explicitly antiapocalyptic, at least insofar as the latter is linked to eschatology. Deconstruction is not prophetic or visionary; it does not announce an imminent end or a new dawning.[7] Indeed, Derrida even characterizes it at times as new form of *Aufklärung*.[8] In that intonation, deconstruction is not a matter of renouncing "the principle of reason" but of interrogating "its meaning, its origin, its goal, its limits," that is, of inquiring after "the grounding of the ground itself."[9] It does not oppose classical logic but calls for another discourse that "accounts for this logic and its possibility" and "for the impossibility of concluding a 'general theory' [of language and meaning]." Indeed, this tone can sound surprisingly like Kant's—at some remove, to be sure, for "the type of 'enlightenment' granted our time" has to be based on a recognition of "the unclarity of the good old *Aufklärung*."[10]

Throughout these changes in tone, however, Derrida's account of deconstruction has remained constant in central respects.[11] To begin with, it involves a radical decentering of the subject in relation to language. As signification is always a function of largely unconscious differential relations (among signifiers, speakers, hearers, situations, contexts, etc.) and as these relations unfold in social spaces and historical times, we are never completely masters of what we say: "The subject, and first of all the conscious and speaking subject, depends upon the system of differences and the movement of *différance*."[12] The process of signification, as Derrida puts it, is a "play of differences" such that "no element can function as a sign without referring to other elements" that are not themselves present, and every element is "constituted on the basis of the trace within it of the other elements of the chain."[13] Because the tissue of relations and differences inevitably leaves its trace in any signifier, we can never achieve simple univocity of meaning. Beyond any present meaning lies the absent, unspoken, unthought, indeed largely uncomprehended network of conditions, presuppositions, and mediations on which it depends. As a result, our meaning always escapes any unitary conscious grasp we may have of it, for language, as "writing," inevitably harbors the possibility of an endless "dissemination" of sense, an indefinite multiplicity of recontextualizations and reinterpretations.

Philosophy is a kind of writing that is essentially predicated on denying all of this, that attempts to uproot meaning from the "relational and differential tissue" in which it is always enmeshed.[14] Throughout its history it has tried one device after another to freeze the play of *différance*: ideal univocal meanings (Forms), an ultimate referent or "transcendental signified" (Being), clear and distinct ideas in self-conscious and self-transparent minds, absolute knowledge, the logical essence of language, and so on—all calculated to call a halt to the dissemination of meaning at the borders of this or that closed system of truth. But such closure is impossible; philosophy cannot transcend its medium. The claim to have done so always relies on ignoring, excluding, marginalizing, or assimilating whatever escapes the grids of intelligibility it imposes on the movement of *différance*. And this repression of what doesn't fit inevitably has its effects, in the forms of the paradoxes, internal contradictions, and systematic incoherencies, which it is the task of deconstructive analysis to bring to light. Its aim in doing so is not to produce a new and improved unified theory of the whole but ceaselessly to undermine the pretense to theoretical mastery, the illusion of a "pure" reason that can gain control over its own conditions, and the dream of a definitive grasp of basic meanings and truths. In short, "It inaugurates the destruction, not the demolition but the de-sedimentation, the deconstruction, of all the significations that have their source in that of the logos. Particularly the signification of *truth*."[15]

This kind of totalized critique of reason has to deal with the paradoxes of self-referentiality that inevitably follow in its wake. How does one deconstruct "all the significations that have their source in the logos," including that of "truth," without at the same time relying on them, at least tacitly? Derrida's response to this dilemma is his well-known "double gesture," combining, roughly, elements of internal and external critique. As his use of this strategy will figure in my remarks about deconstructionist poltical analysis, it will be worthwhile to get clearer here about what it involves. In "The Ends of Man" Derrida writes of "weaving and interlacing" two tactics: the first does not "change terrain" but turns "what is implicit in the founding concepts and the original problematic" against those very concepts and problematic; the second involves a "discontinuous" change of terrain, "placing oneself outside" of, and "affirming an absolute break" with, those concepts and problematic.[16] When the terrain in question is Western logocentrism, the idea of an absolute break is an illusion, for "the simple practice of language ceaselessly reinstates the new terrain on the oldest ground."[17] On the other hand, the first tactic, that of internal critique, has been that of the philosophical tradition, in which each generation of thinkers uncovers and criticizes the presuppositions of the previous generation. "Here, one risks ceaselessly confirming, consolidating, relifting (*relever,* the word Derrida uses to translate Hegel's *aufheben*), at an always more certain depth, that which one allegedly deconstructs."[18] Hence, the appropriate strategy is a "double writing," which combines both internalist and externalist tactics.

If deconstruction is to get a critical purchase on the system it targets, it cannot simply junk the concepts basic to the latter but has to "transform" or "displace" them. The danger in this is that any use of a concept "necessarily assumes, in a non-critical way, at least some of the implications inscribed in its system."[19] The trick, then, is to overturn established conceptual oppositions and hierarchies through patient analysis while *simultaneously* releasing new concepts "that can no longer be and never could be included in the previous regime," thereby "disorganizing the entire inherited order and invading the entire field."[20] I am not interested here in deciding whether this strategy suceeds vis-à-vis the philosophical tradition as a whole, but only in weighing its advantages and disadvantages as a way of thinking about politics.[21] For that purpose, however, we have to understand why Derrida is convinced that deconstructing philosophical concepts and problematics is of decisive poltical import. In what sense is deconstruction itself political intervention?

Despite his own qualifications and the heated denials of his defenders, there can be no doubt that Derrida considers philosophy to be, in Rorty's words, "at the heart of Western culture."[22] In passage after passage he treats it as coconstitutive of Western science and scholarship, language and literature, politics and society, ethnocentrism and imperialism. Thus, for example, he writes that the "metaphysics of phonetic writing" that "always assigned the origin of truth in general to the logos" is "nothing but the most original and powerful ethnocentrism, in the process of imposing itself on the world."[23] The concept of science "has always been a philosophical concept."[24] And there is an "a priori link" between "the essence of the philosophical and the essence of the political."[25] Deconstruction, as a "simultaneously faithful and violent circulation between the inside and the outside of philosophy—*that is of the West*," enables us "to read philosophemes—and *consequently all the texts of our culture*—as kinds of symptoms."[26] He is not referring here only to philosophy's permeation of high culture. Everyday language is also "the language of Western metaphysics," bearing within it "presuppositions inseparable from metaphysics," which are "knotted into a system."[27] It is just this system that is trembling today, and "this trembling is played out in the violent relationships of the whole West to its other," where military and economic violence is "in structural solidarity with 'linguistic' violence."[28]

It is not surprising, on this view, that "what has seemed necessary and urgent to [Derrida], in the historical situation which is our own, is a general determination of the conditions for the emergence and limits of philosophy, of metaphysics, of everything that carries it on and that it carries on."[29] Nor is it surprising that critics should find this estimation of the importance of metaphysics in our culture an overestimation—influenced, perhaps, by Heidegger's view of the modern world. Of course, Heidegger did not articulate his weltanschauung *explicitly* in political terms.[30] But the wholesale rejection of Western rationalism was given a sociopolitical articulation by Max Horkheimer and Theodor Adorno at about the same time.[31] As the dreams of bourgeois culture turned into the nightmare of National Socialism, it was difficult for them to resist Nietzsche's judgment that "nihilism represents the ultimate logical conclusion of our great values and ideas." Western reason, they came to agree, had been from the start keyed to mastery and control. This was true of "enlightened" reason as well; the "dialectic of enlightenment" consumed even the "critical" reason developed from Kant through Marx. In his later philosophy Adorno elaborated this skeptical view of reason into a "negative dialectics" that repeatedly displayed the coercion and distortion at the heart of what passes for reason, the nonidentical in every claimed identity, without offering any positive account of his own: to do so would be only to encourage further the illusion that the truth can be found in theory.

There are more than superficial affinities between Adorno's negative dialectics and Derrida's deconstruction.[32] Like Adorno, Derrida has been characterized as a "post-Holocaust philosopher."[33] And in an interview published in 1983, he does indicate that his youthful experience of Fascism profoundly affected his view of the world.[34] But my topic here is not how Derrida came to his weltanschauung, nor whether he (or Adorno's) life experience gives him (or Adorno) more of a "right" to it than, say, Heidegger. What is at issue is its translation into a philosophicopolitical program. The broad outlines of that program seem clear enough. It can be summed up, very roughly, in the following points, which I tendentiously refer to as Derrida's "Theses on Heidegger."

• "Logocentrism in its developed philosophical sense is inextricably linked to the Greek and European tradition"; it is a "specifically Western response to a much larger necessity" (the structural lure of phonocentrism) that exists in other cultures as well but did not develop into a systematic, logocentric metaphysics in any non-European culture.[35]

• The dominance of "the principle of reason" that marks the modern West is rooted in that original metaphysical response: "Not only does that principle constitute the verbal formulation of a requirement present since the dawn of Western science and philosophy, it provides the impetus for a new era of purportedly 'modern' reason, metaphysics, and technoscience."[36]

• The form this takes is an "interpretation of the essence of beings as objects . . . placed and positioned before a subject . . . who says I, an ego certain of itself, [who] thus ensures his own technical mastery over the totality of what is" (pp. 9–10).

• Progress in the natural and social sciences cannot deliver us from metaphysics, for "philosophy, as logocentrism, is present in every scientific discipline."[37] In particular, the post-Marxian idea of radicalizing the critique of reason by drawing upon the historical and human sciences makes no sense, for these disciplines themselves are "founded on a logocentric philosophical discourse and remain inseparable from it."[38] Consequently, "they never touch upon that which, in themselves, continues to be based on the principle of reason" (p. 16).

• The general "informatization" of knowledge in the present age, which is the culmination of the "original intermingling of the metaphysical and the technical," makes the principle of reason a principle of "integral calculability" (p. 14). It is this total subjection to the "informative and instrumental value of language" that lies behind the "finalization" or "ends orientation" of scientific and scholarly research in all advanced industrial societies: "We know better than ever what must have been true for all time. . . . One can no longer distinguish between technology, on the one hand, and theory, science, and rationality, on the other. The term techno-science has to be accepted" (p. 12).

• The ends orientation built into research in all disciplines—from psychology, biology, and telecommunications to linguistics, hermeneutics, and literature—ultimately serves the interests of the "defensive and offensive security establishment"—the military, the state, and the economy (pp. 13–14). The logocentric metaphysics underlying that technoscience also structures our poltical codes themselves. Its core assumptions are "common to the axiomatics of numerous (perhaps even all) politics in the West, whether of the right or of the left"[39] It is thus internally connected to the violence and repression that mark the history of the West.

• These same factors shape the relations of the West to the non-Western world. Thus, for example, one can view South Africa as a giant screen onto which "Europe, in the enigmatic process of its globalization and of its pradoxical disappearance," projects "the silhouette of its internal war, the bottom line of its profits and loses, the double-bind logic of its national and multinational interests."[40]

• The only way to counter this fateful dispensation is to "think" ourselves beyond the principle of reason. This thought would "unmask—an infinite task—all the ruses of ends-orienting reason," including those of philosophy as it is conventionally practiced (p. 16). It would "raise questions at the level of the foundation or non-foundation of the foundation," not merely by posing "questions that one formulates while submitting oneself . . . to the principle of reason," but also by "preparing oneself thereby to transform the modes of writing" (p. 17). It would, in short, deploy the deconstructionist double gesture: "'Thought' requires both the principle of reason and what is beyond the principle of reason"; between the two "only the enactment of this 'thought' can decide" (p. 19).

• Interrogating the principle of reason, questioning "its meaning, its origin, its possibility, its goal, its limits," leaves us "suspended above a most peculiar void," for a principle of grounding cannot ground itself (p. 9). Thus the practice of deconstruction is risky; "it always risks the worst" (p. 19), but this is "the risk of the future itself" (p. 17). In taking it, one is "playing off one risk against another," the abyss against the barrier (p. 17). The "decision" to do so "exceeds the calculable program that would destroy all responsibility by transforming it into a programmable effect"; it is a "trial and a passage by way of the undecidable," a "response" to a "call," a "new way of taking responsibility."[41]

• The politics of deconstruction is rooted in this response to the call of the other that has been repressed and denied by Western logocentrism: "The rapport of self-identity is itself always a rapport of violence with the other," so that "the notions . . . central to logocentric metaphysics are essentially dependent on an opposition with otherness."[42] More precisely, deconstruction counteracts the "politics of language" that conceals practices of exclusion, repression, marginalization, and assimilation behind the apparent neutrality of "purely theoretical" discourses. Its effects, however, are not confined to language, but "touch all the social institutions. . . . More generally, it touches everything, quite simply everything."[43] Striving to weaken the hegemony of logocentrism for a future deconstruction can neither define nor predict, it is a kind of "responsible anarchy" that serves as "a political ferment or anxiety, a subversion of fixed assumptions and a privileging of disorder."[44]

• The philosophers have only *interpreted* the logos in various ways. The point, however, is to *deconstruct* it.

2

In the second section of this paper I want to examine in more detail the type of political theory and practice that result from Derrida's interrogation of the reason of reason. Are the methods he developed for dealing with questions of language and meaning adequate to moral, social, and political questions? Is it, for instance, merely by accident that his writings contain little analysis of political institutions and arrangements, historical circumstances and tendencies, or social groups and social movements, and no constructions of right and good, justice and fairness, legitimacy and legality? Or is it the case, as Nancy

Fraser has put it, that the politics of deconstruction amounts to little more than the deconstruction of politics?[45]

Derrida's deconstructionism is generally taken to be a skeptical enterprise, a perception nurtured, no doubt, by his characterizations of it. To deconstruct, he has told us, is to "desediment," "destabilize," "uproot," and "overturn" inherited concepts and schemes, "to turn them against their own presuppositions," to "loosen," "undo," "decompose," and "dismantle" them. Questions can be raised about the self-sufficiency of any such wholesale attack on "logocentrism." These questions become all the more pressing in the domains of ethics and politics, for social life cannot be organized solely around the dismantling of graven images. Deconstructive practices seem here to be necessarily complementary to practices of constructing and reconstructing the ideals, norms, principles, laws, and institutions we live by. Thus the more Derrida has insisted on the practical-political import of deconstruction, the more he has been confronted with the objection that it has little to offer in the way of positive ethicopolitical proposals. His standard responses to this objection have not been convincing.[46] If we allow ourselves to be guided by his dictum that deconstruction "'is' only what it does and what is done with it,"[47] we can scarcely avoid the conclusion that it is largely inconoclastic.

The "ethico-political impulse" behind this practice has been interpreted as a commitment to bear witness to the other of Western rationalism: to what has been subordinated in hierarchical orderings, excluded in the drawing of boundaries, marginalized in identifying what is central, homogenized or colonized in the name of the universal.[48] On this reading, deconstruction constantly reminds us that rationalism's constitutive assumption of the fundamental intelligibility of experience and reality has underwritten a history of repression in theory and practice—the repression of the other in nature, in ourselves, in other persons and other peoples. As the bad conscience of an imperialistic logocentrism, deconstruction speaks on behalf of what doesn't fit into our schemes and patiently advocates letting the other be in its otherness. There is undoubtedly something to this reading, but even so, deconstruction can hardly give voice to the excluded other. The wholesale character of its critique of logocentrism deprives it of any language in which to do so. Nonetheless, Derrida apparently wants to have it both ways: to undermine all logocentric concepts and yet to continue to use them for his own purposes. The tactic of using them "under erasure" strikes me as less like being "suspended over an abyss" than like trying to be on both sides of a fence.

We can see how this works in the domain of ethicopolitical analysis by looking at "The Laws of Reflection: Nelson Mandela, in Admiration."[49] All of the analytical and critical work is done via "logocentric" concepts and norms, from which Derrida is at the same time obliged to distance himself. Despite his repeated cautions to the reader, one can't help but notice that he has no other means for conveying the power of Mandela's witness than those same concepts and norms. Mandela is said to have turned "the very logic of the law" against those who wrongfully and scornfully usurped it, to have revealed something in the law that they concealed behind legality, to have brought its true force to bear against them. Derrida is aware that these types of critique are not discontinuous with, but dependent upon Enlightenment conceptions. He brings undecidability into the picture after the feast, as it were, when he raises, without answering, the question of whether Mandela has "let himself be caputed . . . in the view of the West" or rather bears a "promise of what has not yet ever been seen or heard."[50] However, the "promise" is itself identified in terms of a traditional notion of "conscience": it arises from placing "respect for the law which speaks immediately to conscience" above "submission to positive law."[51] The residual undecidability amounts, it seems, to nothing more than our inability to say today how Mandela will be understood in the future.[52] But we do not need the apparatus of deconstruction to make us aware of that.

Consider now a somewhat different case. When Anne McClintock and Rob Nixon criticized Derrida's analysis of apartheid in "Racism's Last Word," his response was laced with appeals to just the sorts of concepts, norms, and standards that he has elsewhere undercut.[53] Presented with this apparent inconsistency, Derrida has responded that it was never his intention to put such concepts as truth, reference, and the stability of interpretive contexts radically into question; rather, he wanted to explore the conditions of their possibility and to show that they are guaranteed never absolutely but only in "pragmatically determined situations."[54] It was, he tells us, only because he considered the context of the apartheid discussion to be pragmatically stable in that sense, that he felt free to appeal to demonstrable ties between words and things and to the difference between true and false. Indeed, he asserts that no research is possible without some "minimal consensus" (p. 146) and that "norms of minimal intelligibility" belong to the requirements of all culture (p. 147). In particular, all "conceptual production," including his own, inevitably involves certain idealizations (p. 117), and this "structural idealism" underlies classical logic and scientific truth (p. 120). The deconstructionist point is only that whatever has been constructed is deconstructible (p. 147), that every contextualization is open to recontextualization (p. 136). There are, he allows, cultural and institutional contexts that exhibit great stability, so great as to appear natural and immutable, but such stabilization is always relative: "The norms of minimal intelligibility are not absolute and ahistorical, but merely more stable than others. They depend upon socio-institutional conditions, hence upon non-natural relations of power that by essence are mobile and founded upon complex conventional structures that in principle may be analyzed, deconstructed, and transformed" (p. 147). The values of "objectivity" and "truth," for instance, "impose" themselves "within a context which is extremely vast, old, powerfully established, stabilized or rooted in a network of conventions (for instance, those of language), and yet still remain a context" (p. 136).

With these remarks Derrida heads in the direction of a pragmatist account of language. The big divide, it seems to me, comes with the negative slant he gives to his recognition of the pragmatic presuppositions of meaning: whatever has been constructed can be deconstructed, destabilized, recontextualized, and so on. True enough, but by the same token, it can also be reconstructed, reformed, renewed, and so forth. Derrida rarely mentions this side of the ledger. His fixation on metaphysics and the pressing need he sees to battle its ideal essences at every turn divert his attention and energies from the real tasks of postmetaphysical thought. The insight that "one cannot do anything, least of all speak, without determining (in a manner that is not only theoretical, but practical and performative) a context" is hardly new (p. 136). Nor is the idea that this signals the end of a certain type of metaphysical thinking. But rather than meditating at the edge of the abyss, pragmatically inclined thinkers try to reconstruct the notions of reason, truth, objectivity, and the like in nonfoundationalist terms. The recognition of the social-practical basis of language and meaning seems to them too to point toward an ethicopolitical thematization of what were traditionally regarded as "purely theoretical" questions. But that project has a positive as well as a negative side. Some of the "vast, old" contexts Derrida remarks on are as old as the human race; others arose historically, but in such a manner as to render alternatives less and less desirable or even possible; others are determined by cultural consensuses that are indeed contingent and particular but that there are good reasons to defend; and, of course, many others are based on relations of force that are disguised by talk of reason, truth, objectivity, and the like—but why suppose all are?

It seems to be an axiom of Derrida's deconstructionism that "norms of minimal intelligibility" always depend upon "nonnatural relations of power" (p. 147) and any determination of context involves "force or irreducible violence" (p. 137). But to use "power," "force," and "violence" in this way—to cover everything from mutual agreement and negotiated compromise to false consciousness and open repression—is to lose sight of all of the differentiations so crucial to social and political theory.[55] It is also to abandon entirely *the participant's point of view* for that of the observer as critic. As participants in social life, we cannot avoid meeting what Derrida refers to as "the minimal requirements of culture." We have to undertake certain idealizations, share certain presuppositions, follow certain rules, be bound by certain norms, and so on. We can and, of course, should interrogate the limits of these undertakings, but not exclusively or at least not without ceasing to be participants:

irony too has its limits. As reflective participants, we can also seek to expand the cooperative bases of our lives together and to reduce the violence and coercion that critical discourse (of many different types) brings to light. To this constructive ethicopolitical task, deconstruction has little to contribute. It produces not pragmatic conceptualizations "for all practical purposes" but constant reminders of the groundlessness of all our basic schemes. This is the reaction, it seems to me, of a disappointed metaphysician still under the sway of the archopposition: all or nothing. The same can be said of Derrida's tendency to hypostatize this lack of ultimate foundations into a *différance* prior not only to subject and object but to all of the oppositions basic to logocentrism, prior even to the distinctions between identity and nonidentity, sameness and difference.[56]

Be that as it may, the deconstruction of our logocentric culture leaves Derrida with nothing substantive to say—at least not without an ironic reminder that he couldn't possibly have meant it. In regard specifically to politics, it places him in the awkward position described in the lines quoted at the start of this essay. Because "all our political codes and terminologies still remain fundamentally metaphysical" on his account, if he wants to express himself politically at all, he has to do so in codes that are incommensurate with his intellectual project. Whenever he does so, however, he must at the same time mark his distance and suspicion with regard to them. The effects of this strategy—wholesale subversion, with no suggestion of remedies or alternatives, combined with a measure of ironic use—are largely skeptical, all assurances to the contrary notwithstanding. To play the skeptic in ethical-political matters is, of course, to adopt an ethicopolitical stance. The warrant for this in Derrida's case seems to be the same sort of pessimistic diagnosis of the modern world that one finds in Hiedegger. If Western reason is in the end nothing more than subjectification and objectification in the service of domination, then some form of *Abbau,* or deconstruction, seems a more appropriate response than any form of *Umbau,* or reconstruction. But this argument supposes that a particular interpretation of Western history, culture, society, politics, technology, etc.—and a very global and undifferentiated one at that—is the correct one, or at least that it is superior to competing interpretations—such as those of Marx, Weber, Durkheim, and Habermas, for example—that stress the ambivalence of rationalization processes, their amalgamation of undeniable achievements and palpable distortions, of growing emancipation and expanded domination. I am arguing that Derrida has in effect deprived himself of the means he needs to enter into that debate. Here I want to note that the poltical stakes between the competing interpretations are quite high. In their various cultural and institutional forms, expectations of reason and truth also play a moderating role in the conduct of social life. Drawing boundaries and setting limits are often what is needed to achieve a common purpose.[57] And while it is necessary to interrogate and revise received notions of liberty, equality, justice, rights, and the like, to disassemble them without reassembling would be to rob excluded, marginalized, and oppressed groups of an important recourse. In short, undercutting the appeal to reason, truth, and justice as presently "coded," without offering alternatives, may harbor not so much the "promise" of a better world as the "danger" of some "monstrous mutation."[58]

Derrida holds the view that an author or signatory must accept responsibility for the effects of his or her text.[59] Thus it is fair to ask Derrida what effects he anticipates for his own texts or, since the effects of a critical practice will be different in different historical situations, what analysis of our contemporary situation lies behind his own estimation of the effects of deconstructionist practice. And what is the evaluative perspective from which he judges those effects to be good? Because of his devaluation of empirical and normative social analysis, we are unlikely to get from him anything more than broad hints regarding our present ills and their possible remedies. But a general reminder of the myriad forms of violence that have accompanied the march of the universal through history is not a sufficient basis for restructuring politics and society. It is sheer romanticism to suppose that uprooting and destabilizing universalist structures will of itself lead to letting the other be, in respect and freedom, rather than to intolerant and aggressive particularism, a war of all against all in which the fittest survive and the most powerful dominate. Enlarging the social space in which otherness can be, establishing and maintaining a multifarious and spacious pluralism, seem, on the contrary, to require that we inculcate universal principles of tolerance and respect and stabilize institutions that secure rights and impose limits. Otherwise, how is the tolerance of difference to be combined with the requirements of living *together* under *common* norms? And in justifying such norms, is there any alternative superior to free and open discussion of matters of public interest? Repeated attacks on the metaphysics of presence, incessant reminders of our finitude, do not at all obviate these familiar questions from political theory. Having placed himself beyond all existing codes, however, Derrida is in no position to answer them.

This is the critical point. As I noted in section 1, Derrida considers all specialized modes of inquiry to be permeated with metaphysics. And it is this "logocentrism present in every scientific discipline" that, in his view, accounts for the complicity of science in the history of Western domination. With this more or less Heideggerian *Zeitdiagnose*, it is perfectly comprehensible that what seems "necessary and urgent to [him], in the historical situation which is our own," is a general deconstruction of philosophy. This diagnosis and the strategy it dictates rest on some rather questionable assumptions. It is, writes Habermas, "as if we were living in the shadow of the 'last' philosophers, as were the first generation of Hegelian disciples," so that we must still battle "against the 'strong' concepts of theory, truth, and system," which have actually "belonged to the past for over a century and a half," for "the fallibilist consciousness of science caught up with philosophy, too, a long time ago."[60]

Derrida has all along insisted on the secondary, derivative status of "scientificity," "objectivity," and "historicity" in relation to *différance* or archewriting: "The very idea of science was born in a certain epoch of writing"; writing is "the condition of possibility of ideal objects and therefore of scientific objectivity"; historicity too is "tied to the possibility of writing," which "opens the field of history." Consequently, "the science of writing should look for its object at the roots of scientificity. The history of writing should turn back toward the origin of historicity."[61] Peter Dews has noted how Derrida adopted from

Husserl the priority of phenomenlogical over empirical inquiry, detranscendentalized it, and made it central to his intellectual project.[62] Like Husserl, Derrida rejected the penetration of the human sciences into the foundational domain reserved to philosophy. When he distanced himself from Husserl's subjectivism, he did so not by moving "downstream towards an account of subjectivity as emerging from and entwined with the natural and historical world," as, say, Merleau-Ponty did, but by moving further "upstream in a quest for the ground of transcendental consciousness itself."[63] The result was to withdraw philosophical thought from the sorts of interdependence with empirical research that it has entered into since Hegel. Deconstruction "cannot learn from its objects, but occupies a position of superior insight. . . . In this way the successor to philosophy continues to evade the exposure of thought to the contingency of interpretation and the revisability of empirical knowledge. But this then raises the question of whether it might not be possible to think the end of metaphysics in a different way—precisely in terms of this exposure."[64]

Derrida continues to pose the issue in terms of a choice between deconstruction and naive objectivism.[65] What gets obscured by this binary opposition are all the nonobjective—e.g., hermeneutical, critical, interpretive, and reconstructive—forms of historical, social, and cultural inquiry that developed alongside of and against positivism and have enjoyed something of a renaissance in recent years. The inadequacy of this oppositional scheme has been registered even within central domains of philosophical inquiry. We have, for example, abandoned the idea of constructing a "logic" of science before and independently of the history and sociology of science. The idea of "deducing" the "essence of the political" before and independently of substantive historical studies is even less plausible. Nancy Fraser has shown how the attempt of French Derrideans to do that—to interrogate philosophically the "constitution and institution of the political (le politique) in Western culture" in a way that was prior yet relevant to politics (la politique)—inevitably came apart from its own inner tensions. Their hope that metapolitical, philosophical reflection could itself produce relevant political insights and thus obviate a need for entering into empirical, normative, and critical debates at the level of politics landed them on the horns of a dilemma: "Either they will try to maintain the rigorous exclusion of politics, and especially of empirical and normative considerations—in which case the political import of their philosophical work will diminish. Or they will cross the line and enter upon concrete political reflection—in which case their work will become increasingly *contested.*"[66]

Derrida's "Politics of Friendship," a text devoted to interrogating *le politique,* shows him to be caught in the same dilemma. It is no accident that he singles out from Carl Schmitt's work the latter's discussion of "the concept of the political" and ignores Schmitt's substantive (and rather unfortunate) views on political institutions, arrangements, and tendencies.[67] It is a commonplace of Schmitt scholarship that his *politics* had a decisive influence on his concept of *the political.* The shift from his early more or less neo-Kantian outlook to his later rather Hobbesian views of human nature and the state, for example, seems to have been infleunced by his views on the history and future of the nation-state and his diagnosis of the post–World War I situation in Germany. A parallel case could be made concerning Heidegger's reflections on the essence of the political.[68] And as I have suggested in section 1, concerning Derrida's as well. Large-scale sociopolitical views and analyses of our present situation are not the special province of philosophical insight. They have to be entered into discursive competition with other accounts, some of which have the virtue of laying their empirical, theoretical, and normative cards on the table for everyone to see and challenge.

The methodological ill effects of Derrida's withdrawal from the specificity of politics and of empirical social research are evident in "The Politics of Friendship." His derivation of "the poltical itself" via a "thinking of *différance*" centers around a "grammar of the response," which, while based on French usage, is, he conjectures, "translatable into the set of European languages," though not perhaps into every language.[69] This, he suggests, will provide a key to "our concept of responsibility."[70] In the same spirit he tells us that Aristotle's whole discourse on friendship is a discourse on language, on the word *philia,* its uses, contexts, etc.[71] But Aristotle could draw upon his reflective participant's understanding of Greek culture and society in fashioning his discourse. If we want now to understand *philia,* we have not just to read Aristotle's texts but to become students of that culture and society, its patterns of interpretation and interaction, its traditions and institutions, its class, race, and gender divisions, and so on. But then we will discover that many of the uses and contexts of key Greek moral and political terms are foreign to us precisely because we no longer live in the world of the *polis.* This awareness may well lead us to wonder how our own grammar of responsibility is interwoven with the fabric of our culture and society, and we may then become interested in historical studies that throw light on the circumstances in which that grammar arose, developed, and was stabilized, or in comparative studies, based on ethnographic materials, which could throw light on the advantages and disadvantages of our own understandings by presenting us with alternatives from other cultures. We might do this partly in the hermeneutic spirit of participating in the conversation of humankind and partly in the critical spirit of unmasking the play of power and interest in and around our received notions of responsibility. The point here is simply that the notion of a "grammar" of responsibility is at best an airy abstraction from the historical, comparative, and critical inquiries relevant to comprehending and assessing the structures of social practice in which that grammar is embedded. It is these inquiries and not that grammar that should serve as the basis for our social and political theorizing. Fraser quotes Gayatri Spivak as calling for a decentering of deconstruction that would open it up to ethical-political contingency.[72] I would add only that this entails an opening to all the modes of inquiry developed to study that contingency and hence to the procedures of evidence, argument, and criticism that they involve.

This is not what we find in Derrida's deduction of the political via the thinking of *différance.* In a manner reminiscent of Heidegger's "essential thinking," his approach devalues the usual procedure of empirical and normative inquiry as being, one and all, shot through with the metaphysics of presence. Their place is taken by the deconstructive reading of selected texts, in this case "the great philosophical and canonical discourses on friendship."[73] To be sure, Derrida at the same time distances himself from the notion of a "canon," but the canon performs its usual functions. One might well ask why a reading of Aristotle, Montaigne, Nietzsche, Schmitt, Heidegger, and Blanchot on friendship should serve as the basis for "thinking the essence of the political" or even of friendship. Why not some other selection of classical texts? Why not discourses that never achieved classical status for a variety of reasons? Why confine oneself to analyzing discourse in the first place? To the charge of "textual idealism" Derrida's standard response has been that his infamous dictum "There is nothing outside the text" refers not to books and the like but to "con-texts," to "the entire 'real-history-of-the-world'"; it does not, then, "suspend reference to history, to the world, to reality, to being."[74] The question at this point is whether he draws the appropriate *methodological* conclusions from this. If attending to con-text is compatible with approaching political theory via a deconstructive reading of selected texts, it is difficult to see how it constitutes a response to the charge of "textualism."[75] The only effective response would be to make "the real history of the world," in the form of the vast array of materials generated by studying it, figure prominently in one's thinking about politics.

The normative implications of Derrida's approach are no less problematic than the methodological. "No politics without *différance*," he declares.[76] One might say as well say, No politics without language. But it is obvious that the latter declaration points us in no *particular* direction, whereas Derrida asserts that *différance* points us in the direction of democracy. He hastens to add, however, that this is a "democracy to come" and "not the one we think we know." It is, rather, a democracy beyond "formality" and "calculable relations." I think it is fair to ask for more specificity before setting our sights beyond any known ethicopolitical horizon in this way. What sorts of social, political, legal, economic institutions of democracy does he see superseding those we have experienced or imagined? What replacements does he envision for received notions of rights, justice, tolerance, respect and other such "edifying humanist" conceptions? Derrida does not attempt to satisfy us on such matters, nor is he likely to do so. As we have seen, deconstruction aims at "a language and a political practice that can no longer be comprehended, judged, deciphered by [existing] codes." In view of this ambition, in what terms could he possibly discuss the new order of things? Although he explicitly eschews any idea of a radical break, the politics of friendship gestures toward a transformation so radical that we cannot say anything about what lies beyond it. I have found nothing in Derrida's writings to persuade me that his quasi-apocalyptic, near-prophetic mode of discourse about politics should displace the more prosaic modes available or constructible in our tradition.[77] Even if his heart is in the right place and even if his "anarchy" is meant to be "responsible," we know from experience that the devaluation of these modes opens a space, or rather creates a vacuum, that can be filled in quite different ways, for instance, by Heidegger's call for submission to some indeterminate authority.

Derrida's discourse, it seems to me, lives from the enormous elasticity, not to say vagueness and ambiguity, of his key terms.[78] In the case at hand, much of what he says about "minimal friendship," the "friendship prior to friendship," makes sense only if friendship is roughly equivalent to social interaction, viewed from a perspective that highlights allocution and response.[79] On the other hand, his quasi-normative deployment of friendship in relation to politics—for example, in the idea that the democracy to come should, as he put it, no longer be an insult to friendship but should rather be a respectful test of it—makes sense only if "friendship" signifies some yet to be specified ideal of true friendship, which, as he uses it, has to be higher than any "political friendship" or concord.[80] If the "allocution" involved in minimal friendship, as minimal community, refers to modes of address and response constitutive of "being together" socially at all, it is doubtful that it can bear the freight of the apostrophe "O my friends" as set forth earlier in the paper.[81] Rather, the structure of what Derrida calls "waiting, promise, or commitment" seems to have been imported into the ontology from a normative perspective, which is then said to be founded upon it. The figures of recall and appeal, memory and waiting, community and commitment are, of course, familiar from our religious tradition, especially when they are connected, as they are by Derrida, to "infinite heterogeneity" and "infinite alterity."[82] At one point he asks, "And what politics could one found upon this friendship which exceeds the measure of man, without becoming a theologem?" To that question I can find no answer in his work.[83]

Postscript

The Politics of Friendship

A general question raised by Derrida's "The Politics of Friendship" is how best to be postmetaphysical in thinking about ethics, law, and politics.[1] Is it by pursuing a deconstructionist strategy that remains at the level of metaphysics in order to disrupt and displace it? I have argued against that approach and want here only to add a brief suggestion of another reading of the phenomena Derrida alludes to: a reading drawing on just those domains of social research and practical philosophy that as Derrida notes, Heidegger devalued in relation to ontology (p. 637, n. 5).

We become individuals in and through being socialized into shared forms of life. In this sense, "the Other" does indeed "come before autonomy" (p. 634). Because we become who we are by growing into a network of social relations, we are always "already caught up in . . . a curvature of social space" (p. 633). This is, however, "prior to any organized *socius*" (pp. 633–634) only in the sense that the lifeworld is prior to formal law and formally organized spheres of life. But everyday life is itself highly organized and structured, and it is our shared understanding of its structures that informs the normative expectations we bring to social situations. To pick up on Derrida's example (p. 633), it is our knowledge of what it means to be invited to address a scholarly organization, to assemble for that purpose, to present a formal response to a paper, etc. that informs what we do in that situation. We orient our behavior to these shared schemes of interpretation and expectation, mutually attributing understanding of them to one another and holding one another responsible in terms of them. In short, at the level of our everyday interactions we normally believe ourselves to be, and take others as being, knowledgeable subjects confronted by real choices, for which we and they will be held accountable.

But this means that the network of reciprocally connected and temporally generalized expectations that Mead called *the generalized other* has a mechanism for individuation built right into it. It is the individual actor who must "answer to the other," must meet or fail to meet the other's expectations in more or less standard or novel ways, who can answer yes or no to the claims made by others to and upon him or her. Thus, it is not only in friendship but also in social interaction generally that the "singularity of the other" is intimately interconnected with the "generality of the law" (p. 641), in the sense of generalized normative expectations. And though the individual is related "asymmetrically" to the *generalized* other, which is always "anterior," the socially generalized patterns of behavior that the latter comprises are themselves typically structured as relations of reciprocity with *individual* others: the actor is entitled to expect certain kinds of behavior from others in certain situations and is obligated in turn to meet their legitimate expectations. Moreover, we are typically expected to justify behavior that deviates from what is legitimately expected. From this perspective, what is built into "the sharing of a language" and "being together" is not so much a "minimal friendship" (p. 636) as a minimal ethics of reciprocity and accountability. Moreover, inasmuch as individuation and socialization are two aspects of the same process, personal identity is interwoven with a fabric of relations of mutual recognition. This brings with it a reciprocal vulnerability that calls for guarantees of mutual consideration to preserve both the integrity of individuals and the web of interpersonal relations in which they form and stabilize their identities. Both of these concerns—with the dignity and inviolability of the person and with the good of the community as a whole—have been at the heart of traditional moralities. It is our intuitive grasp of the minimal ethics built into the structure of social interaction and of the complementary role played

by morality that philosophical eithics seeks reflectively to articulate, refine, and elaborate.

In the Kantian tradition, equal respect has been tied to autonomy—the freedom of moral subjects to act upon laws they
themselves accept as binding on the basis of their own insight—
and concern for the common good has been tied to the impartiality of laws that could be accepted by everyone on that
basis. Contemporary neo-Kantians typically retain this dual
thrust but shift the frame of reference from Kant's solitary
reflecting moral consciousness to the community of moral subjects in dialogue. In Habermas's discourse ethics, for example,
whether a norm is justified cannot be determined monologi-
cally but only by discursively testing its claim to be justified
through the informed, uncoerced, reasoned agreement of
those affected by it. In this representation of the moral point
of view, equal respect for individuals is reflected in the requirement of rationally motivated agreement, where each has the
right to respond with a yes or no to the reasons offered by way
of justification; concern for the common good is reflected in
the requirement of general and reciprocal perspective taking,
where in seeking mutual agreement, each attempts to get beyond the egocentric viewpoint by taking the situations of others
into account and giving them weight equal to his or her own.
This is, of course, a highly idealized account of moral and legal
relations, and so it is meant to be. In the Kantian tradition,
regulative ideas are marked by the same sort of "promise,"
"commitment," and "responsibility to the future" that Derrida
sees in the notion of "friendships that are 'the most perfect of
their kind'" (p. 636). Though never fully actual, regulative
ideas are nonetheless actually effective in structuring our practices—in guiding our efforts to fashion just laws and institutions, in shaping our perceptions and criticisms of injustice,
and so forth.[2]

As this brief sketch of an alternative to "the politics of friendship" suggests, the "curvature of social space" is not only "asymmetrical and heteronomical" (p. 633); "originary sociality" is
also marked by relations of symmetry, reciprocity, and mutual
recognition. Mastering such relations belongs to the repertoire
of competent social actors, e.g., to the competence to play social

roles of any sort, and this entails an intuitive mastery of the rudiments of the moral point of view. It is true that general norms justified from the standpoint of impartial judgment will require abstracting from the concrete circumstances of specific cases and in this sense will necessarily be unheeding of difference and in violation of singularity. But it should also be noted that the point of view of fairness is at the same time respectful of the other and tolerant of difference; it functions precisely to place limits on egocentric violations of the other by forcing a decentering of perspective. Furthermore, the process of applying general norms *fairly* requires at least a partial reversal of the abstractions required to justify them, for example, by requiring attention to the specifics of individual cases to determine whether they are really alike in relevant respects.

Treating friendship as "a privileged place" for reflecting on law, morality, and politics (p. 638) can serve to remind us that universalizing theories of justice do not exhaust the domain of the ethical. But Derrida's basic motivation for taking it as paradigmatic lies elsewhere, I think, namely in the link he sees between "reciprocity" and the "homological, immanentist, and finitist" (p. 644) tendencies of Western logocentrism, whose dominance the practice of deconstruction is designed precisely to disrupt. In this context, friendship can serve as an allegory for what gets left out of totalizing systems of representation, for "heterogeneity, asymmetry, and infinity" (p. 644). The costs of approaching law by this route are very high, however; the "heteronomical" can appear to be its "very essence" (p. 634), and any attempt to name the law to be a violation of an ancient proscription.[3] I have wanted to suggest that a better way of being postmetaphysical in ethics, law, and politics is to stop doing metaphysics, even of a negative sort, when thinking about them. If we do that, talk of reciprocity, symmetry, mutual recognition, and the like will seem no longer to be a hybristic attempt to say the unsayable but rather a necessary effort to explicate the very ideas of respect, tolerance, and solidarity that antiuniversalist invocations of otherness and difference generally take for granted.

II

Reconstruction and Critical Theory

5

Reason and Rationalization: Habermas's "Overcoming" of Hermeneutics

The debate between Habermas and Gadamer in the late 1960s and early 1970s came to a provisional close on Habermas's side with a series of promissory notes.[1] While he agreed with Gadamer on the necessity for a *sinnverstehenden* access to social reality, he insisted that the interpretation of meaningful phenomena need not, indeed could not, be restricted to the type of dialogic understanding characteristic of the hermeneutic approach. He held out instead the possibility of a theoretically informed analysis of symbolically prestructured objects and events, which, by drawing on generalized empirical knowledge, would reduce the context dependency of understanding and leave room for both quasi-causal explanation and critique. The types of empirical-theoretical knowledge in question, he suggested, included

• a general theory of *communication* that would reconstruct the "universal-pragmatic infrastructure" of speech and action,

• a general theory of *socialization* in the form of a theory of the acquisition of communicative competence,

• a theory of *social systems* that would make it possible to grasp objective interconnections going beyond what was subjectively intended or expressly articulated in cultural traditions,

• a theory of *social evolution* that would make possible a systematic reconstruction of the historical situations of the interpreter (or critic) and the object of interpretation (or criticism).

In some ways this appeared to signal a break with Habermas's earlier program, which had stressed the historical and practical dimensions of a critical theory aimed at unmasking ideological distortions and promoting the realization of a just society.[2] And there is no doubt that the need to distance himself from hermeneutics once they had jointly dealt with their common positivist opponents did push him in a more emphatically theoretical direction. For philosophical hermeneutics stresses that the interpreter of social phenomena is always already a member of a life world and thus occupies a specific historical, social, and cultural position from which she tries to come to terms with the beliefs and practices of others. The understanding achieved is, as a result, inexorably situation-bound: an understanding from a point of view that is on the same level as what is understood. There are no privileged positions outside of or above history from which to view human life. And there is no such thing as *the* correct interpretation: "Each time will have to understand . . . in its own way. . . . One understands otherwise if one understands at all."[3] The interest behind hermeneutics is not an interest in bringing a certain object domain under theoretical control or submitting it to a critique of ideology; it is an interest in coming to an understanding though dialogue—with others in my own culture, with alien cultures, with the past—about the common concerns of human life. The social inquirer is not, as may be mistakenly supposed, a neutral observer, explainer, predicter, nor is she a sovereign critic who may safely assume her own cognitive or moral superiority. She is, however virtually, always also a partner in dialogue, a participant, even when observing or criticizing.

It was in part to contain what he saw as the relativistic implications of this and related views that Habermas stressed the need for a theoretically informed analysis of social phenomena. The fronts of the *Methodenstreit* in the theory of the human sciences had begun to shift. The positivist and empiricist views that had dominated the scene for so long were gradually yielding to the interpretative approaches they once barely tolerated.[4] Thus Wittgenstein's *Tractatus* gave way to his *Investigations* and thence to trenchant attacks by post-Wittgensteinians on the unity of scientific method. Husserl's transcendental phenomenology generated its detranscendentalized progeny as well: the phenomenological and ethnomethodological approaches to social inquiry flowing from Alfred Schutz and others and the interpretive, hermeneutic approaches inspired by Heidegger and Gadamer. In consequence of this shift, the universalism associated with the positivist emphasis on logic and mathematics, on universal laws and general theories, came increasingly under attack. A new front was forming along contextualist versus universalist lines. Fundamental challenges to the idea of a critical theory of society no longer came solely from the direction of positivism; more and more they issued from post-Heideggerian and post-Wittgensteinian streams of historicism and culturalism.

The theoretical approach to social inquiry that Habermas proposed did not, however, rest on a rejection of the detranscendentalization of philosophy since Kant. On the contrary, a central theme of *Knowledge and Human Interests* was precisely the progressive radicalization of epistemology that led to the idea of a theory of knowledge as social theory. Here and elsewhere Habermas traced the decline of the conception of the subject that had dominated modern philosophy from Descartes through Kant. He argued that the transformation in the course of the nineteenth century to a view of the subject of knowledge and action as inherently social, historical, embodied, and laboring relegated irretrievably to the past the idea of a presuppositionless "first philosophy," whether in ontological or epistemological guise. At the same time, however, he argued that the fall of the transcendental subject was not per se incompatible with salvaging certain of the universalistic claims of transcendental philosophy, though these would now have to be reformulated in conjunction with the human sciences. He hoped, in particular, to salvage by way of reconstruction Kant's claim that there are universal and unavoidable presuppositions of theoretical and practical reason, as well as his conception of *Mündigkeit*, autonomy and responsibility, as the essence of rational personality. But he also wanted, thinking here more with Hegel, to present a reconstructed conception of the *Bildungsprozesse*, the self-formative processes of the individual and the species that have rational autonomy as their telos, a kind of systematic history of reason.

In this essay I would like to examine the types of arguments that Habermas employs to make his case, to clarify their status, and to offer tentative evaluations of their philosophical cogency and empirical plausibility. Considerations of space will make it impossible to lay out the individual arguments in any detail.[5] Instead, I shall focus on the general strategy of argumentation that he pursues and the kinds of considerations to which he appeals so as to make clearer both what the force of his arguments would be if they were successful and the sorts of evidence that might count against them.

1 Variations on Kantian Themes

The Kantian aspect of Habermas's program might be represented as an analogue to the question, How is experience possible in general? The corresponding question for Habermas would then read, *Wie is Verständigung überhaupt möglich?* How is mutual understanding (among speaking and acting subjects) possible in general?[6] And just as Kant's analysis of the conditions of possibility of experience was at the same time an analysis of the object of experience, Habermas's investigation of the "general and unavoidable presuppositions of achieving understanding in language" is meant to elucidate the structures of communicative interaction itself.[7] Having said this, I should note that he explicitly distances himself from the claims and procedures of transcendental philosophy. His project is empirical not in the sense of the nomological sciences of nature but rather in the sense of the "reconstructive" approaches that have been developed above all in linguistics and cognitive developmental psychology.[8] As Habermas sees it, the basic idea behind this type of approach is that speaking and acting subjects know how to achieve, accomplish, perform, and produce a variety of things without explicitly adverting to, or being able to give an explicit account of, the structures, rules, criteria, schemata, and the like on which their performances rely. The aim of rational reconstruction is precisely to render explicit what underlies such practically mastered, pretheoretical know-how, the tacit knowledge that represents the subject's competence in a given domain. Thus it differs from hermeneutic understanding in that its goal is not a paraphrase or a translation of an originally unclear meaning but an explicit knowledge of the "deep" structures and rules, the mastery of which is implicit in the competence of a subject to generate meaningful symbolic configurations.

If the tacit, pretheoretical mastery to be reconstructed represents a universal know-how and not merely that of a particular individual, group or culture, the task becomes the reconstruction of a species competence. Such reconstructions can be compared in their scope and status with general theories (for example, of language or cognition). From another point of view, they can also be compared with Kant's transcendental logic. But the differences are critical here. Rational reconstructions of universal or species competences cannot make the strong a priori claims of the Kantian project. They are advanced in a hypothetical attitude and must be checked and revised in the light of the data, which are gathered a posteriori from the actual performances and considered appraisals of competent subjects. Any proposal must meet the empirical condition of conforming in a mass of crucial and clear cases to the intuitions of competent subjects, which function ultimately as the standard of accuracy.

Adopting this approach, Habermas advances a proposal for a universal or formal pragmatics, which is based on the idea that not only language (*langue*) but also speech (*parole*) admits of rational reconstruction in universal terms, that "communicative competence" has as universal a core as linguistic competence. The competence of the ideal speaker must be regarded as including not merely the ability to produce and understand grammatical sentences but also the ability to establish and understand those modes of communication and connections with the world through which speech becomes possible. Pragmatic rules for situating sentences in speech acts concern the relations to reality that accrue to a grammatically well-formed sentence in being properly uttered; they are general rules for arranging the elements of speech situations in relation to the external world of objects and events (about which one can make true or false statements), the inner world of my own experiences (which can be expressed sincerely or insincerely, authentically or inauthentically), and the social world of shared norms (with which an act can conform or fail to conform and which are themselves either right, i.e., justifiable, or wrong). From this pragmatic point of view it becomes clear that communication involves (even if often only implicitly) the raising, criticizing, and redeeming of validity claims, claims to the truth of statements, to the sincerity or authenticity of self-presentations, and to the rightness of actions and norms of action.

Habermas's analyses of communication focus on *verständigungsorientierte Sprechhandlungen,* i.e., on "pure" cases of communication oriented to reaching understanding in the following strong sense: "The goal of coming to an understanding (*Verständigung*) is to bring about an agreement (*Einverständnis*) that terminates in the intersubjective mutuality of reciprocal understanding, shared knowledge, mutual trust, and accord with one another. Agreement is based on recognition of the corresponding validity claims of comprehensibility, truth, truthfulness [or sincerity], and rightness."[9] It is obvious—and Habermas readily acknowledges the fact—that a great deal of everyday social interaction does not fit this idealized model. In addition to cases of overtly strategic and covertly manipulative interaction, of conscious deception and unconscious self-deception, of insincerity and inauthenticity, there is the whole range of interaction in which these and other elements are combined in a variety of ways to constitute the "organized artful practices of everyday life," "relations in public," "games people play," and the like, which have been so extensively studied in recent years. The point here is simply that if, as appears to be the case, instances of "pure" communicative action in Habermas's sense are, at least in many spheres of life, the exception and not the rule, there is the question of why the reconstruction of putatively "universal and unavoidable" structures of communication should start with this idealized case.[10]

In defense of his starting point, Habermas maintains that action oriented to reaching understanding is not just one type of social action among others but is "fundamental," in the sense that other forms of social action—e.g., conflict, competition, deception, manipulation—are "derivative" from it and have to be reconstructed as such.

The sphere of possible action does not coincide with the sphere of possible speech with a communicative intent. But I would like to reconstruct the universal conditions of employing language from the original mode thereof, . . . speech for the purpose of coming to an understanding. Wittgenstein was right to find fault with this way of putting it; it is not possible to define "speech" in terms of the purpose of achieving understanding, because one cannot explain what it is "to reach an understanding" if one does not know what it is "to speak." The telos of reaching understanding is inherent in the concept of speech. The class of actions with which I begin my analysis is not chosen arbitrarily; it is the class of those speech actions that are carried out in an attitude oriented to achieving understanding. We can construct the normative content of possible understanding by stating which universal presuppositions have to be met for understanding to be achieved in an actual case.[11]

In addition to such conceptual arguments, Habermas advances empirical-theoretical considerations on the importance of mutual understanding in social life. They center on the claim that unconstrained agreement in language is a fundamental medium of social cooperation, which can be replaced with other, strategic or coercive options only to a limited degree and within limited spheres of life: "In my view, it belongs to the form of life of a species that reproduces itself through labor and through understanding in language that motives are shaped primarily in communicative relationships."[12] Moreover, the shift from unconstrained consensus to coercion or manipulation exacts its price:

Acknowledged universal validity claims have a motivating force that does not derive from power or institutions. If one decides to behave strategically, one does not have all the advantages that come with behaving consensually. As the saying goes, "lying won't get you very far." Because it is possible to give a structural description of the built-in burdens that one takes on in detaching oneself from validity claims so that one does not follow a command of reason, it is possible on the empirical level to speak in a trivial sense of the motivating force of validity claims.[13]

Perhaps these general arguments, conceptual and empirical, could be sufficiently developed to make Habermas's starting point plausible before the fact, that is, before research based on the program is sufficiently far along to permit an appraisal after the fact. But I shall turn instead to a line of questioning that arises from Habermas's specific proposals in regard to the basic universal-pragmatic structures of communication. These are represented concisely in his model of communicative action (action oriented to mutual understanding) and the distinctions it embodies among different types of validity claims (truth, rightness, sincerity/authenticity), among different attitudes in which one can use language (objectivating, norm-conformative, expressive), and among different "worlds" or domains of reality to which speech relates (the objective world, our social world, each person's own inner world). Now it is rather evident that this way of setting out the fundamental structures of communication reflects the influence of epistemological and ontological distinctions characteristic of modern Western culture. And this, of course, raises the question of whether the model succeeds in capturing *universal* conditions of reaching understanding in language, that is, *general* and *unavoidable* presuppositions of communicative action, or whether it represents instead a thinly disguised Eurocentrism.

To be sure, this is not a problem of which Habermas is unaware:

When one pursues no longer transcendental philosophy ... but rather research into universals, one must be aware of the dangers that lie in seizing upon historically limited and rather variable capabilities for cognition, communication, and action and stylizing them as universal competences or in reconstructing what is actually a universal pretheoretical knowledge from a culturally and historically distorted perspective, so that the reconstructive proposals are caught up in provincialism. It goes without saying that one must allow for such possibilities of error.[14]

The claimed universality of the structures Habermas singles out cannot be established inductively, for it is quite clear that they are not characteristic of communication in all cultures and in all historical epochs, nor even of all communication in advanced industrial societies. The abilities to differentiate the "worlds" of external nature, internal nature, and society, to distinguish the "validity claims" of propositional truth, moral-practical rightness and sincerity/authenticity, to deploy these distinctions in communicative action and, at a reflective level, in argumentative discourse are not, as a matter of empirical fact, to be met with universally. Even if we keep separate, as Habermas suggests, the question of "empirical generalities" and that of "universals discovered by way of rational reconstruction," the problem remains.[15] If formal pragmatics is an empirical-reconstructive science that seeks knowledge a posteriori, if reconstructions are supposed to capture just those structures and rules that are actually operative in the domains under investigation, and if, finally, the structures of communicative action and discourse that Habermas singles out are to be found with significant frequency only in certain spheres of certain cultures at certain times, how then is it possible to defend the view that these structures are universal-pragmatic features of communication as such?

It is here that Habermas's thought takes a Hegelian turn: reason does not appear at one blow; it has a history, both in the individual and in the species. The passage quoted above on the dangers of provincialism continues,

On the other hand, I do not see how this admission amounts to an objection in principle to a research strategy directed at universals. We are normally quite prepared to regard the forms of objectivating thought as universal even though they gained institutional relevance, so to speak, only with the establishment of modern science. I assume that the forms of moral-practical insight are just as universal. This does not mean that such cognitive structures could appear all at once, whether in ontogenesis or in social evolution.[16]

Viewed in a developmental perspective, Habermas's universalist claims appear less immediately implausible than they would from a purely inductive standpoint. Problems remain, but they are of a different kind. To put it succinctly, he has to show that the ability to act communicatively (in his strong sense) and to reason argumentatively and reflectively about disputed validity claims is a developmental-logically advanced stage of specieswide competences, the unfolding of potentialities that are universal to humankind. To anyone familiar with the "rationality" debates that have accompanied the development of cultural anthropology from the start, and more particularly with the turn they have taken in recent years, it will be clear that the burden of this proof is considerable.

2 Variations on Hegelian Themes

The contrasts between "mythicomagical" and "modern" modes of thought and action have been characterized in a number of different ways. Very often "modern" is read as equivalent to "scientific-technological" and the contrast takes the form of exhibiting the "pre-" or "proto-" or "unscientific" character of the "savage mind." Habermas rejects this starting point as based on too narrow a conception of rationality. He starts instead from the model of communicative action developed in his universal pragmatics and, taking Lévi-Strauss and Godelier as his guides, characterizes the mythicomagical understanding of the world in a series of contrasts suggested by that model.[17] Thus, he singles out for attention the "leveling" of the different domains of reality: nature and culture are projected onto the same plane. This results in an anthropomorphized nature and a naturalized culture; techniques of magically influencing the world connected with this "confusion" and with the attendant failure to recognize the distinction between instrumental control of things and intersubjective relations among persons, between moral and physical success/failure, between good/evil and the harmful/advantageous; the inadequate distinctions between language and the world, between names and the named, between external relations of objects and internal relations of ideas, between the validity of symbolic expressions and physical efficacy; the lack of differentiation among diverse validity claims such as propositional truth, normative rightness, and expressive sincerity; the absence of self-awareness *as* a worldview, as an interpretation of the world that is subject to error and open to criticism and revision; the lack of clear demarcations of a domain of subjectivity, of intentions and motives from actions and their consequences, of feelings from normatively fixed stereotyped expressions; the binding of identity formation to the details of myth and the prescriptions of ritual; and thus the absence of ego identity in the strict sense. In other words, mythicomagical worldviews are marked, in Habermas's view, by insufficient differentiation of the objective, social, and subjective domains of reality, of the fundamental attitudes towards them, and of the validity claims proper to them, as well as by a lack of reflexivity that prevents their recognizing themselves as interpretative systems constituted by internal relations of meaning, symbolically related to reality, connected with validity claims, and thus open to criticism and revision. In this formal-pragmatic sense, they are by comparison "closed" systems.

It is obvious that this characterization is drawn from "our" (or Habermas's) perspective. It presupposes rather than proves *quod est demonstrandum*: the universal significance of the categories and assumptions on which it is based. Only when this has been demonstrated is the description above warranted as more than a particular, culturally biased account of an alien form of life. This is a special case of a problem facing social inquiry generally, as Habermas is well aware:

If *some* concept of rationality is unavoidably built into the action-theoretical foundations of sociology, then theory-formation is in danger of being limited from the start to a particular, culturally or historically bound perspective, unless fundamental concepts are constructed in such a way that the concept of rationality they implicitly posit is encompassing and general, that is, satisfies universalistic claims. The demand for such a concept of rationality also emerges from methodological considerations. . . . The experiential basis of an interpretive sociology is compatible with its claim to objectivity only if hermeneutic procedures can be based at least intuitively on general and encompassing structures of rationality. From both points of view, the metatheoretical and the methodological, we cannot expect objectivity in social-theoretical knowledge if the corresponding concepts of communicative action and interpretation express a merely particular perspective on rationality, one interwoven with a particular cultural tradition. . . . The rational internal structure of processes of reaching understanding . . . would have to be shown to be *universally valid* in a specific sense. This is a very strong requirement for someone operating without metaphysical support and no longer confident that a rigorous transcendental-pragmatic program, claiming to provide ultimate grounds, can be carried out.[18]

Habermas's account of the contrasts between modern and mythicomagical thought makes it clear that he does not regard this "rational internal structure" as everywhere and always characteristic of social interaction. How, then, can it be shown to be "universally valid" if not empirically (i.e., inductively) or through metaphysical or transcendental argument? As we have seen, Habermas's approach to justifying such universal claims is "rational reconstruction" in the broad sense that includes developmental studies. What has to be shown is the empirical and theoretical adequacy of the reconstructive model of communicative action. Several lines of research suggest themselves: formal-pragmatic analysis of general structures of communication; investigation of pathological or distorted patterns of communication in the light of the standards and conditions established for normal communication by formal pragmatics; application of formal-pragmatic perspectives to studies in the ontogenesis of communicative competence; and their application to the theory of anthropogenesis, the process of hominization from which the sociocultural form of life emerged, as well as to the theory of social evolution itself.[19] The structures of communicative rationality singled out by Habermas would have to prove themselves adequate to the empirical materials available in all these areas. Since, as we saw above, their universal significance cannot be established solely by the "horizontal" reconstructions of formal pragmatics, it would have to be established principally in the "vertical" reconstructions of developmental theories; that is, the mastery of these structures would have to be shown to represent the developmental-logical unfolding of specieswide competences.

Turning the argument in this way to considerations of empirical and theoretical adequacy and fruitfulness, and thereby to the present state and future course of research in the areas mentioned, clearly takes it beyond the scope of individual reflective virtuosity. But Habermas has tried to make his (hypothetical) claims plausible with reference to existing materials in the study of ontogensis and social evolution.[20] I am not in a position to offer an overall evaluation of the ways in which he appropriates these materials, but I would like to make a few very general points concerning the use he makes of cognitive-development psychology.

Charges of ethnocentrism and of scientistic and rationalistic bias have, of course, been leveled against cognitive-development paradigms in general. Habermas has not given adequate consideration to these charges, nor indeed to the host of other criticisms—metatheoretical and methodological, empirical and theoretical—that have been directed against the Piagetian and Kohlbergian programs in particular. And yet it is clear that his empirical-reconstructive approach to universals must prove itself precisely in the face of these sorts of objections.

The Piagetian model was developed on the basis of studies carried out with urban, middle-class schoolchildren in Switzerland and, subsequently, in several other advanced Western societies. It is only more recently that cross-cultural research has been carried out to any great extent, and this has consisted largely of cross-sectional studies of concrete-operational thought that have focused on different aspects of conservation (of quantity, weight, volume, etc.).[21] There have been significantly fewer cross-cultural investigations of the other stages and longitudinal studies tracing particular individuals throughout the course of their development. Thus the results to date are very incomplete and open to different interpretations. Nevertheless, a number of general problems and questions have emerged that bear directly on this inquiry.

1

The end-state toward which the developmental process is construed as heading is clearly Western in conception. Indeed, it has been characterized as "the development of a Western scientist." And this construal of the telos in terms of abstract, formal cognition affects, in turn, the conception of the earlier stages leading to it: "The most important thing is not so much what the child can do in the concrete world as how quickly he can do without it"; the tests of concrete-operational thought "do not track the skills of concrete science . . . but progress toward formal abstraction."[22] The problems this raises for cross-cultural research are obvious:

The typical research demonstrates either the presence of a certain structure or its absence (but negative results are clearly non-interpretable), and there is little room to find an alternative structure. . . . The demonstration that all individuals are able to reason according to a certain structure does not prove that this is their usual or preferred mode of reasoning. In fact we may not be adequately sampling the culturally relevant skills. What we may be asking is the question, "How well can *they* do *our* tricks?" whereas what we should be asking is, "How well can *they* do *their* tricks?"[23]

The point is that without an adequate understanding of the "end states" of development in other cultures, and thus the modes of thought and types of knowledge valued by those socialized in other cultures, we are determined before the fact to construe their performances as exhibiting a more or less deficient mastery of our competences rather than as expressing a mastery of a different set of skills altogether. The question of whether there are alternative cognitive structures more adaptive in a given environment and more culturally valued, and thus of whether there are alternative lines of development, cannot be adequately explored within the limits of the standard design for cross-cultural Piagetian research. And yet it seems quite possible that different domains of activity might call for different types of thinking or different types of knowledge and that in such domains Western thought might be rather "primitive" by comparison—*we* can't do *their* tricks very well either.

2

Until such questions as these are convincingly resolved, the results of cross-cultural research seem to be open to divergent assessments. In the usual interpretation, the development of the Western middle-class child is taken as the norm, and the "time lag" discovered for development in other cultures is seen as a "deficit" or "retardation." That is, human reason is viewed as following the same course of development in different societies, but at a faster or slower pace and with a more or less early arrest, depending on the social environment. Thus the proportion of different populations ever attaining to formal operations, and even to some aspects of concrete operations, is subject to wide variation. This variation is linked to a variety of social, cultural, and economic factors: an urban versus a rural setting, the extent of contact with Western culture and technology, the existence and nature of formal schooling, the degree of industrialization, the structure of workaday activities, and so on.[24] There are, for example, studies indicating that children from pottery-making families in Mexico perform better on conservation of substance than do their peers from non-pottery-making families; that nomadic, hunting populations develop spatial concepts more rapidly than do sedentary, agricultural groups, whereas the latter attain concepts of conservation of quantity, weight, and volume more rapidly; that among Australian Aborigines performance on concrete-operational tasks is directly proportional to the extent of contact with the dominant culture; in general, that the *structure d'ensemble* or intertask consistency posited by Piaget for the concrete-operational thought of the Genevan child apparently does not hold in different cultures ("Two concepts that develop congruently in the average Genevan child may develop at very different rates in another culture if one of those concepts is highly valued in that culture . . . and the other is not");[25] further, that the development of formal-operational thought is heavily dependent on schooling; that children with formal schooling that emphasizes symbolic thinking generally develop formal thought processes faster and further than those without it; and that there is a high degree of variability in performance across different materials and situations. "This limitation creates a paradox: the formal operations which were supposed to be independent of context are in fact situation-bound. . . . What [are] lacking . . . are studies of operational thinking in culturally relevant, real-life situations."[26]

Results such as these inevitably raise questions of the extent to which patterns of cognitive development are determined by environmental factors; of whether such factors affect only the "quantitative" aspects (ages) of development or the "qualitative" (structural) aspects as well; of how to distinguish "competence" conceived as universal from "performance," clearly dependent on such factors; or indeed, whether this distinction is at all possible. Until such problems are satisfactorily resolved, the question of cultural retardation versus cultural difference remains an open one. Do the observed differences in task performance reflect the nonuniversality of Piagetian theory, merely quantitative differences in the rate of acquisition of universal competences, or simply the inadequacies of cross-cultural research design?

3

Specifically Kohlbergian cross-cultural research is in an unhappier state: the number of cultures in which such studies have been carried out is still relatively small; the conceptions of the higher stages of moral consciousness (as reflected in the various editions of the *Standard Form Scoring Manual*) have frequently changed; and the results obtained seem to indicate a high degree of cultural variability, which might be expected, since the structures in question develop from interacting with features of the social environment. More particularly, "principled morality" appears to occur in significant proportions only in Western or Westernized populations, and even here the occurrence of stage 6 morality is "exceedingly rare."[27] This is, of course, what one would expect to find for the "social contract reasoning" of stage 5—justifying moral prescriptions or evaluations by appeal to social-contract rights, values, and principles—and for the "ideal role-taking" of stage 6—justifying moral prescriptions or evaluations by decisions of conscience in accord with self-chosen ethical principles appealing to logical comprehensiveness, universality, and consistency. In general, then, the questions I raised above in relation to Piagetian cross-cultural research—about different developmental end points and alternative cognitive structures, about disentangling competence from performance, and about the influence of environmental factors—are even more pressing here. And there is the added problem of metaethical disagreement among the principled moralists of the Western philosophical tradition as to which is really the most adequate style of moral reasoning. The assessment of the transition from contractarianism and utilitarianism to justice-as-fairness as an advance to a higher stage would scarcely meet with universal agreement (not to mention the view that the first two are developmental-logical presuppositions of the last).

4

This points up a larger methodological problem: even if we grant the general fruitfulness of developmental approaches, it is questionable whether the highest stages of development can be investigated and established with the same methods as the lower stages. As long as we are dealing with modes of thought that are, in Habermas's formal-pragmatic sense, not "open," there is some plausibility to the model of reconstructing the intuitive, pretheoretical knowledge underlying the performances of competent subjects. In such cases there is an asymmetry presupposed between the insufficiently decentred thought of an individual or a culture and the differentiated, reflective thought of the investigator. And this asymmetry provides a foothold for the conception of explicating an intuitive know-how, of knowing "better" in this sense the structures and rules underlying a subject's performance. Further, if the competence in question concerns basic features of human life as we know it, or even as we can possibly conceive it, there is some plausibility to the claim of universality as well. This seems to be the case, for example, with the progressive formation of a conception of the permanence of objects and of their invariance under certain operations; it seems also to hold for the child's developing ability to coordinate social perspectives in interpersonal relations to the extent required for role taking in family and society. In such cases, it seems, we are dealing with the acquisition of unreflectively mastered kinds of know-how—in relation to the external and social worlds—that are constitutive of the human form of life. To the degree that they can be characterized formally, we might claim to have identified universal structures of human reason.

The attainment of the "highest" cognitive stages—of formal operations and principled morality—by contrast, requires a certain break with the "here and now," that is, with the unreflective character of the "theories in action" that underlie performance at the lower stages. Thus in Kohlberg's view, the attainment of stages 5 and 6 involves questioning the conventional morality absorbed in socialization during an adolescent "moratorium" marked by metaethical reflection on the origin, function, and validity of received ethical sentiments. This view raises certain difficulties for the claim that we are dealing with "natural" stages of development. It is not merely that the requisite experience of disembedding oneself from an implicit worldview and adopting a detached and questioning posture in an environment that favors the move to principled morality is hardly typical of coming of age in all societies. More to the present point, even when this does occur, "Kohlberg's description of these orientations as natural stages seems improbable in the light of the essential role played by reflective metaethical thought in their construction, since natural stages are theories-in-action presumably constructed through implicit interactive processes."[28] The suggestion I would like to advance is that Kohlberg's account places the higher-stage moral subject, at least in point of competence, at the same reflective or discursive level as the moral psychologist. The subject's thought is now marked by the decentration, differentiation, and reflexivity that are the conditions of entrance into the moral theorist's sphere of argumentation. The asymmetry between the prereflective and the reflective, between theories in action and explications, that underlies the model of reconstruction begins to break down.[29] The subject is now in a position to argue with the theorist about questions of morality. This discursive symmetry might help to explain why Kohlberg's attempt to get from "is" to "ought" by establishing the "naturalness" of the higher stages has struck moral philosophers as questionable. He has to adopt and defend a specific position on the very metaethical issues they spend their careers debating; the appeal to empirical-psychological consideration brings no dispensation from participation in this debate. This is not to deny the significance of such considerations for moral theory; it is only to say that they will have to make themselves felt *within* moral-theoretical argumentation.[30]

One might advance a similar, if perhaps more controversial, suggestion in relation to Piaget's studies of cognitive development. He views the underlying functioning of intelligence as unknown to the individual at lower stages of cognition. At superior levels, however, the subject may reflect on previously tacit thought operations and the implicit cognitive achievements of earlier stages; that is, she may engage in epistemological reflection. And this places the subject, at least in point of competence, at the same discursive level as the cognitive psychologist. Here too the asymmetry between the subject's prereflective know-how and the investigator's reflective know-that begins to break down. The subject is now in a position to argue with the theorist about the structure and conditions of knowledge. One reason this does not emerge as clearly as it might from Piaget's own work is his focus on natural-scientific thought, on the development of those concepts (space, time, causality, number, etc.) and operations requisite for hypothetical deductive reasoning about objectified states and events. And there is considerable agreement about these in our culture. If we shift our focus from the development of a Western scientist to the mastery of the structures underlying the type of reflective thought in which the cognitive psychologist is engaged, however, the presumed asymmetry becomes less plausible. As the subject's thought itself becomes more reflective, particularly in an epistemological vein, the subject is increasingly in a position to argue with the psychologist about the latter's own presuppositions, standards, procedures, appraisals, etc. And again, this discursive symmetry suggest the implausibility of any empirical approach that assumes that epistemological issues are settled. The appeal to empirical-psychological considerations does not exempt the developmental psychologist from engaging in epistemological debate; rather, such considerations contribute to the debate.

3 Kant versus Hegel

I shall conclude this discussion with some general remarks on a central feature of Habermas's developmentalist approach. It seems to me that in this context he is working with a conception of the end point of the history of reason that fails to account for some of his own insights. As we saw, in contrasting mythical and modern modes of thought, he characterizes the latter primarily in terms of a differentiation of the objective, social, and subjective worlds, of the fundamental attitude toward them, and of the validity claims proper to them. The differentiation theme is stressed as well in his characterization of the telos of ontogenesis in terms of ego autonomy:

By that I mean the independence that the ego acquires through successful problem-solving, and through growing capabilities for problem-solving, in dealing with (a) the reality of external nature and of a society that can be controlled from strategic points of view; (b) the nonobjectified symbolic structure of a partly internalized culture and society; and (c) the internal nature of culturally interpreted needs, of drives that are not amenable to communication, and of the body.[31]

This stress on differentiation and the autonomy of the self in relation to external nature, internal nature, and society represents a conception of reason strongly reminiscent of Kant—a conception of *Verstand*, as Hegel would say, rather than of *Vernunft*. Yet in other contexts Habermas has in effect sided with Hegel against Kant. In regard to the relation of self and society, for instance, he explicitly rejects all monadological views in favour of a notion of coconstitution. Individuation, he maintains, can be comprehended only as a process of socialization; in formative processes, the subject is inextricably involved in a network of interactions that enable her to develop a personal identity on the basis of mutual recognition:

No one can construct an identity independently of the identifications that others make of him. . . . [The ego] presents itself to itself as a practical ego in the performance of communicative actions; and in communicative action the participants must reciprocally suppose that the distinguishing-oneself-from-others is recognized by those others. Thus the basis for the assertion of one's own identity is not really self-identification, but intersubjectively recognized self-identification.[32]

Habermas also rejects conceptions of ego autonomy that are based on the suppression of inner nature:

The dual status of ego identity reflects . . . an interdependence of society and nature that extends into the formation of identity. The model of an unconstrained ego identity is richer and more ambitious than a model of autonomy developed exclusively from perspectives of morality. . . . Need interpretations are no longer assumed as given, but are drawn into the discursive formation of will. . . . Inner nature is rendered communicatively fluid and transparent to the extent that needs can, through aesthetic forms of expression, be kept articulable (*sprachfähig*) or be released from their paleosymbolic prelinguisticality. But that means that internal nature is not subjected, in the cultural preformation met with at any given time, to the demands of ego autonomy; rather, through a dependent ego it obtains free access to the interpretive possibilities of the cultural tradition. . . . Naturally this flow of communication requires sensitivity, breaking down barriers, dependency—in short, a cognitive style marked as field-dependent, which the ego, on the way to autonomy, first overcame and replaced with a field-independent style of perception and thought. Autonomy that robs the ego of a communicative access to its own inner nature also signals unfreedom.[33]

Oddly enough, Habermas does not adopt the same dialectical stance in the third dimension, that is, the relation of self to nature. Here we are left with a subject-object relationship characterized in terms of prediction and control. Thus in *Knowledge and Human Interests* he maintains that the conditions of instrumental action "bind our knowledge of nature with transcendental necessity to the interest in possible technical control over natural processes."[34] I have argued elsewhere that this position is incompatible with his Marxian thesis that nature is the ground of spirit and with his notion of a "nature preceding human history" in the sense of a "natural process that, from within itself, gives rise likewise to the natural being man and the nature that surrounds him."[35] In that perspective, nature is "at the root of laboring subjects as natural beings";[36] social labour, and the technical objectivation of nature that it entails, are "founded in a history of nature that brings about the toolmaking animal as its result."[37] Nature is, in short, also a *natura naturans* and thus not merely an object of technical domination. Habermas, who dealt extensively with Schelling's *Naturphilosophie* in his earlier writings, is certainly aware of what is at stake here. And he several times alludes to the possibility of a science of nature that would not be categorically rooted in an interest in technical controllability:

A theory of evolution which is expected to explain emergent properties characteristic of the sociocultural life-form—in other words, to explain the constituents of social systems as part of natural history—cannot, for its part, be developed within the transcendental framework of objectifying sciences. If the theory of evolution is to assume these tasks, it cannot wholly divest itself of the form of a reflection on the prehistory of culture that is dependent on a prior understanding of the sociocultural life-form. For the time being these are speculations which can only be confirmed by a scientific clarification of the status enjoyed by the contemporary theory of evolution and research in ethology.[38]

This suggestion of a nonobjectivistic, reflectively cast theory of evolution certainly relativizes the dichotomy of an autonomous ego and a technically controllable nature that Habermas builds into his conception of autonomy. But in later writings he admits to being sceptical that such a project could actually be carried through. His position is, "While we can indeed adopt a performative attitude to external nature, enter into communicative relations with it, have aesthetic experiences and feelings analogous to morality with respect to it, there is for this domain of reality only one *theoretically fruitful,* attitude, namely the objectivating attitude of the natural-scientific, experimenting observer."[39] And the reasoning behind this limitation is the following:

It does not make sense to demand of a reason separated into its moments a reconciliation at the level of the scientific system, or at the level of the cultural tradition generally. We cannot expect to use the experiential potential gathered in non-objectivating dealings with external nature for purposes of knowledge and to make them theoretically fruitful. Precisely from the perspective of the theory of knowledge, which has to orient itself to successful examples of theory formation, the internal obstacles become visible which modern science places in the way of all attempts to reestablish the unity of reason in the theoretical dimension. Such attempts would have to lead back to metaphysics, and thus behind the levels of learning reached in the modern age into a reenchanted world.[40]

There are two important assumptions underlying this argument: first, that any theoretical attempt to articulate a perspective of reconciliation with nature inevitably leads back to metaphysics, and second, that any such philosophy of nature has to compete with the modern sciences of nature—in vain. But we have models for reconceptualizing nature that do neither. Most prominent among them, perhaps, is Kant's "Critique of Teleological Judgment." In that model, teleological explanations of nature do not compete with causal explanations but are complementary to them; nor are teleological judgments of purpose in nature "metaphysical" in any precritical sense, for the principles governing them are maxims only of reflective judgment. I do not wish to go into the details of Kant's approach here, nor to suggest that it is a fully adequate model for contemporary attempts to rethink our relations to nature. My only point is that there is *no conceptual necessity* for the philosophy of nature to take on the form of a metaphysics of nature claiming a validity independent of and prior to science, that is, the form of an *Ursprungsphilosophie.*[41] It is possible to envision a philosophy of nature constructed after the transcendental turn as a nonfoundationalist, falliblistic attempt to conceive of nature as a *natura naturans* that gave rise to, among other things, a species capable of communicating in language and thereby of giving its intraspecific relations the form of a moral order. Of course, this attempt would have to be constantly renewed in the light of our historically changing scientific and moral experience.

While this approach remains fundamentally anthropocentric and thus unsuited for the restoration of a cosmological ethic based on a teleology of nature in itself,[42] it might provide a view of our place in nature that could complement and relativize the objectivating view of a nature to be dominated. As noted, Habermas denies not that we can take up a nonobjectivating *attitude* toward nature but only that *knowledge* can be gained in this attitude "at the same level . . . that Newton attained in his objectivating knowledge of nature."[43] But it seems rather arbitrary to judge the rationalizability of one actor-world relation by the standards of another.[44] If we were to ask instead whether specialized forms of discourse could develop that were sufficiently productive from the standpoint of acquiring knowledge to be fruitful for political action and social change, it is not at all clear that the answer must be negative. The view of the human species as in and of nature that we would get from this perspective would be quite different from the view of the human species as set over against nature that we adopt in the objectivating sciences. And this change in viewpoint from domination to harmonization might well have consequences for our sense of obligation to nature and for the norms governing our interactions with it.[45]

I shall close with a few tentative remarks concerning what, in my view, the preceding considerations do and do not entail.

• These considerations do not of themselves entail a rejection of the ideas of structurally different, hierarchically ordered modes of thought and of sociocultural learning processes.[46] But they do suggest that once the level of discursive thought has been attained and reflective argumentation plays an important role in the development of rational practices, the empirical-reconstructive methods of Piaget and Kohlberg become increasingly blunt. At this level the model of the prereflective subject versus the reflective investigator gradually loses its foothold. In the end we are all participants in the debate as to what is higher. To be sure, explicit reconstructions of implicit kinds of know-how retain their point, but only as contributions to this debate. They cannot by themselves settle it.

• These considerations do not imply a rejection of differentiation as a mark of cognitive development. The dissolution of a comparatively undifferentiated unity of thought does appear to be a necessary step in the progress of rationality. But the separation of domains of reality and types of validity claims, of an ego that stands over against nature, society, and its own feelings and desires, must eventually allow for a nonregressive reconciliation with self, others, and nature if the "dialectic of enlightenment" is to lose its sway over our lives.[47]

• These considerations do not entail a wholesale renunciation of theoretical and critical distancing in favor of heremeneutic participation. The interpretation of meaningful phenomena need not be restricted to dialogic understanding. It can be theoretically informed by a systematic conception of reason and its history and thus be joined to explanation and critique. But if differentiation itself is not the last chapter in that history, we have things to learn from traditional cultures as well as they from us—not only things we have forgotten or repressed but something about how we might put our fragmented world back together again. This is not a matter of regression, but of dialogue, dialogue that is critical, to be sure, but not only on one side. From this point of view as well, "in a process of enlightenment there can only be participants."[48]

6

Complexity and Democracy: The Seducements of Systems Theory

There is a specter haunting *The Theory of Communicative Action*, a close relation to the totally reified world that haunted Western Marxism's original reception of Max Weber. In the 1940s Horkheimer and Adorno in effect abandoned Marx for Weber on the question of the emancipatory potential of modern rationality. The spread of instrumental reason represented for them the core of a domination generalized to all spheres of life. Habermas agrees that the basic distortions of modern life can be traced to processes of rationalization. However, he stands with Marx in regarding them as due not to rationalization as such but to the peculiar nature of capitalist modernization, and thus in regarding them as remediable by transforming basic social structures. In this respect, his position is closest to that of Lukács, who attempted to integrate Weber's analysis of rationalization into a Marxian framework. Reconceptualizing rationalization in terms of *reification* and tracing this back to the universalization of the commodity form in capitalist society, Lukács viewed the pathologies of modernity as specifically capitalist in origin and thus as reversible. It is, in fact, one of the principal aims of *The Theory of Communicative Action* to develop a more adequate version of the theory of reification. This "second attempt to appropriate Weber in the spirit of Western Marxism" has three major ambitions:

• To break with the philosophy of consciousness in favor of a theory of *communicative rationality*, which is no longer tied to and limited by the subjectivistic and individualistic premises of modern philosophy and social theory

• To go beyond the primarily action-theoretic conceptualization of *rationalization* in Weber and his Marxist heirs and back to Marx in order to recapture the systems-theoretic dimension of his analysis of capitalist society—in less historical terms, to reconnect action theory with systems theory by constructing a "two-level concept of society" that integrates the lifeworld and system paradigms

• To construct on this basis a critical theory of modern society that reconceptualizes *reification* as a "colonization of the lifeworld" by forces emanating from the economic and political subsystems, that is, that traces fundamental sociocultural deformations back to the growing subordination of the lifeworld to systemic imperatives of material reproduction.

• In this paper I would like to examine several of the ideas basic to the second and third endeavors with the aim of identifying some potentially troublesome weakspots. I shall be particularly concerned with problems stemming from Habermas's appropriation of systems theory. In his early essays he was already concerned to dispel the specter of a cybernetically self-regulated organization of society, a "negative utopia of technical control over history" in which humans no longer occupy the position of *homo faber* but rather occupy that of *homo fabricatus*, totally integrated into their technical machine.[1] This same concern came to the fore in his debate with Luhmann, in the last part of *Legitimation Crisis*, and in his Hegel Prize lecture of 1974.[2] And it has been at least a subtext of most major publications since. It is this specter that he seeks to come to terms with in *The Theory of Communicative Action*.[3] His strategy is to enter into a pact of sorts with social systems theory; certain areas are marked out within which it may move about quite freely on the condition that it keep entirely away from others. I want to argue that the terms of this pact are sometimes unclear, that it cedes too much territory to systems theory, and that as a result, critical theory is left in an unnecessarily defensive position.

1

The main lines of Habermas's proposal for connecting the lifeworld and system paradigms are first sketched out with reference to Durkheim's account of how the forms of social solidarity change with the division of labor.

It directs our attention to the empirical connections between stages
of system differentiation and forms of social integration. It is possible
to analyze these connections by distinguishing mechanisms for co-
ordinating action that harmonize the *action orientations* of participants
from mechanisms that stabilize the non-intended interconnections of
action by way of functionally intermeshing *action consequences*. In the
one case, the integration of an action system is established by a
normatively secured or communicatively achieved consensus, and in
the other case, by a non-normative regulation of individual decisions
that extend beyond the actors' consciousnesses. This distinction between *social integration* and *system integration* . . . calls for a corresponding differentiation in the concept of society itself. [On the one hand,]
society is conceived from the perspective of acting subjects as the
lifeworld of a social group. In contrast, from the observer's perspective
of someone not involved, society can be conceived only as a *system of
actions* such that each action has a functional significance according
to its contribution to the maintenance of the system. (p. 117)

Generally speaking, the problem of "integration" concerns
the mutual adjustment of diverse parts to form a unified whole.
It moved to the center of sociological theory with Durkheim's
discussions of organic and mechanical solidarity. The latter was
rooted in collective consciousness, in shared values and norms,
beliefs and sentiments, in individuals' agreement with and acceptance of the group's basic goals, ideals, practices. The former was based on the interdependence of specialized roles in
such a way that the diverse activities of different individuals
complemented one another and fit together into a harmonious
whole. It was clear to Durkheim that the degree of sociocultural
homogeneity required for mechanical solidarity was increasingly improbable in modern society. And yet he was not willing
to view organic solidarity as a full functional equivalent to
sociocultural homogeneity demanded by the division of labor.
Thus he rejected Spencer's idea of a wholly spontaneous integration of individual interests brought about entirely through

mechanisms like the market, that is, not through a conscious harmonizing of value orientations but through a functional coordination of the aggregate effects of action. For Durkheim, organic solidarity also needed to be anchored in a basic normative consensus. It seemed evident, however, that capitalist modernization destroyed traditional normative foundations without generating suitable modern replacements. The inevitable result was anomie, against which he could in the end only campaign.

Like Durkheim, Habermas rejects the idea of a society integrated solely via the unintended functional interdependence of consequences of action, beyond the consciousness of actors, so to speak, rather than in and through it. He wants to argue instead that every society needs to be integrated in both ways, socially and systemically, and thus he is confronted with the fundamental problem of how to combine them. It is this problem that dominates volume 2 of *The Theory of Communicative Action*. The role of Spencer is played for Habermas by Niklas Luhmann, who has argued at length that modern societies have to develop alternatives to normative integration, which is hopelessly inadequate for dealing with high levels of complexity. The "world society developing today," Luhmann insists, faces problems that can be solved only at the level of system integration. "The basic reality of society can no longer be said to lie in its capacity to generate and sustain interaction systems. As a consequence modern society cannot be grasped as the sum of personal encounters. This is expressed, for example, in the gulf separating the ethics of face-to-face interaction from objective social requirements in (say) economics, politics or science. In view of this discrepancy, moralistic demands for more 'personal participation' in social processes are hopelessly out of touch with social reality."[4] If this is so, Habermas noted in his Hegel Prize lecture, then "individuals henceforth belong only to the environment of their social systems. In relation to them society takes on an objectivity that can no longer be brought into the intersubjective context of life, for it is no longer related to subjectivity."[5] This "dehumanization of society" is the systems-theoretic version of the totally reified society that Western Marxists had projected in terms of the philosophy of consciousness. To counter it, Habermas undertakes to demonstrate that society cannot be represented exclusively, or even fundamentally, as a boundary-maintaining system. It must be grasped also and primordially as the lifeworld of a social group. The central problem of social theory thus becomes how to combine the two conceptual strategies, that is, how to conceive of society as at once socially and systemically integrated.

In earlier writings Habermas made clear the problems that the system paradigm poses for empirical social analysis, which depends importantly on our ability to identify boundaries, goal states, and structures essential for continued existence. In *Legitimation Crisis*, for example, he wrote, "The difficulty of clearly determining the boundaries and persistence of social systems in the language of systems theory raises fundamental doubts about the usefulness of a systems-theoretic concept of social crisis. For organisms have clear spatial and temporal boundaries; their continued existence is characterized by goal values that vary only within empirically specifiable tolerances. . . . But when systems maintain themselves by altering both boundaries and structural continuity, their identity becomes blurred. The same system modification can be conceived of equally well as a learning process and change or as a dissolution process and collapse of the system."[6] Any adaptive system has to be able to mediate the relations among parts, whole, and environment via "information flows" so as to "select" and "code" stimuli from the environment and to direct its responses to them. What distinguishes societies from organisms is the peculiarly symbolic form of the linkages between the system, its parts, and the environment. It is with this in mind that Luhmann introduced *meaning* as a fundamental category of *social*-systems theory, but with a functionalist twist, to be sure: meaning is a mode of reducing the complexity peculiar to social systems. Habermas criticized this bit of conceptual legerdemain at some length.[7] He in fact argued that it is precisely the dimension of meaning that sets the limits to the application of systems theory to society. For one thing, the whole notion of self-maintenance becomes fuzzy, even metaphorical at the sociocultural level, where self-preservation is not merely a physical matter. "The 'clearly defined' problem of death and a corresponding criterion of survival are lacking because societies never reproduce 'naked' life but always a culturally defined life."[8] That is to say, the definition of life "is no longer pregiven with the specific equipment of the species. Instead, continual attempts to define cultural life are a necessary component of the very life process of socially related individuals."[9] Yet functionalist analysis requires a reliable determination of essential structures and goal states if there is to be an "objective" problem to serve as its point of reference. It is for this reason, among others, that the empirical usefulness of the system paradigm at the sociocultural level has been quite limited and, according to Habermas, can be enhanced only by combining it with the lifeworld paradigm. Only in this way can we get at the historically variable interpretive schemes in which societies understand themselves, secure their identities, and determine what counts for them as human life.

Meaning causes problems not only for the identification of goal states but for the identification of the boundaries of systems as well. The boundaries of sociocultural systems are blurry "because the determination of symbolically constituted limits of meaning brings with it fundamental hermeneutic difficulties," and this obviously causes problems for empirical-systems analysis. In this respect too, if it is not connected with action theory, social-systems theory is of limited empirical use, a play of cybernetic words that only serves to produce reformulations of problems that it does not really help to resolve.[10] The same holds true for the structural features of social systems. What are usually referred to as social structures are patterns of interaction that are relatively stable at a given time. But these patterns may be altered or dismantled as well as sustained by the ongoing interactions of members. This has motivated theorists of various stripes to focus attention on the *microprocesses* underlying not only the structuring but also the restructuring and destructuring of social systems. "Process" here refers to "the actions and interactions of the components of an ongoing system in which varying degrees of structuring arise, persist, dissolve or change."[11] Seen in this light, "society becomes a continuous morphogenic process." The implications for the study of social order are not difficult to draw: "Social order is not simply normatively specified and automatically maintained but is something that must be 'worked at,' continually reconstructed."[12] This holds for formal organizations as well. For example, summarizing the results of "The Hospital and Its Negotiated Order," Walter Buckley writes,

The hospital, like any organization, can be visualized as a hierarchy of status and power, of rules, roles and organizational goals. But it is also a locale for an ongoing complex of transactions among differentiated types of actors. . . . The rules supposed to govern the actions of the professionals were found to be far from extensive, clearly stated or binding; hardly anyone knew all the extant rules or the applicable situations and sanctions. Some rules previously administered would fall into disuse, receive administrative reiteration, or be created anew in a crisis situation. As in any organization, rules were selectively evoked, broken and/or ignored to suit the defined needs of the personnel. Upper administrative levels especially avoided periodic attempts to have rules codified and formalized, for fear of restricting the innovation and improvisation believed necessary to the care of patients. . . . In sum, the area of action covered by clearly defined rules was very small. . . . The rules ordering actions to this end [patient care] were the subject of continual negotiations—being argued, stretched, ignored or lowered as the occasion seemed to demand. As elsewhere, rules failed to act as universal prescriptions, but required judgment as to their applicability to the specific case.[13]

This is indicative of a general line of attack on mainstream organization research taken by action-theorists in the phenomenological, ethnomethodological, and symbolic-interactionist traditions, among others. Their studies have shown formally organized domains of action to be "transactional milieux where numerous agreements are constantly being established, renewed, reviewed, revoked and revised." The formal framework of rules and roles does serve as a point of reference for actual transactions; it is a central element in the "daily negotiations" through which it is *at the same time maintained and modified*. Far from adequately depicting actual patterns of interaction in the organizations to which they refer, formal organizational schemes are used by participants as "generalized formulae to which all sorts of problems can be brought for solution. . . . [They] are schemes of interpretation that competent and entitled users can invoke in yet unknown ways whenever it suits their purposes. . . . When we consider the set of highly schematic rules subsumed under the concept of rational organization, we can readily see an open realm of free play for relating an infinite variety of performances to rules as responses to these rules. In this field of games of representation and interpretation, . . . extending to the rule the respect of compliance, while finding in the rule the means for doing whatever need be done, is the gambit that characterizes organizational acumen."[14]

Habermas agrees, to be sure, that the question of actual behavior in organizational settings is a matter for empirical investigation, and he acknowledges that existing studies have shown the classical model of bureaucracy to be strongly idealized. But he seems to suppose that the systems-theoretic model can escape this fate; at least he does not draw the same conclusions with regard to it as, it seems to me, he might. Are the membership rules (boundaries) and legal regulations defining formal organizations any different in these respects from other rules and laws? There is no obvious reason for thinking that they should be. Habermas insists that, however fluid, fleeting, and flexible action within organizational settings may be, it always transpires "under the premises" of formal regulations, which can be appealed to by members. While this *is* certainly a ground for distinguishing behavior within organizational settings from behavior outside of them, it does not of itself warrant interpreting this distinction as one between a system and its environment. The action-theoretic accounts to which we have referred suggest that the "buffer zone" of organizational "indifference" to personality and individual life history, to culture and tradition, to morality and convention is such that some of what is to be kept out is already within, and much of the rest can enter as the need arises. If organizations are systems, they are, unlike organisms, systems with porous and shifting boundaries, and if they are constituted by positive law, the legal regulations in question are not merely ideal presuppositions but important elements in the representations and interpretations that members deploy, at times with strategic intent, at times in the search for consensus. My point, then, is *not* that there are no important differences to be marked here but that these systems-theoretic concepts may not be the best way to mark them.

2

There may be some plausibility to characterizing the market as "norm-free," as an ethically neutralized system of action in which individuals interrelate on the basis of egocentric calculations of utility, in which subjectively uncoordinated individual decisions are functionally integrated. The question I wish to raise in section 2 is whether anything like this description fits *political* life in modern society. Whereas capitalist economic relations were institutionalized as "a sphere of legally domesticated, incessant competition between strategically acting private persons" (p. 178), political relations were grounded on the rule of law, basic human rights, popular sovereignty, and other "moral-practical" consensual foundations. What is it about contemporary capitalism that would suggest a theoretical assimilation of economics and politics?

It is surprising that Habermas has little to say in *The Theory of Communicative Action* about the political system as such, since its inclusion in the "basic" functional domain of material reproduction is central to his reconceptualization of Marx. But what he does say seems consistent with what he has said before, e.g., in *Legitimation Crisis,* and it is thus possible to reconstruct his position, at least in broad outline. The first thing to note is that he usually refers to the "political system" only when he is discussing problems of legitimation in mass, welfare-state democracies (see, for example, pp. 344 ff.). Outside of that context he typically talks of the "administrative system," "state apparatus," "government administration," and the like. And the colonization diagnosis is consistently rendered in terms of the subordination of the lifeworld to the economic and *administrative* subsystems. What is at play here, it appears, is a version of the distinction, familiar among system theorists, between administration and politics in the narrow sense. Thus Parsons specifies the function of the political system in terms of effective attainment of collective goals. The medium of interchange specific to this system is power, "the generalized capacity to secure the performance of binding obligations by units in a system of collective organization when the obligations are legitimized with reference to their bearing on collective goals and where in case of recalcitrance there is a presumption of enforcement by negative situational sanctions."[15] The political function is centered in the specific role of office, elective and appointive, with the power to make and implement collectively binding decisions. The political (elective) and bureaucratic (appointive) components of the political system are differentiated out as complementary subsystems, the elected component supplying the "nonbureaucratic top" of a bureaucratic organization. This administrative bureaucracy responsible to elected officers stands in relation to other parts of society via the interchange of inputs and outputs across its boundaries. In particular, it requires from the public generalized support and the advocacy of general policies, while it supplies to it effective leadership and binding decisions.[16]

Similarly, we find in Luhmann a basic differentiation of the political system into politics and administration. The enormous complexity of modern society has to be reduced through authoritative decision making. Power, a reduction of complexity binding on others, is a medium of communication that enables decisions to be transmitted—the power holder's decision is accepted by subordinates as a premise for their own decision making.[17] In modern political systems there is a fundamental differentiation of roles for bureaucratic administration, on the one hand, and electoral politics with its specifically political organizations such as parties and interest groups, on the other. The former is specialized in "elaborating and issuing binding decisions according to politically predetermined criteria"; the latter in "building political support for programs and decisions."[18] Luhmann regards the public, in certain of its complementary roles (e.g., "taxpayer, proponent of resolutions, legal complainant, voter, writer of letters to the editor, supporter of interest groups"), as part of the political system.[19] In complex societies, politics and administration must be kept structurally and functionally separated. Political parties specialize in securing a diffuse mass support for elected leaders, the state apparatus in carrying out their programs and decisions.

In *Legitimation Crisis* Habermas explicitly takes issue with Luhmann's insistence on a strict separation of administration from politics.[20] But his own descriptive model of advanced capitalist societies seem to concede that some such separation does in fact obtain.[21] Thus, he distinguishes the administrative system, which is primarily responsible for regulating, complementing, and substituting for the economic system, from the "legitimation system," which ensures mass support for this while shielding the administrative system from effective democratic participation. "Formally democratic" institutions and procedures secure both a diffuse mass loyalty and the requisite independence of administrative decision-making processes from the specific interests of the public. They are democratic in form but not in substance. The public realm, whose functions have been reduced largely to periodic plebiscites, is "structurally depoliticized."

We find a similar picture in *The Theory of Communicative Action*. The state apparatus is said to be functionally specialized in attaining collective goals via the medium of binding decisions or power (p. 171). Central to its tasks in advanced capitalist societies is that of complementing the market and, when necessary, filling the functional gaps therein. This it must do while preserving the primacy of private investment and the dynamic of capital accumulation. Under these circumstances, state intervention in the economy takes the *indirect* form of manipulating the boundary conditions of private enterprise and the *reactive* form of crisis-avoidance strategies or of compensating for dysfunctional side effects (pp. 343–344). At the same time, the modern capitalist state requires legitimation through democratic electoral processes involving competition among political parties. There is, Habermas maintains, an "indissoluble tension" between these two principles of societal integration: capitalism and democracy. For the normative sense of democracy entails that "the fulfillment of the functional necessities of systematically integrated domains of action shall find its limits in the integrity of the lifeworld," whereas specifically capitalist growth dynamics can be preserved only if "the propelling mechanism of the economic system [is] kept as free as possible from lifeworld restrictions as well as from demands for legitimation directed to the administrative system" (p. 345). These opposing principles or imperatives clash head-on in the public sphere, where, according to Habermas, "public opinion" and "the will of the people" are a result *both* of communication processes in which values and norms take shape *and* of the production of mass loyalty by the political system (p. 346). But he clearly continues to regard the latter as predominant: "As the private sphere is undermined and eroded by the economic system, so too is the public sphere by the administrative system. The bureaucratic disempowering and desiccation of spontaneous processes of opinion- and will-formation expands the scope for mobilizing mass loyalty and makes it easier to uncouple political decision-making from concrete, identity-forming contexts of life" (p. 325). The possibilities of participation legally contained in the role of citizen are neutralized. The political content of mass democracy shrinks to social-welfare programs necessitated by the disparities, burdens, and insecurities caused by the economic system. These are compensated for in the coin of economically produced value. As long as capital continues to expand under political protection, as long as there is an adequate supply of compensatory use values to distribute, political alienation does not develop explosive force. Thus the dual task of the state is to "head off immediately negative effects on the lifeworld of a capitalistically organized occupational system as well as the dysfunctional side effects thereupon of economic growth that is steered through capital accumulation, and it is supposed to do so without encroaching upon the organizational form, the structure, or the drive mechanism of economic production" (pp. 347–348).

The correspondences between this assessment of the functions and limits of politics in modern society and those put forward by many system theorists are evident. On the other hand, Habermas's diagnosis is also broadly consistent with leading Marxist theories of the state. The reduction of politics in the narrow sense to the generation of nonspecific mass support and the competition for top administrative positions, of the manifest content of politics to the social-welfare state agenda, and of the basic tasks of the state to securing the conditions of capital accumulation while compensating for its dysfunctional side effects have been discussed in both systems-theoretic and Marxist traditions.[22] Of course, in the one case this is meant to be only a description, in the other it is also a denunciation. In Habermas it is both a description of basic *tendencies* within advanced capitalism and a critique of the consequent disempowering of democratic institutions and processes. The normative standpoint of his critique is *not* a complete absorption of the system into the lifeworld, for in his view, every complex modern society has to give over certain economic and administrative tasks to functionally specified and media-steered domains of action.

There are, broadly, two sorts of questions we might raise in connection with the view of politics expressed in *The Theory of Communicative Action:* questions regarding its adequacy as an account of actually existing political systems and questions regarding its implications for the utopian content of the critical-theoretical tradition. I am not in a position to deliver a final verdict on the theoretical and empirical adequacy of Habermas's account of the state and politics in capitalist society, but I would like to register some doubts. Recall that for the social-systems theorist, the differentiation of the political system into bureaucratic administration, party politics, and the public is a differentiation among functionally specialized *subsystems,* that is to say, the conceptual tools of systems theory are used for analyzing all domains and their interconnections. For Habermas, by contrast, the public sphere belongs to the *lifeworld,* which is indeed uncoupled from the administrative system, but not as a subsystem within the political system. Accordingly, we require different categories and principles for analyzing these different domains. In one domain, interaction is systemically integrated, formally organized, and media-steered, in the other it is oriented to mutual understanding, whether traditionally secured or communicatively achieved. Thus one clue that might be followed in checking the adequacy of Habermas's characterization of the political system is the part that one or the other type of action coordination plays in that domain.

Is interaction in the political sphere systemically rather than socially integrated?[23] Even if we grant for the moment the very reduced systems-theoretic and Marxist conception of politics in advanced capitalism to which Habermas more or less subscribes, and further confine our attention to its administrative side, the matter seems ambiguous at best. For one might still ask, Is interaction within large administrative bureaucracies coordinated via functional interconnection of its effects *rather than* via the orientations of actions? Is it integrated, like the market, via the "nonnormative" steering of subjectively uncoordinated individual decisions *rather than* via normative consensus? The question only has to be posed in this way, it seems to me, to raise doubts about any either/or answer. Obviously, much of the activity of such bureaucracies typically involves conscious planning to achieve organization goals. These goals are at least sometimes known to and accepted by organization members. In fact, Habermas, following Parsons, designates the "real value" in terms of which power is to be redeemed as "achieving collectively desired goals"; "effectiveness of goal-attainment" is the corresponding "generalized value" (p. 268). It is difficult to see why interaction within such organizations is not socially integrated to the degree that the collective goals really are collective (or at least are thought to be) and the interest in attaining them is broadly shared by members.

Habermas is at pains to show that "power needs to be legitimated and therefore calls for a more demanding normative anchoring than money" (p. 271). Whereas the exchange relation does not obviously disadvantage either of the participants and is apparently in each's interest, subordinates are structurally disadvantaged in relation to power holders—one gives orders, the other obeys. If the authority of office is not to rely solely on the threat of sanctions (which, according to Habermas, is an inadequate basis for stability) a sense of obligation to follow orders is required. Subordinates must be able to examine the goals themselves and determine whether they are legitimate. The differences from the money medium are evident. "Whereas no agreement among parties to an exchange is needed to make a judgment of interest, the question of what lies in the general interest calls for consensus among the members of a collectivity. . . . Power as a medium evidently retains something of the power to command that is connected with the authority behind commands in contrast to simple imperatives" (pp. 271–272). In volume 1 of *The Theory of Communicative Action* the contrast between normatively authorized and simple imperatives is presented as an example of the difference between communicative and strategic action, and in volume 2, in the discussion of steering media the issuing and acceptance of orders is again referred to as an example of communicative interaction (p. 262). If this is so, it is difficult to understand why interaction mediated by legitimized power is systemically rather than socially integrated.[24]

There is another respect in which Habermas grants the premises but resists the conclusion: the relation of formal and informal organization. It is now a generally accepted fact that the formal aspects of social organizations—the rationally ordered systems of norms and roles, rules and regulations, programs and positions—are only one side of the coin. The other side consists of the informal aspects: the concrete norms and values, rituals and traditions, sentiments and practices that inform interpersonal relations within organizations. Habermas notes this fact but does not permit it to affect his judgment that "organizations not only disconnect themselves from cultural commitments and from attitudes and orientations specific to given personalities, they also make themselves independent from lifeworld contexts by neutralizing the normative background of informal, customary, morally regulated contexts of action" (p. 309). He acknowledges that "even within formally organized domain of actions, interactions are still connected via the mechanism of mutual understanding," without which "formally regulated social relations could not be sustained, nor could organizational goals be realized" (p. 310), and he grants that the question of the extent to which formal organization actually structures action and interaction within organizations is an empirical question that can by no means be answered deductively. He even cites approvingly an empirical study showing that in government organizations the discrepancies between the idealized model and actual behavior were considerable (p. 429, n. 6). Yet he insists that socially integrative mechanisms are put out of play in formal organizations where "action falls under the premises of formally regulated domains" and "forfeits its validity basis" (p. 310). That is, mem-

bers act communicatively only "with reservation." They know
that "they *can* have recourse to formal regulations," that "there
is no necessity of achieving consensus by communicative
means" (pp. 310–311). It seems clear, however, that there are
also situations in which organizational superiors can act au-
thoritatively only "with reservation," that is, in which they know
they cannot achieve their goals without collegiality, cooperation, mutual understanding. The ratio of power to agreement
in the actual operation of administrations seems, in short, to
be a thoroughly empirical question that allows of no general
answer either in regard to what is the case or with regard to
some single ideal of what ought to be the case.

Even if we restrict ourselves to the most bureaucratically
hierarchical forms of organization, it is not obvious that the
contrast of system integration versus social integration captures
what is specific to them. Recall that system integration was said
to stabilize unintended interdependencies by way of functionally interconnecting the results of action. Correspondingly, systems analysis is supposed to get at these counterintuitive
interdependencies by way of discovering the latent functions
of action. But this is not at all the same thing as "just taking
orders" within organizations. We need a stronger theoretical
link between "formally organized" and "systemically integrated"—stronger, that is, than the fact that the systems-theoretic paradigm has established itself in organization theory. To
say that interaction within organizations is not primarily coordinated by traditionally preestablished consensus or by communicatively achieved consensus (in Habermas's strong sense)
is *not* to say that it is not coordinated via actors' orientations at
all, e.g., via the giving and taking of orders, the threat and
fear of sanctions.[25] Of course, the orientations are different in
important respects from those that prevail outside hierarchical
organizations. But getting at that difference is essential to understanding the type of action coordination within them. The
integration of action orientations via everybody's following orders seems no less an alternative to normative consensus than
integration via latent functions. It is also clear that they need
not coincide. I am trying here not to resurrect a pure Weberian
model of bureaucratic administration against the now domi-

nant functionalist models but only to suggest that something of both is needed, that neither is by itself adequate, and thus that we cannot talk of formal organizations as being systemically integrated *rather than* socially integrated.

Consider, finally, an even more extreme case, a strongly hierarchical, formally organized setting in which the actors have no clear idea of why they are ordered to do what they do. Are their actions then integrated via the stabilization of latent functions? This is not the most obvious answer. If the top generals, managers, bureaucrats, or whatever have worked out and implemented a plan of action, successful coordination of the actions of diverse members might in part be attributed to the planners' astuteness and the efficiency of their organization. This is at least as plausible as attributing it to the working of anonymous control mechanisms. Habermas often equates the fact that the objective sense of an action in not intuitively present to the actor with its being a matter of latent functionality. It could also be present to other actors who have the authority or power to direct his or her actions.[26] All of this is meant merely to say that system integration and social integration, as they are defined by Habermas, seem to be extremes of possibilities rather than alternatives that exhaust the field of possibilities: the denial of one does not entail the other. Moreover, if softened to correspond to the inside/outside differences in methodological perspectives, it seems clear that most, if not all, domains of social action can be looked at in both ways. Organizations, whether government bureaucracies or industrial corporations, can certainly be viewed in action-theoretic terms as well as in systems-theoretic terms—or rather certainly in action-theoretic terms, very likely in functionalist terms, and possibly in systems-theoretic terms as well.[27] It goes without saying that all of this would apply a fortiori to the specifically political (in contrast to the administrative) side of the "political system."

There are also normative reasons why Habermas should be wary of conceptualizing administrative organizations in systems-theoretic terms. He maintains that any complex society will require a high degree of system differentiation, that is, will have to rely in part on mechanisms of coordination other than building consensus in language, which, as he says, can be very time-consuming and is in many situations a "luxury" that can be ill afforded. Surely he does not mean by this that we should aim to construct institutions whose functions are kept latent and in which members just take orders without regard to the legitimacy of goals and the like. In fact, Habermas strongly criticized Luhmann's Gehlenesque dictum "The latency of basic problems has the function of protecting structural decisions against insight and variation."[28] He critically contrasted this "counterenlightenment" view with the enlightenment goal of maximizing our self-understanding and our ability to "make history with will and consciousness."[29] It represents, he said, the most refined form of the technocratic consciousness that today serves to insulate practical questions from public discussion.[30]

Habermas has retreated, it is true, from the overly strong conceptions of self-consciousness and self-determination that informed many passages of *Knowledge and Human Interests*. He has found a systematic place in his thought for the inevitably incomplete transparency of lifeworld backgrounds and the substrata of psychic life. *The Theory of Communicative Action* argues something similar, it seems to me, with respect to economic and administrative mechanisms whose operation does not depend on communicatively achieved consensus. In regard to politics, this implies that we should not think of direct or council democracy and workers' self-management as the only legitimate possibilities. We may well need forms of representative democracy and forms of public administration. If one accepts this, the decisive question becomes, What forms? And hear I fear that Habermas has taken over so much of the conceptual arsenal of systems theory that he risks not being able to formulate an answer to this question compatible with his professed political ideals. I shall come back to this below. For now I want only to look further at the question of latent versus manifest functions. As noted above, Habermas emphatically distances himself from Luthmann's arguments for the necessity of keeping basic problems latent. In his view, that is a paradigmatically counterenlightenment approach to politics. He proposes instead that all problems of general societal significance be submitted to open, unrestricted discussion in a democratic public sphere. Collective goals would be agreed upon in such discussions and implemented through existing organs of administration. There is no room in this model for keeping functions that are manifest at one level latent at lower levels. So systems-theoretical analysis—which, on Habermas's view, is necessary only to get at latent functions—presumably would exist only to transcend itself continually, that is, to make latent interdependencies manifest and thus open to discussion and reasoned acceptance or rejection. Perhaps Habermas wants to maintain that latent functions, like background, assumptions, are unavoidable and can never be made manifest all at once. Then systems analysis, like presuppositions analysis, would be an ongoing, unending *task* of self-clarification. While this analysis does not answer the question raised above concerning the type of administration that would be desirable in a genuinely democratic society, it does suggest that, in light of Habermas's political ideals, the answer should not be "systemically rather than socially integrated."

The normative inadequacy of system concepts for characterizing the institutions of a genuinely democratic society becomes even clearer when they are viewed in the light of Habermas's earlier discussions of complexity and democracy. In *Legitimation Crisis* he criticized elite theorists (from Pareto and Michels through Schumpeter and Weber to Lipset and Truman) in these words:

Democracy in this view . . . counts only as a method for selecting leaders and the accoutrements of leadership. . . . It is no longer tied to political equality in the sense of an equal distribution of political power, that is, of the chances to exercise power. . . . Democracy no longer has the goal of rationalizing authority through the participation of citizens in discursive processes of will-formation. It is intended instead to make compromises possible between ruling elites. Thus, the substance of classical democratic theory is finally surrendered. . . . Pluralism of elites replaces the self-determination of the people.[31]

If self-determination, political equality, and the participation of citizens in decision-making processes are the hallmarks of true democracy, then a democratic government could not be a political *system* in Habermas's sense, that is, a domain of action *differentiated* from other parts of society and preserving its *autonomy* in relation to them while regulating its interchanges with them via delinguistified steering media like money and power. The idea of democratic participation in government decision making can be spelled out in a number of different ways, from pyramidal council systems to competitive, participatory party systems in which leaders are effectively made responsible to the rank and file.[32] But each of them entails a loss, through "dedifferentiation," of "autonomy" of the political system. Why, then, does Habermas insist on the continued need for system differentiation in this domain?

One consideration seems to be practicality: How could participatory democracy operate in pluralistic societies with millions of members sharing no common worldview? There would, it seems, have to be *some* form of representative democracy, *some* type of party system, *some* way of selecting leaders with *some* measure of latitude for decision making, *some* administrative apparatus for carrying out decisions, etc. This is the point, I take it, of characterizing schemes in which all of this is simply thought away as "utopian" in a negative sense. Even if this is granted, however, the size and shape of the "some" in each case cannot be determined in an a priori manner. As Habermas himself has stated, this is an open question that can only be decided through learning processes that test the limits of the realizability of the utopian elements of the democratic tradition. Against Luhmann he argued that even on grounds of effectiveness there is no conclusive argument for shielding the administrative system from democratic participation.[33] Numerous studies have shown that there are very real and rather narrow limits to centralized administrative planning. They may well be inherent in it. This raises the question of whether participation might not actually enhance planning capacity under certain conditions. As Habermas noted, the rationalizing effect "is difficult to determine, for democratization would, on the one hand, dismantle the avoidable complexity . . . produced by the uncontrolled inner dynamic of the economic process. But at the same time it would bring the unavoidable (i.e., not specific to a system) complexity of generalized discursive processes of will-formation into play. Of course the balance does not have to be negative if the limits to complexity . . . built into administration are reached very soon. In this case, one complexity that follows unavoidably from the logic of unrestrained communication would be overtaken, as it were, by another complexity that follows as unavoidably from the logic of comprehensive planning."[34] In short, there is no general answer to the question of where and when and how participatory planning may be more effective than nonparticipatory planning. It can only be answered by testing and learning in different and changing circumstances.

Furthermore, even where it is less effective in an instrumental sense, we may favor it on other grounds. System complexity is merely one point of view from which to judge "progress."[35] Even in the realm of natural evolution, the degree of complexity is not a sufficient criterion for the level of development, since "increasing complexity in physical organization or mode of life often proves to be an evolutionary dead-end."[36] In the case of social evolution, growth of system complexity must, on Habermas's own principles, be subordinated to the communicative rationalization of life as a measure of progress. Realistically, there will have to be compromises and trade-offs. The "selection pressure on complex systems of action in a world that is contingent," that is, the problem of survival, cannot be wished away.[37] However, for critical social theory, the "utopian" idea of self-conscious self-determination must remain a regulative idea, in light of which we may at least recognize when we are compromising and why.

3

Social-systems theory represents today, no less than it did in 1971, "the *Hochform* of a technocratic consciousness" that militates against any tendencies toward democratization and promotes a depoliticization of the public sphere by defining practical questions from the start as technical questions.[38] Why, then, does Habermas now regard it as desirable, or perhaps even necessary, to integrate it into critical theory?

The reason clearly cannot be the proven fruitfulness of this approach as a framework for *empirical* social research. Nothing has happened since 1967 to remedy the apparent "fetishism of concepts" or the "ridiculous imbalance between the towering heap of empty categorical containers and the slight empirical content housed in them."[39] Nor has Luhmann's conceptual imperialism improved matters in this regard. Even in the home territory of social-systems analysis, the theory of formal organizations, the question of its empirical fruitfulness is, at best, an open one. The disproportion between the complex conceptual arsenal, on the one hand, and our ability to operationalize and actually use the notions of "input" and "output," "feedback loops" and "control mechanisms," "environments" and "adaptive capacity," on the other, is generally conceded, even by its proponents.[40] The abstractness, vagueness, and empirical indeterminacy of such concepts have rendered the predictive power of system models questionable, to say the least.[41] One of the problems is the neglect of internal factors—structures, processes, problems—by organizational systems theorists. In their reaction to classical organization theory's overemphasis on such factors and its neglect of the impact of an organization's environment on how it is structured and operated and on what goals it pursues, they have too often gone to the opposite extreme: "Rational planning and decision-making appear almost not to exist . . . , and little if any attention is given to interpersonal relations among members."[42] In short, social-systems theory does not recommend itself on grounds of empirical-analytical fruitfulness and predictive power, even in the favored setting of formal organizations.

On what grounds, then, does it recommend itself? Why has systems theory proved to be so popular in the theory of complex organizations? Part of the answer might be its appropriateness to "the type of problems that management encounters in the newer, more technologically complex industries. Here the issue has shifted from efficient task fulfillment to the consideration of structures with the necessary flexibility to ensure system 'survival' in the face of rapid change."[43] Be that as it may, the use of systems theory in the study of formal organizations has in fact been largely normative-analytic rather than empirical-analytic. Though boundaries and goal states cannot be empirically *ascertained*, they can be stipulated or *set*. Systems analysis can then be used as an aid in planning. It provides what Habermas once called second-order technical knowledge. But *this* cannot be what recommends it to *him*.

Its seductiveness for him derives, I think, from its perceived theoretical virtues. Thus, he explains the role that Parson's work plays in *The Theory of Communicative Action* by praising it as "without equal in its level of abstraction and differentiation, its social-theoretical scope and systematic quality, while at the same time it draws upon the literatures of specialized research" (p. 199). Similarly, it seems to be Luhmann's conceptual and theoretical virtuosity that Habermas admires above all else. There is, of course, always the possibility that these virtues are just the other side of the coin of the vices mentioned above, in particular of the "ridiculous imbalance" that Habermas noted in 1967. In what follows, I shall try to arouse some suspicion concerning the supposed virtues of systems theory by refurbishing the familiar objections to functionalism that Habermas himself once raised. It seems to me that they have lost nothing of their power.

In the first section, I mentioned the lower degree of structural fixity in social as contrasted with biological systems. A change of structure can as well be regarded as a regeneration of the original system as its transformation into a new system. There seems to be no objective way of deciding which description is correct. In *Legitimation Crisis* Habermas suggested that this problem might be overcome if we combined systems analysis with lifeworld analysis in the framework of a theory of social evolution that took account of both the expansion of steering capacity and the development of worldviews. The idea seemed to be that we could then get at the historically variable interpretations of social life in a systematic way and thus ascertain the goal states of social systems in a nonarbitrary manner. Without going into great detail, I would like simply to register my doubt that the problem can be solved in this way. A developmental logic of worldviews and normative structures is not going to help fix the goal states of social systems in a precise empirical manner, since at any given formal stage of development, countless different material conceptions of the good (social) life are possible. Nor will concrete lifeworld analysis do the trick if members' conceptions of social life and its essential structures are multifarious, fluid, flexible, tailored to varied situations, and so forth—as they typically are in modern societies. It seems obvious, furthermore, that members of social organizations that are undergoing change may themselves strongly disagree as to whether or not they are also "in crisis."

Systems theory is sometimes thought (by Habermas too, apparently) to have overcome at least one central problem of classical functional analysis, which one of its practitioners, Emile Durkheim, expressed as follows: "To show how a fact is useful is not to explain how it originated or why it is what it is. The uses which it serves presuppose the specific properties characterizing it, but do not create them. The need we have of things cannot give them existence, nor can it confer their specific nature upon them. It is to causes of another sort that they owe their existence."[44] Thus the contributions made by the consequences of patterns of action to the maintenance of a social system can't of themselves explain why these patterns exist. If the functional consequences are manifest (intended), the explanation presents no particular problems, but if they are latent (unintended, unrecognized), we still have to wonder why such useful patterns of activity ever arose and why they continue to exist. The systems theorist has an answer ready: like any cybernetic process, social processes have their feedback loops, through which the results of each stage of a cycle are the causes of the next. As Hempel and Nagel pointed out some time ago, however, there are very demanding logical requirements on this type of explanation, and they are not met in social-systems research. One might point, in particular, to the unsatisfied requirement of specifying empirically and with some degree of precision the feedback and control mechanisms that are supposedly at work to keep the system directed toward its supposed goals. Without this, social-systems theory can "achieve little more than a translation of old ideas into a new jargon."[45]

It has generally made sense to approach biological systems as unified, integrated, adapted systems that have been naturally selected, and thus to treat their structures and processes as contributing somehow to system maintenance (though doubts have arisen about the usefulness of systems theory here as well). Does the same approach make sense with respect to social systems? Is biocybernetics going to be any more fruitful a model of society than classical mechanics was? It has some of the same drawbacks, for instance, the traditional ideological twist of treating what is social, and thus potentially the object of human will, as natural and thus purely a matter of objectified relations, processes, and events. Habermas hopes to dissolve this solidity in the waters of action theory, but it may just prove to be insoluble. As I have tried to show, traces of systems-theoretic objectification can be detected in his description of "the political system." And as I shall now suggest, they are also present in his projection of political processes in a genuinely democratic society: the latter are represented in terms of the relations between a government administration conceived of as *system* and a public sphere conceived of as *lifeworld*. The categories remain the same, but the direction of control changes.

This approach, which was already suggested in Habermas's Hegel Prize lecture (1974) and in *The Theory of communicative Action* (1981),[46] has become more explicit in recent essays:

If curbs and indirect regulation are now to be directed against the internal dynamics of public administration as well, the necessary potentials for reflection and steering must be sought elsewhere, namely in a completely altered relationship between autonomous, self-organized public spheres on the one hand and domains of action regulated by money and administrative power on the other. This leads to the difficult task of making possible a democratic generalization of interest positions and a universalist justification of norms *below* the threshold of party apparatuses that have become independent complex organizations and have, so to speak, migrated into the political system. . . . By this I mean that the integrative social force of solidarity would have to be able to maintain itself in the face of the "forces" of the other two regulatory resources, money and administrative power. . . . A political will-formation that was to have an influence on the boundaries and the interchange between communicatively structured spheres of life on the one hand and the state and the economy on the other would have to draw from this same source. . . . Autonomous public spheres would have to achieve a combination of power and intelligent self-restraint that could make the self-regulating mechanisms of the state and the economy sufficiently sensitive to the goal-oriented results of radically democratic will-formation."[47]

This may or may not be a possible way of securing democratic decision-making processes. I shall not attempt to answer that question here but shall only try to prevent another way—democratization through dedifferentiation of economy and state—from being metatheoretically ruled out by appeal to systems-theoretic injunctions.[48] Here again the question arises of whether differentiation is the last word or whether it should be superseded by nonregressive forms of dedifferentiation.

Habermas is certainly correct in arguing that *some* type of functional analysis is essential to the reconstruction of the Marxian project. The idea that history has not been made with will and consciousness, that unplanned consequences, unrecognized interdependencies, uncomprehended systemic dynamics hold sway over our lives like a second nature, is quite naturally spelled out by this means. The question is, what type of functional analysis?

We do not need the paraphernalia of social-systems theory to identify unintended consequences. Nor do we need them to study the "functions" that an established social practice fulfills for other parts of the social network, for these are simply the recurrent consequences of this recurrent pattern of social action for those other parts. If the consequences for a given institution support its continued existence—the status quo, more or less—they are usually said to be functional for that institution; if the consequences are destablizing for a given institution—if they necessitate change, more or less—they are usually said to be dysfunctional for that institution. Whether stabilizing or destabilizing, functional or dysfunctional, causal interconnections of this sort can be investigated with comparatively meager theoretical means. Perhaps the need for systems theory arises in the attempt to comprehend the inner dynamics of expansive subsystems like the economy and the state? I do not know whether this is the case in the final analysis, but it does not serve this function in Habermas's argument, for he more or less takes the expansive dynamics of these systems for granted in his analysis of colonization. There is no attempt to provide the type of analysis of inner dynamics that Marx was concerned with in *Capital*. And in fact, there is some question as to whether this is even on the systems-theoretic agenda. Marx was concerned with the internal workings and endogenously generated problems of the economic system. Systems theory directs our attention rather to problems generated by the environments of systems. In fact, one of its virtues, according to Habermas, is that it gets us beyond the strongly idealized models that resulted from focusing on the inner dynamics of a system in isolation. But it is, I think, fair to say that the question of whether and how systems theory can also be used to reconstruct the expansive inner dynamics of the economic and administrative systems is still open. Until this is resolved, we do not know whether the processes of colonization that Habermas singles out will need to be understood in specifically systems-theoretic terms. There are alternative frameworks for dealing with phenomena of monetarization and bureaucratization, from Marxist theories of commodification to neo-Weberian accounts of the bureaucratic state. And much of what he has to say about "mediatization" could be rendered in action-theoretic terms. In short, it is not clear just where the need for systems theory arises.

If we look to Habermas's favored formulations, they usually stress the ideas of "objective purposiveness," the "system rationality" of unplanned adaptive responses, objective (unintended) responses to objective challenges to system survival. But these holistic ways of talking bring us right back to the simple fact that the "needs" of social systems cannot be empirically established because "survival" is not a matter of objectively specifiable parameters.

To deal with this global level of analysis, Habermas in the 1960s developed the idea of a "theoretically" or "systematically" generalized history with practical intent."[49] He argued that the inadequacies of functionalist social theory are insuperable so long as it is understood as a form of empirical-analytic inquiry: goal states are not simply given. On the other hand, if we do not wish to rest content with using it as a form of normative-analytic inquiry, we cannot simply stipulate goal states. What alternative is there? They can, Habermas proposed, be hypothetically anticipated as the outcome of a general and unrestricted rational discussion among members based on adequate knowledge of limiting conditions and functional necessities: "Given such criteria, a state of equilibrium would be determined by whether the system of authority in a society realized utopian contents and dissolved ideological contents to the degree made objectively possible by the given state of productive forces and technological progress. In that case, however, society can no longer be conceived exclusively as a system of self-preservation. . . . Rather, the meaning in terms of which the functionality of social processes is measured is now linked to the idea of communication free from domination."[50] A functionalism of this global sort would no longer be understood on the model of biology. It would rely, rather, on a "general interpretive framework" analogous in important respects to the systematically generalized history used as a narrative foil in psychoanalysis.

In place of the goal state of a self-regulating system, we would have the anticipated end-state of a formative process. A functionalism that is hermeneutically enlightened and historically oriented has as its aim not general theories in the sense of strict empirical science, but a general interpretation of the kind we examined in the case of psychoanalysis. . . . For a historically oriented functionalism does not aim at technologically exploitable information. It is guided by an emancipatory cognitive interest that has reflection as its aim and demands enlightenment about its own formative process. . . . The human species is constituted as such through formative processes that are embodied in the structural transformation of social systems and that can be reflected upon, in other words, narrated systematically from the perspective of an anticipated later point in those processes. For this reason, the framework of a general interpretation, however saturated it may be with prior hermeneutical experience and however much it may have been confirmed in individual interpretations, retains a hypothetical moment. The truth of historically oriented functionalism is confirmed not technically but only practically, in the successful continuation and completion of a formative process.[51]

This notion of a theoretically generalized narrative drawing upon both hermeneutical and functional modes of analysis was the developed form of Habermas's idea of a historically oriented theory of society with practical intent. It retained an intrinsic relation to practice: guided by an emancipatory interest, social analysis was undertaken from the standpoint of realizing, to the extent possible at a given stage of development, a form of organization based on unrestricted and undistorted communication. The truth of such analyses could be confirmed in the end only through the successful continuation of *Bildungsprozesse.*

After the 1960s Habermas's thought moved in a more strongly theoretical direction. It is because he now wants a *theory* of contemporary society that the systems approach seems so appealing. Habermas once criticized Marx for succumbing to the illusion of rigorous science and traced a number of Marxism's historical problems with political analysis and political practice to this source. The question I have wanted to pose here is whether, in flirting with systems theory, he does not run the danger of being seduced by the same illusion in more modern dress.

7

Practical Discourse: On the Relation of Morality to Politics

From his earliest writings on the public sphere to his most recent writings on law, politics, and morality, Jürgen Habermas has been concerned to rethink the foundations of democratic theory.[1] Though there have been shifts in his conception of the appropriate political institutions and processes, his basic normative ideas have remained largely constant. Like Kant, he seeks to ground the principles of justice in notions of practical reason and autonomous self-legislation. Unlike Kant, he wants to do this without relying on supraempirical ideas of reason and autonomy, though he does retain a variant of the distinction between *Wille* (i.e., the rational general will) and *Willkür* (i.e., the aggregation of particular wills). And as with Kant, it is not possible to understand Habermas's legal and political theory without also examining his moral theory. They are, in fact, so closely interconnected that one might, with some justification, view his moral theory as a theory of "political morality"—of social justice rather than of moral virtue, character, feelings, and judgment, or of ethical life, community, and the good—and his political theory as being, at least at the core, a "moral politics"—as privileging strictly universal laws over the conflict and compromise of interests.

In what follows, I want to examine Habermas's conception of practical discourse with the aim of showing how a residue of the Kantian dichotomy between the phenomenal and the noumenal persists there in the form of a tension between situated reasoning and the transcendence of situatedness required by his model of rational consensus. I will then briefly indicate how that tension figures in his conception of the public sphere. Kant once wrote that the problem of a just political order could be solved for a race of devils, but only because a providential nature brought about the juridical condition that morality demanded. As Habermas does not rely on a providential nature, political justice can only be achieved for him through the discursive unification of empirical wills. The basis of political legitimacy becomes what all could will not as noumenal selves but as participants in practical discourse, whose adoption of the moral point of view enables them to transcend not only interest-oriented perspectives but also value-based perspectives. The question arises whether this is a realistic normative ideal for democratic theory.

I should make clear at the start that I will not be dealing with Habermas's attempt to ground his conception of procedural justice in universal pragmatic features of communication. Questions concerning his explication and justification of the moral point of view are bracketed in what follows.[2] My concern is only with whether his conceptions of practical discourse and rational consensus are appropriate models, however idealized, for political debate and collective decision making. It is also worth mentioning that I shall be pursuing a strategy of immanent critique. Rather than confronting Habermas's ideas with objections from competing theoretical traditions, I hope to bring out the tensions in those ideas themselves. In particular, I want to show that what he has to say about needs, interests, and values pulls against what he says about rational consensus, and it does so in ways that suggest a more flexible and politically serviceable conception of rationally motivated agreement.

1

In Habermas's discourse ethics, the rationally motivated consensus that expresses practical reason in the sphere of justice concerns the general acceptability of the anticipated consequences of a norm for the legitimate satisfaction of needs. If we are to understand more precisely the problems this approach faces, we shall have to take a close look at what he means by "needs." He is not referring to anything that can be attributed to individuals prior to or independently of social relations (in a way that society or the state could then be based on some form of contractual agreement to meet them). In his view, we have access to our needs only under culturally shared interpretations. Nor is he referring to needs in contrast to mere preferences, desires, feelings, or the like. He uses *Bedürfniße* in the very broad sense captured in the following passage:

Needs have two faces. They are differentiated on the volitional side into inclinations and desires, and on the other side, the intuitive, into feelings and moods. Desires are oriented toward situations of need satisfaction; feelings "perceive" situations in the light of possible need satisfaction. Needs are, as it were, the background of partiality that determines our subjective attitudes in relation to the external world. Such predilections express themselves both in the active striving for goods and in the affective perception of situations. The partiality of desires and feelings is expressed at the level of language in interpretations of needs, that is, in evaluations for which evaluative expressions are available. . . . These evaluative, need-interpreting expressions serve to make a predilection understandable . . . and at the same time to justify it, in the sense of making it plausible by appeal to general standards of evaluation that are widespread at least in our own culture. Evaluative expressions or standards of value have justificatory force when they characterize a need in such a way that addresses can, in the framework of a common cultural heritage, recognize in these interpretations their own needs.[3]

Thus the articulation of needs in practical discourse will draw upon existing standards of value; as interpreted, needs are internally related to, and thus inseparable from, cultural values.

At first sight, the implications of this for the possibility of rational consensus seem disastrous. If the evaluative expressions used to interpret needs have "justificatory force" only within "the framework of a common cultural heritage," how can we reasonably expect to arrive at universal (i.e., transcultural) agreements on the acceptability of the consequences of a norm for the legitimate satisfaction of needs? Or to bring the argument closer to our present concerns, how can we hope to achieve rational political consensus in a pluralistic society?

The first thing to note is that Habermas's understanding of "the general will," "the common interest," and the like has a Rousseauean strain. He is not talking of the aggregation of individual interests but of the transcendence of merely particular interests in a search for the common good. He differs from Rousseau, however, in stressing the *argumentative* nature of that search. The public deliberation that leads to the formation of a general will has the form of a debate in which competing particular interests are given equal consideration. It requires of participants that they engage in "ideal role-taking" to try to understand the situations and perspectives of others and give them equal weight to their own. This adoption of the standpoint of impartiality is what distinguishes an orientation toward justice from a concern merely with one's own interests or with those of one's group. And it is only from this standpoint, the moral point of view as Habermas reconstructs it, that we can draw a distinction between what is normatively required of everyone as a matter of justice and what is valued within a particular subculture as part of the good life.

In traditional societies the legal and political orders are interwoven with the tacit background certainties of an inherited form of life. Social institutions and intersubjectively binding norms belong to the taken-for-granted totality of the lifeworld. In modern societies the unquestioned validity of what is socially established becomes increasingly open to discussion. According to Habermas, when existing norms are subjected to examination from the standpoint of fairness, a key differentiation is introduced into the domain of social practice. On the one hand, there are matters of justice to be regulated by norms binding on all alike; on the other, there are questions of the good life, which are not susceptible of general legislation but have to be considered in connection with diverse life forms (*Lebensformen*) and life histories.[4] It is only after the specifically moral point of view has come to be distinguished from concrete forms of *Sittlichkeit*, or ethical life, that normative questions concerning what is right can be adequately distinguished from evaluative questions concerning what is good, which can *also* be rationally discussed but only within the context of a shared form of life.

How, then, are the two types of questions related? Valid

norms, on Habermas's account, "claim to express, in relation to some matter requiring regulation, an interest common to all those affected" and thus "must be capable in principle of meeting with the rationally motivated approval of everyone involved."[5] The practical discourses in which such claims are examined will, then, have an internal relation to participants' interpretations of their interests and hence to their values.[6] So just as the analysis of needs led us to consider the values in terms of which needs are interpreted, the analysis of what is involved in ascertaining a common interest carries us in the same direction. But this means that discourse concerning the legitimacy of general norms, inasmuch as it concerns the acceptability of their consequences for the satisfaction of participants' needs and interests, will not admit of closure with respect to discussions of the appropriateness or adequacy of the value standards in the light of which needs and interests are interpreted. More generally, as Habermas acknowledges, it is in principle open to participants in practical discourse to call into question the language that frames debate, that is, the terms in which problems are identified and posed, data selected and described, reasons formulated and weighed, warrants proposed and assessed, and so forth.[7] Questioning the very terms of debate, particularly with regard to the adequacy or appropriateness of standards of value, is the sort of thing that regularly occurs in the political discourse of pluralistic societies. In such cases, normative disagreements turn on value disagreements. And, as Habermas realizes, we need not presuppose that rational agreement on values is possible: cultural values, though more or less widely shared, "do not count as universal"; they "can be made plausible only in the context of a particular form of life."[8]

The same can be said of the type of hermeneutical self-reflection that Habermas refers to as "ethical" (in contrast to "moral") deliberation. Pushed far enough, the discussion of "strong evaluations" can lead to a consideration of who we are and who we want to be, of what kind of life we want to lead. And these questions neither require nor permit the same distancing from the context of action that, according to Habermas, questions of justice do. In deliberating about who we are and examining the strong evaluations involved in our idea of the good life, "the roles of participant in argumentation and social actor overlap." We cannot "jump out of the particular life history or form of life in which (we) actually find (ourselves)" and with which our identities are "irrevocably bound up."[9]

If this meant that evaluative frames cannot be challenged and changed with reasons, that they have to be accepted as given in practical discourse, the orientation of the latter to universal validity would be an illusion. Thus, it is crucial for Habermas that value standards can be rationally criticized and revised. But the forms he envisages for such discussions again set them off from discourse: "critique" and "criticism" remain tied to the context of action and experience in ways that discourse does not.[10] One may challenge, for instance, the truthfulness of an agent's expression of desires, preferences, feelings, and so forth. When this goes beyond questions concerning insincerity, conscious deception, manipulation, or the like to questions of inauthenticity, self-deception, false consciousness, and the like, we may enter into a form of discussion whose paradigm case, in Habermas's view, is therapeutic critique. The aim of this mode of communication is to get an individual or group of individuals "to adopt a reflective attitude toward [their] own expressive manifestations," to "see through the irrational limitations" to which they are subject, to "clarify [their] systematic self-deception."[11] Of course, using psychotherapy as a model for the critique of false consciousness raises questions of its own, but I shall not consider them here. In the present context I am interested only in noting Habermas's acknowledgment that these modes of communication do not involve the idealizing presuppositions of practical discourse but remain closely tied to the context of action and experience.

The adequacy or appropriateness of standards of value can also be challenged in forms of communication for which aesthetic criticism serves as a paradigm. As Habermas understands it, this may involve an indirect challenge to our evaluative language by getting us to see a work or performance as "an authentic expression of an exemplary experience." Grounds or reasons serve here "to guide perception and to make the authenticity of a work so evident that this aesthetic experience can itself become a rational motive for accepting the standards" according to which it counts as such.[12] The general idea here seems to be that our wants, needs, feelings, emotions, attitudes, sentiments, and the like are not normally shaped *directly* by the force of arguments. But discussion can serve to "open our eyes" to the values disclosed or discredited in certain exemplary experiences. Habermas focuses on aesthetic experience, but a case could also be made for the transformative power of experiences of significant others, life crises, alien cultures, countercultures, nature, and the sacred, among other things. Modes of reflective discussion are, in these matters too, no substitute for experience but function to articulate guide and it. Thus they too remain bound to the context of action and experience in a way that, according to Habermas, discourses do not. But perhaps it is time now to examine this latter claim more closely.

2

It is fundamental to discourse ethics that rightness claims have cognitive and not merely volitional significance. Their validity, like the validity of truth claims, is based not on de facto acceptance but on the soundness of the reasons that can be offered in support of them. Warranted commands, like warranted assertions, require justification. Having insisted on this basic similarity between truth and rightness, Habermas is then at pains to point out some basic differences. For one thing, we do not conceive the normative order of society as existing independently of validity claims, as we do nature. Social reality is intrinsically linked to validity in a way that natural reality is not. "Consequently, the results of practical discourses in which it is demonstrated that the validity claim of de facto recognized rules cannot be vindicated . . . can stand in a critical relation to reality (i.e., the symbolic reality of society), while theoretical discourse can be directed not against reality itself (i.e., nature), but only against false assertions about it."[13] This is reflected in the types of argument and evidence relevant to the two cases. As we saw, the reasons advanced in practical discourse have to do with the anticipated consequences of proposed norms for the satisfaction of needs and interests. And this means that they will eventually refer to desires and feelings rather than to perceptions—which raises the question of whether desires and feeling can be standardized for purposes of normative consensus in the way that perceptions can (through measurement) for purposes of theoretical consensus. In terms of the previous discussion of values, the problems can be stated as follows. The backing for norms comes not in the form of demonstrative arguments but in the form of "casuistic evidence" regarding consequences for need satisfaction. The "cogency" or "consensus-generating power" of this kind of reason is, as we saw, inherently dependent on the sociocultural contexts in which they are mobilized.[14] Because of the diversification of ways of life in modern societies, which Habermas regards is irreversible, different sorts of reasons will obviously possess different degrees of cogency or power for different groups. What is more, the heightened individualism of modern life means that differences in individual temperament, experience, and situation can also translate into differences concerning the relative cogency of different sorts of reasons for action. In short, the selection and weighing of casuistic evidence for norms will itself reflect the pluralism and individualism of modern life. Furthermore, since Habermas cedes a certain privilege to subjects as regards the interpretation of their own needs, there can be no question of prescribing or dictating their needs to them.[15] We can at most try to convince others, by using arguments that run the spectrum from aesthetic to therapeutic, that their understanding of their own needs is inadequate, inauthentic, or what have you. But as we saw, these arguments themselves remain tied to specific contexts of action and experience and thus are not able wholly to transcend the struggle between Max Weber's warring gods and demons.

Habermas is aware of this situation and in fact conceives of discourse ethics as a *response* to it: "The fact that modern societies are differentiated into life forms and interest positions, and will increasingly be so, does not mean that action oriented to mutual understanding ceases to be effective. Our need to reach understanding increases to the same degree, and this need has to be met at higher and higher levels of abstraction.

Consequently, the norms and principles that we can agree upon become more and more general."[16] As a rule of argumentation, Habermas's universalization principle is meant precisely to bridge the gap between different individual and group wants and feelings, and norms whose validity everyone accepts on the grounds that they are in the general or common interest—the gap, that is, between the many particular wills and the general will. But how does this work if, in contrast to Rousseau, Habermas builds into his sociocultural starting point not only solidarity but also pluralism and individualism? His answer is, By argumentatively convincing everyone to accept the foreseeable consequences and side-effects that the general observance of a proposed norm can be expected to have for the satisfaction of each person's interests. But how do we do this if those interests are typically not only different but competing? It is of decisive importance for Habermas's political theory that he does not answer, By negotiating a compromise. This is not to say that he rejects bargaining and compromise as reasonable means for dealing with conflicts of interests. Quite the contrary. But as his debate with Ernst Tugendhat makes clear, he subordinates them to the achievement of consensus in practical discourse.[17] Compromise is, so to speak, a second-best alternative that we can turn to when discourse has shown there to be no common interest. Even if negotiated under conditions of a balance of power ensuring participants an equal opportunity to push their own interests, compromise fails to capture the core of our sense of justice: it "cannot account for an intuition that is very difficult to deny, the idea of impartiality, . . . of impartially judging the interests of all concerned."[18]

From the standpoint of impartiality, we seek not to maximize our own interests but to discover a general or common interest. There are two quite different ways of understanding this, and Habermas is not always clear about the difference. On the one hand, through discourse we may find or shape particular interests that are distributively shared by all participants. In this sense, for example, if security against violent attack turned out to be in each's own particular interest, then it could be said to be a common or shared or "generalizable" interest. But most of the matters that require regulation in complex, highly differentiated societies are not of this sort. They impinge on a diversity of life situations and life projects in a diversity of ways so that consequences are different for different individuals and groups. Discovering a general interest in such cases will require that participants distance themselves from particular "first-order" interests in a different sense from that required in the other case. This is why, according to Habermas, we can argumentatively agree on what is in the general interest only if every participant adopts an impartial standpoint from which his or her own particular interests count for no more nor less than those of any other participant. That is to say, "the impartial consideration of all interests affected already presupposes a moral standpoint. . . . We have to consider what general interest all those involved would agree upon if they were to adopt the moral standpoint of impartiality, taking into account all the interests affected."[19]

This is a lot to ask of participants in political debate, but it is not yet enough. For not only will the consequences differ among individuals and groups, the interpretation and assessment of those consequences will differ among them as well.[20] So the "ideal role taking" in which participants must engage will require each participant to put him- or herself in the place of every other participant in the very strong sense of coming to understand and appreciate the consequences from all of their interpretive and evaluative perspectives. Under ideal conditions this would be backed by the requirement that each have the opportunity to present his or her own point of view and to seek to make it comprehensible and plausible to others. Nevertheless, even if we outfit our good-willed participants with the intelligence and sensitivity to understand and appreciate the needs, interests, and points of view of others, we are still far from rationally motivated consensus. For one thing, participants' interpretations of their needs cannot simply be taken at face value. Though they have a "privileged access" to their own feelings and desires, they are by no means the sole and final arbiters regarding them. "Kant and the utilitarians . . . reduced the motives and aims of actions, as well as the interests and value orientations on which they depended, to inner states and private episodes. . . . In fact, however, motives and ends have something intersubjective about them; they are always interpreted in the light of a cultural tradition. . . . [Thus] the individual actor cannot be the *final* instance in developing and revising his interpretations of needs. Rather, his interpretations change in the context of the lifeworld of the social group to which he belongs; little by little, practical discourses can also gear into this quasi-natural process."[21] To the extent that this happens, the cultural interpretations in the light of which different participants understand their needs and values, interests and aims are also up for discussion. So consensus could be achieved only if all participants could come to agree on the authentic interpretation of each's needs, and they would have to do so from the very different hermeneutic starting points afforded by a pluralistic and individualistic culture. This would presumably entail criticizing and rejecting value orientations that are too self- or group-centered to permit the proper weighting of other participants' needs, as well as value orientations imbued with racism, sexism, ethnocentrism, homophobia, or any other less than universalistic outlook. In a word, only those value differences compatible with a postconventional moral orientation can survive practical discourse.

But we still have a way to go before we can arrive at rationally motivated consensus. For we now have somehow to "synthesize" all of the various consequences, variously interpreted and variously assessed, into one unified judgment of rightness or wrongness. We are, remember, dealing with the case in which particular "first-order" needs and interests are different. How, then, do we weigh x's feelings and desires against y's, or negatively affecting the intensely felt needs of a few against inconveniencing the less intensely felt needs of many, and so on? After hearing the arguments of everyone, each will have to judge for him- or herself which normative regulation seems fairest to all of the different—and differently interpreted, assessed, and weighted—interests involved. On what grounds should we suppose that everyone would, even under ideal conditions, agree in a judgment of this sort?[22]

The success of Habermas's universalization principle in getting from multifarious "I want"s to a unified "we will" depends on finding "universally accepted needs." The argument just sketched suggests that this may not be possible when there are fundamental divergences in value orientations. The separation of formal procedure from substantive content is never absolute: we cannot agree on what is just without achieving some measure of agreement on what is good. But practical discourse is conceived by Habermas to deal precisely with situations in which there is an absence of such agreement, that is, when there is a need to regulate matters concerning which there are conflicting interests and values, competing conceptions of the good.

3

In recent essays Habermas has proposed a multidimensional model of discourse in the democratic public sphere. It comprises a variety of types of "rational collective will-formation" in both the resolution of conflicts and the pursuit of collective goals.[23] What is common to these types is the neutralization of power differentials attached to conflicting interest positions or concealed in traditional value constellations. In addition to practical discourses in which laws and policies are justified as being in the general interest, the model includes deliberations in which general norms are applied to particular situations, ethical-political discussions concerning basic values and collective identity, the negotiation of compromises under fair bargaining conditions, and pragmatic discourses concerning the means of implementing policies and attaining goals. In a society organized along radical democratic lines, Habermas claims, this "whole web of overlapping forms of communication" would have to be effectively institutionalized.[24] But the institutionalization of practical discourses of justification remains central, for the integrity of the whole web depends on them: the conditions for negotiating fair compromises would have to be agreed to in practical discourse; the impartial application of general laws yields just results only if the laws themselves have stood the test of discursive justification; pragmatic discourses about means presuppose that we know what we want or should want; and ethical self-clarification itself cannot get us beyond the value differences that may result from it. Thus, despite these differentiations, the question still remains whether practical discourse is suitable as a normative ideal for discourse in the public sphere.

This question can be put in more concrete terms if we take a brief look at Habermas's account of the conditions of democratic politics.[25] He grants that large complex societies cannot do without markets and administrative bureaucracies and argues that the democratic ideal should be to bring these under the control of the will of the people as formed in open and public debate. For various reasons, which I shall not go into here, he does not think that this can be accomplished within the formal organizations of the economy and the state, or within formally organized political parties, interest and pressure groups, or the like. Having abandoned the hope that he earlier placed in the democratization of all governmentally relevant and publicly influential organizations, he now pursues the rather different line that locates rational collective will formation *outside* of formal organizations of every sort.[26] In this view, it is the variegated multiplicity of spontaneously formed publics engaged in informal discussions of issues of public interest that is the core of the democratic public sphere. The "nodal points" of this "web of informal communication" are voluntary associations that organize themselves and secure their own continued existence. "Associations of this kind concentrate on generating and disseminating practical convictions, that is, on discovering themes of relevance to society as a whole, contributing to the possible solution of problems, interpreting values, providing good reasons and discrediting others. They can only be effective in an indirect manner, that is, through changing the parameters of constitutional will-formation by way of widely influential changes in attitudes and values."[27]

I won't raise here the important question of how effective voluntary associations and social movements can be in monitoring and influencing the formal decision-making processes of a systemically integrated economy and state. I shall confine myself instead to pointing out that the tension between the reality of multiple value-perspectives and the ideal of rationally motivated consensus shows up in this account as well. Habermas acknowledges the sociostructural differentiation that goes along with a complex market economy and a bureaucratic state administration, and he welcomes the heightened pluralism of forms of life and individualism of personality structures characteristic of modern cultures. But the concomitant differences in background, situation, experience, training, and so forth regularly translate into basic differences in value orientation. And these differences get reflected in the voluntary associations and social movements that comprise the public sphere.[28] As a result, under the conditions specified in his model, the "democratic generalization of interests" and the "universalistic justification of norms" would encounter all the obstacles spelled out earlier in this essay.

Moreover, if judgments of the relative cogency of reasons that cite needs, interests, feelings, sentiments, and the like vary with interpretive and evaluative standpoints, and if there is no common measure by which to assess the relative weights of reasons articulated in different evaluative languages, then the distinction between argument and rhetoric, between convincing and persuading becomes less sharp than the discourse model allows. Habermas's interpretation of Freud holds out the promise of raising to consciousness unconscious determinants of behavior. This has to be understood in process terms, that is, not as an actually realizable state of affairs but as an orientation for what must always be an ongoing effort. The same can be said of the "cultural unconscious" that hermeneutics has unearthed and the "sociostructural unconscious" that systems theory tries to conceptualize. In all of these cases, even if we grant that it is possible in principle to bring any particular unconscious factor to consciousness, this by no means implies the possibility of making all of them conscious all at once. But this means that at every moment and in every situation, unconscious factors will play a role in shaping interpretive and evaluative perspectives and thus that the symbolic force of language will inevitably figure in judgments of cogency. As there is no Archimedean point from which to judge whether what democratic majorities regard as the better argument is really better, dissenters can only continue the debate. If minorities regularly fail to convince majorities or to be convinced by them, we may well conclude that judgements of better and

worse in this domain are intrinsically susceptible to considerable variation, that unanimity on practical-political issues is not
always attainable, and that democratic institutions should not
be constructed on the supposition that it is.

4

Understanding why Habermas insists on the supposition that
rational consensus be possible is the key to understanding his
approach to practical reason. As he sees it, this supposition is
not merely a normative or regulative *ideal* of argumentative
discourse but one of its constitutive *presuppositions*. If participants in discourse did not make this supposition, if they were
to assume instead that reaching agreement solely on the basis
of reasons is impossible, their linguistic behavior would have a
significance other than that of rational argumentation. More
generally, if we were (*per impossible*) to drop the pragmatic
presupposition that we could convince others of the validity of
claims by offering good reasons in support of them, most of
our rational practices would lose their sense, and this, it goes
without saying, would entail far-reaching changes in our form
of life. In Habermas's view, it would mean the elimination of
our main alternative to violence, coercion, and manipulation
as a means of conflict resolution and social coordination.

Be that as it may, I want to suggest that the participant's
perspective, the underlying presuppositions of which Habermas's pragmatics aim to reconstruct, has to be consistently
combined with the perspective of the observer. Assume for the
sake of argument that the latter reveals something like the
irreducible plurality of evaluative and interpretive standpoints
that I sketched above. Assume further that this pluralism is
found, from the observer's perspective, to be at the root of
many intractable political disputes. Can we reconcile this finding with the participant's spontaneous supposition that rational
agreement is possible? In dealing with similar situations, Habermas has introduced a notion of "reflective participation," of
participants whose previously unreflective behavior comes to
be informed by what they learn upon reflection to be the case.
We might extend that notion here to participants in political

discourse whose linguistic behavior is informed by the knowledge that irreducible value differences regularly give rise to intractable disagreements on normative questions. What pragmatic presuppositions might such participants bring to political discourse that would not simply transform it into more or less refined forms of symbolic manipulation? Or to bring this line of thought back to our original problem, is there a conception of public debate that is compatible both with this knowledge and with the supposition that some form of rationally motivated agreement, agreement based on good reasons, is possible?

I can do no more here than to suggest a line of reasoning. To begin with, we have to modulate the idea of rationally motivated agreement beyond Habermas's basic distinction between a strategically motivated compromise of interests and an argumentatively achieved consensus on validity. If the ultimate *moral-political* significance of agreement based on reasons is to provide an alternative to open or latent coercion as a means of social coordination, there is room for more than these varieties. Here I shall only mention two additional types.

(a) Owing to differences in evaluative and interpretive perspective, well-intentioned and competent participants may *disagree about the common good* (e.g., in the multitude of situations where the preservation of traditional values conflicts with economic expansion). In this familiar case the dispute is not about competing particular interests but about what is "really" in the general interest. If the parties to the dispute want genuinely to debate the point, they will, as Habermas maintains, have to suppose that it is in principle possible to convince and be convinced by good reasons. As reflective participants, however, they may at the same time doubt that in the case at hand complete consensus is achievable. Being good-willed members of the same political community, they will also keep in mind that if their *experimentum argumentationis* does fail to produce a consensus, they will have to reach a reasoned agreement of another sort if they want to do more than simply to vote. If that agreement is to serve as a stable basis for social cooperation, it will have to be some form of compromise, not among strategically acting utility maximizers, but among community-minded consociates who want to live together in harmony even when they disagree about the common good. The point I am getting at is that *rationally motivated* agreement as a moral-political alternative to coercion may well involve elements of conciliation, compromise, consent, accommodation, and the like. Argument, including argument about what is in the general interest, can play a role in shaping any and all of them.[29] And thus the expectation that they will figure in the outcome of political debate, as well as consensus in Habermas's strict sense, can itself give sense to participants' argumentative practices. The only supposition that seems necessary for the genuine give and take of rational discourse is that the force of the better argument can contribute to the final shape of *whatever* type of agreement is reached.

(b) I was assuming in (a) that disagreement concerned only what was good for a particular political community and not what was right for human beings generally. In Habermas's terms, that could be called an "ethical-political" dispute in contrast to a "moral-political" one.[30] The second type of disagreement I want briefly to mention has to do with *norms that at least one party takes to be moral* in Habermas's sense—that is, to be binding on all human beings (e.g., in connection with abortion, euthanasia, pornography, animal rights). There are a number of subcases here. For example, what one party considers to be a moral issue, another party may regard merely as a pragmatic issue or as a question of values open to choice or as a moral issue of another sort, or the opposing parties may agree on the issue but disagree as to the morally correct answer. These types of disagreement are usually rooted in different "general and comprehensive moral views," to borrow a phrase from Rawls.[31] For instance, members of different religious communities may have conceptions of the significance and value of human life that differ from one another and from those of secular interpretive communities.[32] If not even moral philosophers have been able to agree on the nature and scope of morality, any realistic conceptualization of the democratic public sphere will have to allow for disagreement in this regard too. Furthermore, since political discourse always takes place under less than ideal conditions, it will always be open to dissenters to view any given collective decision as tainted by de facto limitations and thus as not acceptable under ideal conditions.[33] Disagreements of these sorts are likely to be a permanent feature of democratic public life. They are in general not resolvable by strategic compromise, rational consensus, or ethical self-clarification in Habermas's senses of these terms. All that remains in his scheme are more or less subtle forms of coercion, e.g., majority rule and the threat of legal sanctions.

But we might rescue a sense of "rationally motivated agreement" even for situations of this sort. Reflective participants will be aware of the "particularity" of general and comprehensive moral views, of their rootedness in particular traditions, practices, and experiences. If they are fallibilists and if they consider the basic political institutions and procedures of their society to be just, they may well regard collective decisions arising from them as legitimate, and hence as "deserving of recognition," even when they disagree.[34] That is, their background agreement with the operative political conception of justice may *rationally motivate* them to consent to laws they regard as unwise or unjust in the hope, perhaps, that they will be able to use the same resources eventually to change them. In such situations, arguments may be used to convince others of the justice or injustice of a norm, for example by getting them to adopt the view of human life from which its consequences appear acceptable or unacceptable. The expectation that *some* participants, perhaps even a majority, could be convinced by these means seems a sufficient basis for genuine debate.

None of these considerations is new to political theory. I mention them here only to show that Habermas's conception of practical discourse is too restrictive to serve as a model, even as an ideal model, of rational will formation and collective decision making in the democratic public sphere.[35] There are alternatives to coercion not captured by his notions of negotiated compromise and rational consensus, forms of reasoned agreement among free and equal persons that are motivated by good reasons in ways different from the way singled out by his strong conception of argumentation. In pursuit of such agreements, citizens may enter public debate with a variety of expectations, of which the possibility of unanimity is only one. And this diversity in types of agreement and expectation is reflected in the diversity of forms of political conflict resolution. A public sphere whose institutions and culture embodied this diversity would, I have wanted to suggest, be a more realistic ideal than one embodying, in however detranscendentalized a form, Kant's insufficiently contextualized notion of the rational will.

Critical Theory and Political Theology: The Postulates of Communicative Reason

Doubts about the possibility of grounding critical social theory in a detranscendentalized, intersubjectivist theory of reason arise not only from post-Nietzschean and post-Heideggerian quarters. On quite a different front, political theologians have maintained that social inquiry undertaken with the practical intent of exposing and criticizing injustice in all its forms requires *stronger* normative foundations than a theory of reason can provide. One of the central arguments for this position starts from Kant's reflections on the limits of his own critique of practical reason.

In answering the third of his three basic questions of philosophy, For what may I hope? Kant gave a historically important twist to the philosophical foundations of religious belief. He made the answer to that question depend directly on the answer to the second of his basic questions, What ought I to do? and only indirectly on the answer to the first, What can I know? In contradistinction to the mainstream of traditional philosophical theology, Kant regarded speculative proofs of the freedom of the will, the immortality of the soul, and the existence of God as one and all spurious. To attempt to establish such propositions on theoretical, i.e., cosmological and metaphysical, grounds was hopeless, for *knowledge* of these things lay beyond the bounds of theoretical reason, as he established to his satisfaction in the First Critique. At the same time, these limits ensured that speculative *disproofs* of such propositions were ruled out of court as well. In fact, by confining our knowledge to the phenomenal realm, the realm of appearances, while insisting on the necessity of thinking—not knowing—a noumenal realm, a realm of things-in-themselves, Kant's Critique of Pure (Speculative) Reason had left open a space that might be occupied by other means. He filled this space in the Second Critique by means of not theoretical but practical reason. There Kant proposed *moral* arguments for religious belief to replace the disqualified cosmological and ontological arguments. He attempted to justify a *moral* faith in a *moral* religion, which he distinguished sharply and consistently from any metaphysically or historically based faith. In contrast to speculative theology, which Kant regarded as shot through with error and confusion, a *moral* theology he thought to be quite possible. In a nutshell, for him, to adopt the religious attitude was to regard moral duties as if they were divine commands.

I shall not be concerned here with the thorny exegetical debates about just how to interpret Kant's idea of a moral religion, nor will I be concerned to evaluate the arguments he presents on its behalf. I want to give only a brief account of these arguments as a prelude to my principal topic, which might be adumbrated as follows. A number of contemporary political theologians have approached the tasks of fundamental theology in a way reminiscent of Kant; that is, they have discussed the philosophical foundations of religious belief from the point of view of *practical* rather than theoretical reason and have conceptualized its essential content from the same point of view. There is, to be sure, one very important difference from Kant: whereas he starts from the experience and practice of individual morality, they start from the experience and practice of social-political morality. In one case we get a moral theology, in the other a *political* theology. Yet the structures of at least some of the central philosophical arguments are strikingly similar. What I would like to do here is to examine one such argument, the original of which is to be found in Kant's discussion of the postulates of pure practical reason in the dialectic of the Second Critique. Of the several variations on this theme in contemporary political theology, I shall consider that developed by Helmut Peukert in *Science, Action, and Fundamental Theology*, for it is one of the more philosophically self-conscious versions of the argument for what might be called a "political faith" in God.[1] My remarks will fall into three parts: first, an account of the general structure of Kant's postulate arguments; second, a brief look at the general perspective of political theology for the purpose of comprehending why and how this sort of argument might prove attractive to it; third, a reconstruction and assessment of Peukert's version of the argument.

1

Roughly, Kant's postulate arguments seek to establish that morality makes no sense unless we postulate the immortality of the soul and the existence of God. The relation of freedom to morality is somewhat different, for it is a direct presupposition of moral agency. By comparison, the arguments for God and immortality are indirect. Their form is something like the following: we are commanded by the moral law to pursue certain ends that would be impossible to achieve if God did not exist and the soul were not immortal. The inherent tension between our moral-rational duties and aspirations, on the one hand, and our finite limitations, on the other, would lead to moral despair without God and immortality. Thus, it is a practical necessity that we postulate them; not to do so would be to commit moral suicide. Moral faith is thus a practically rational response by finite rational beings to their inability to fulfill the moral demands of their nature on their own. Its mode of conviction is not logical but moral certainty. Kant warns us not even to say "*It is* certain that there is a God, etc." but only "I am morally certain, etc."[2] This faith is not, however, irrational. The postulate arguments justify a certain religious conviction as, in Kant's terms, "the most reasonable obinion for us men" to hold.[3] Allen Wood sums up their status as follows: "On the basis of practical considerations holding for each man personally as a moral agent, Kant proposes to justify and even rationally to require of each man the personal conviction that there exist a God and a future life."[4] Let us briefly turn now to the argument for the existence of God.[5]

Kant locates the moral worth of an action in its intention

and not in its results. Since one of the distinguishing marks of rationality is universality, I act rationally and hence morally only if the maxim of my action exhibits that property. As Kant put it, I only have to ask myself the single question of whether I could will that my maxim become universal law, governing not merely this particular action of mine but the action of anyone in similar circumstances. In other words, as moral judgments must hold without distinction of persons in order to be universal, an action can be morally right for me only if it would be right for anyone in my situation. The moral law is impartial. Accordingly, Kant distinguishes the concern of morality not only from the egoistic pursuit of narrow self-interest but also from the prudential consideration of overall happiness or well-being. Questions of duty are strictly separated from questions of happiness, whether in the short run or the long run, whether for an individual or for a community.

On the other hand, we are finite creatures of need, who naturally seek happiness. What Kant calls the antinomy of pure practical reason has its roots in our situation: we are, as it were, inhabitants of two worlds at once, rational beings who are commanded to act universally without regard to our own self-interest and natural beings who are urged by nature to seek happiness, the fulfillment of our own purposes. For such beings, the "highest good" is neither virtue by itself nor happiness by itself; it consists rather in a proper combination of the two: happiness conditioned by or in proportion to virtue, the happiness we morally deserve. This, writes Kant, is the only reasonable state of affairs: "Virtue [is not] the entire and perfect good as the object of the faculty of desire of rational finite beings. For this, happiness is also required, and indeed not merely in the partial eyes of a person who makes himself his end but even in the judgment of an impartial reason, which impartially regards persons in the world as ends-in-themselves. For to be in need of happiness and also worthy of it and yet not partake of it could not be in accordance with the complete volition of an omnipotent rational being."[6]

And yet, as we know only too well, the separation of virtue and happiness is the way things are in this vale of tears. Because nature and morality are distinct orders, there is no necessary connection, let alone just proportion, between moral virtue and earthly happiness. As rational beings we are commanded to do our moral duty regardless of whether it conflicts with our own happiness or that of others; on the other hand, as rational beings we could not choose a state of affairs in which those in need of happiness and deserving of it fail to achieve it. Thus our object as rational beings must be a combination in which happiness is proportioned to virtue. This Kant calls the "highest good." We are, then, commanded by reason to pursue the highest good. And yet it is not in our power to achieve it, for happiness is not merely a matter of the will but also of natural causes and effects. Hence, even the most meticulous observance of the moral law cannot be expected to produce happiness. So we have a problem, which Kant put this way: "Since, now, the furthering of the highest good . . . is an a priori necessary object of our will and is inseparably related to the moral law, . . . if the highest good is impossible, . . . then the moral law which commands that it be furthered must be fantastic, directed to empty, imaginary ends, and consequently inherently false."[7]

The only way to avoid moral despair, which we have a moral duty to avoid, is to assume the possibility of the highest good. As it is beyond the power of finite moral beings to bend nature to the demands of morality, we have to postulate the existence of an infinite moral being who has the power to produce the necessary harmony between the two orders. In Kant's words, "Now it is our duty to promote the highest good; and it is not merely our privilege but a necessity connected with duty to presuppose the possibility of this highest good. This presupposition is made only under the condition of the existence of God. . . . Therefore, it is morally necessary to assume the existence of God. It is well to notice here that this moral necessity is subjective, i.e. a need, and not objective, i.e. duty itself. . . . As a practical need it can be called *faith,* and even pure *rational faith,* because pure reason alone is the source from which it springs."[8] So here we have it: there is a pure practical need to assume the existence of God, for without it the moral life to which we are called as rational beings is threatened by moral despair in the face of nature's indifference.

2

Perhaps the central objection to Kant's argument was formulated already in his lifetime by a certain Thomas Wizenmann, who disputed simply the right to argue from a need to the objective reality of what meets that need.[9] Kant tried to get round this objection by stressing the difference between particular, natural needs and a need of pure practical reason as such. I shall not go into the pros and cons of that debate, since the political theologians with whom I am concerned do not hold to these Kantian dualisms.[10] If one were to classify them philosophically, they are probably closest to the left Hegelians. Just as Marx castigated the philosophers for trying to understand the world rather than change it, political theologians typically give short shrift to traditional speculative theology. They are after a "theology of the world" that engages and transforms its orders rather than withdrawing from them and contemplating them, a theology articulated in terms of political practice. Let me note briefly a few of the general features of this reorientation.

• It involves a new relationship to the Old Testament and a rehabilitation within Christian theology of the Jewish sense for history and narrative as against the long-dominant Hellenistic tendencies to cosmology and logocentrism, and it involves a reading of revelation as a history of God's promises, a past that announces a future calling for a present practice.

• As this future is essentially open, it cannot be captured in the categories of a philosophy of history or a theology of universal history. In fact, it escapes the grasp of pure theory altogether, for what the future will hold is essentially dependent on our practice in the present. Correspondingly, the task of a political theology is not merely to interpret the world but to change it. It must become a type of practical and critical thinking that informs and is informed by practice. The traditional primacy of doctrinal theory thus gives way to a primacy of practice, or at least to a constant mediation of theory and practice.

• The sort of practice in question is indicated by the gospel of love, by its fundamental identification with the poor and the oppressed of this world. As Moltmann, for example, reads it, the Bible is a revolutionary and subversive book; the hope it holds out is for the hopeless, the weak, the downtrodden, the destitute and deprived. We must, he says borrowing the words of Theodor Adorno, learn to see the "messianic light" that shines from the eyes of the victim onto the "faults and fissures" of our own situation.[11] Thus political theology is not a sacralizing legitimation of the status quo, a domesticated civil religion, but a theology of emancipation and liberation.

• As this liberation is essentially social in nature, political theology challenges overly individualistic traditional interpretations of Christian eschatalogical symbolism. It attempts to recover the social and political meaning of such symbols as "covenant," "kingdom," "peace," "reconciliation." In a world in which the conditions of individual existence are largely determined by social, political, and economic structures, the religious practice of alleviating human misery can be effective only by addressing the causes of that misery, that is, by becoming politically engaged. For political theologians, the meaning and validity of religious faith proves itself not through doctrinal assertion but through the social practice of uplifting the downtrodden and liberating the oppressed.[12]

Even from this brief sketch it is not difficult to see the general affinity of political theology to the Western Marxist tradition of social thought. What I am interested in, however, is a particular relation to Kant's moral view of religion. To put the matter somewhat crudely, the bridge from a usually atheistic, or at least nontheistic, Marxism to a theology of the world is often framed in terms reminiscent of Kant's postulate arguments: roughly, without religious faith we cannot avoid moral-political despair; solidarity with the victims of history makes sense only on the assumption of a just God who reconciles virtue and happiness.

There are numerous versions of this argument, some looser

and some stricter. I want to focus here on one of the more clearly spelled-out versions advanced by Helmut Peukert in his *Science, Action, and Fundamental Theology.* There he attempts to apply this type of argument to an influential stream of Western Marxism, namely the critical social theory of the Frankfurt School. His point of departure is a discussion between Max Horkheimer and Walter Benjamin, which began with an exchange of letters and continued, implicitly, in their subsequent works.[13] Reacting to Benjamin's idea that the historical materialist cannot regard the past as *abgeschlossen*—finished, closed, over and done with—Horkheimer wrote to Benjamin, "The supposition of an unfinished or unclosed past is idealistc if you don't incorporate a certain closedness into it. Past injustice has happened and is over and done with. Those who were slain were really slain."[14] And he adds in a published work from the same period, "What happened to those human beings who have perished cannot be made good in the future. They will never be called forth to be blessed in eternity. Nature and society have done their work on them and the idea of a Last Judgment, which the infinite yearning of the oppressed and the dying has produced, is only a remnant from primitive thought, which denies the negligible role of the human species in natural history and humanizes the universe."[15] In the same vein he writes elsewhere, "While the religious thinker is comforted by the thought that our desires [for eternity and for the advent of universal goodness and justice] are fulfilled all the same, the materialist is suffused with the feeling of the limitless abandonment of humanity, which is the only true answer to the hope for the impossible."[16] Benjamin of course continued to be concerned with the redemption of the past. And to Horkheimer's charge that this was, in the end, theology, he responded that history is not merely a science but a form of remembrance, of empathetic memory (*Eingedenken*), that can transform what is closed, finished, over and done with (e.g., past suffering) into something that is open and unfinished. "In empathetic memory," he writes, "we have an experience that prohibits us from conceiving history completely nontheologically, which is not at all to say that we can write history in directly theological concepts."[17] It is clear as well from Benjamin's "Theses on the Philosophy of History" that he resists any approach to universal history that has as its implicit principle empathy with its victors rather than its victims and thus becomes incapable of grasping "history as the history of the suffering or passion of the world."[18] He wants instead to develop an approach to history based on an "anamnestic solidarity" with its countless generations of oppressed and downtrodden. Horkheimer acknowledges the roots of this impulse but regards the approach to history it entails as unjustified: "The thought that the prayers of those persecuted in their hour of direct need, the prayers of the innocents who die without comprehending their situation, the last hopes for a supernatural court of appeals—are all to no avail, and that the night in which no human light shines is also devoid of any divine light—this thought is monstrous. Without God, eternal truth has just as little footing as infinite love—indeed they become unthinkable concepts. But is monstrousness ever a cogent argument against the assertion or denial of a state of affairs? Does logic contain a law to the effect that a judgment is false when its consequence is despair?"[19] This last phrase recalls the drift of Kant's postulate arguments, but Horkheimer, like Wizenmann 150 years before him, stoically (or pessimistically) notes that need and despair are not forms of logical validity.

Though this debate serves as a point of departure for Peukert's fundamental theological reflections on critical social theory, he mounts his central argument in terms of another, later development in this tradition, Habermas's theory of communicative action. The reasons for his choice are not hard to divine. The theory of communicative action is an attempt to construct post-Kantian ideas of reason and rationality that might serve as a basis for political and social theory.[20] Thus Peukert can plumb the depths of Habermas's notion of practical reason and try to discover in it a foothold for his reconstituted version of the postulate arguments. Following Kant, he will argue that practical reason, even in the form of communicative rationality, requires a background of hope if it is to make moral-political sense. And this background of hope cannot simply be projected into the future, as it is in the Marxist tradition. A just society that might be established by human beings in the indefinite future is no substitute, he will argue, for a reconciliation with the past grounded in religious belief. In the political sphere, as in the moral sphere, the question For what may I hope? has to be given a religious answer.

There is no need to go into Habermas's theory of communicative rationality in any great detail to catch the point of Peukert's argument. Generally, the theory shifts the center of gravity of the concept of reason from the Cartesian point of subjectivity to communicative forms of intersubjectivity.[21] Kant, who still operated within the horizon of individual consciousness, could capture objective validity only in terms of the structures of transcendental subjectivity. For Habermas, validity is tied to reasoned agreement concerning defeasible claims. Claims to the truth of a statement or the rightness of an action can be contested and criticized, defended and revised. There are any number of ways of settling disputed claims, such as appeals to authority, to tradition, or to brute force. One way, the giving of reasons for and against, has traditionally been regarded as fundamental to the idea of rationality. And it is precisely to the experience of achieving mutual understanding in discussion free from coercion that Habermas looks in developing his idea of communicative reason. The key to this idea is the possibility of using reasons and grounds—the unforced force of the better argument—to gain universal recognition for contested validity claims.

Habermas is by no means the first to attempt to detranscendentalize Kant's notion of reason while retaining universal agreement as a regulative idea. In the heyday of American philosophy this line of thought reached a high point: Peirce tied truth to agreement in the unlimited, i.e., potentially infinite, "community of investigators"; Royce to the "community of interpretation" of all human beings; Mead to the "community of universal discourse." The underlying idea is simple: "true" means true for everyone, "right" means right for everyone. Truth and rightness, insofar as they are dealt with on a rational basis, are internally related to the idea of universal agreement.

Habermas's idea of a communicative ethics can be viewed as a corresponding revision of Kantian ethics. From this perspective, his discourse model represents a procedural reinterpretation of Kant's categorical imperative. Rather than ascribing as valid to all others any maxim that I can will to be a universal law, I must submit my maxim to all others for purposes of discursively testing its claim to universality. The emphasis shifts from what each can will without contradiction to be a general law to what all can will in agreement to be a universal norm. A rational will is not something that can be secured and certified privately; it is inextricably bound to communication processes in which a common will is both discovered and formed.

For Kant, the autonomy of the will requires the exclusion of all "pathological" interests from the choice of maxims of action. If the particular ends of action (which can be summed up as "happiness") are not excluded from its determining grounds, its maxim will be ipso facto unsuitable for universal legislation, for if a maxim is to be universalizable, valid for all rational beings, then it must be independent of my particular inclinations. This constellation alters perceptibly when we shift to Habermas's intersubjective (communicative) framework. The aim of practical discourse is to come to a consensus about which interests are generalizable. Individual wants, needs, and desires need not, indeed cannot, be excluded, for it is precisely concerning them that agreement is sought; they belong to the content of practical discourse. What that content concretely is depends, of course, on the historical conditions and potentials of social existence at a given time and place.

3

This abandonment of the Cartesian paradigm in ethics in favor of a proceduralism that does not set reason against inclination in the way in which Kant did clearly narrows the gap between justice and happiness: happiness belongs to the content of justice. It might seem, then, that we have no foothold here for renewing Kant's postulate arguments in relation to communicative ethics. Peukert thinks otherwise. Even if we put to one side for the moment the pain and suffering, loneliness and guilt, sickness and death that seem to be inevitably associated with the contingencies of human life in any society, there is, he argues, an antimony built into the deep structure of communicative practical reason, an antinomy that points irresistibly to a background of hope that must be postulated if our moral-practical lives are to make sense. He locates the antinomy in the tension between the universalism of communicative ethics and "the annihilation of the innocent other" in history. The ideal of communicative rationality entails that discussions in which validity claims are decided upon cannot be arbitrarily restricted. It implies a community of discourse that is in principle unlimited. If, now we look at human history from the standpoint of some anticipated future state of perfect justice, the results are unsettling. Peukert puts the problem of a hypothetical, blessed generation in this future as follows:

It has achieved the end-state of happiness; its members can live with one another in perfect solidarity. But how is their relation to previous generations to be determined? They must live with the consciousness that they owe everything to the oppressed, the downtrodden, the victims of the whole historical process of human emancipation. This generation has inherited everything from past generations and lives on what *they* paid for. . . . The happiness of the living consists in the expropriation of the dead. Is happiness at all conceivable under these presuppositions? Is it not a presupposition of their happiness that the unhappiness of those who went before them be simply forgotten? Is amnesia, the utter loss of historical memory, the presupposition for their happy consciousness? But then is not the life of these future human beings inhuman? . . . How can one hold on to the memory of the conclusive, irretrievable losses of the victims of history—to whom one owes one's entire happiness—and still be happy? . . . The dream of "perfect justice" can, then, be only a nightmare. . . . Here we reach the extreme point of despair and, if despair does not kill, the point of inconsolable grief.[22]

We have come back to the exchange between Benjamin and Horkheimer, but now there is a third voice more unequivocally religious then Benjamin's. And it speaks in tones reminiscent of Kant. Without a rational faith in God and immortality to supply a background of hope to practical reason, moral-political practice in solidarity with the victims of history makes no sense; it can only lead to despair. How convincing is this argument? If it is to succeed, Peukert will have to deal with Horkheimer's version of Wizenmann's objection to Kant: the monstrousness of a state of affairs is no argument against its obtaining; no law of logic says that a judgment that leads to despair is false. Kant tried to deal with the original objection— that need cannot establish existence—in terms of a strict distinction between the pure needs of reason and the empirical needs of nature. This avenue is not open to Peukert, since the theory of communicative rationality makes no such strict separation. How, then, can he defend himself against Horkheimer's Schopenhauerian pessimism? He does not attempt to do so in any detail but rests content, more or less, with having exhibited the worm at the heart of the apple of perfect justice and with developing its theological implications. But we can imagine how the argument might proceed from here.

For one thing, Peukert might resist Horkheimer's framing of the question in terms of the "laws of logic." Recall that for Kant, the dialectic that gave rise to the postulates was a dialectic of *practical* reason. And the postulates themselves are not claims to knowledge but justifications of *faith*. In the *Critique of Judgment*, published two years after the *Critique of Practical Reason*, he put the matter thus: the moral law unconditionally prescribes to rational beings like us a final end that we ourselves are incapable of attaining, indeed, that—in light of the moral indifference of nature and the self-interestedness of human beings—we must despair of attaining by our own efforts.[23] To be rationally called to strive for an end that we rationally take to be impossible to attain places us in a dialectical perplexity from which we can escape only by "assuming" the possibility of the *summum bonum* and the reality of the conditions of its possibility. Thus there is a "pure moral ground" for postulating a moral world cause. This is not an "objectively valid proof" of God's existence but a "subjective argument sufficient for moral beings."[24] It establishes not the "objective theoretical reality" of a moral world order but its "subjective practical reality."[25] As Allen Wood has put it, pure rational faith is primarily not an assent to certain speculative propositions but a "belief about the situation of moral action," an "outlook" or "attitude" in virtue of which we may continue *rationally* to pursue a goal marked out for us by reason: the establishment of a just world order.[26] If all efforts toward this goal are doomed to failure, the rationality of moral action comes into question. Moral faith as a trust in God to supply our deficiencies if we do all that is in our power is then a condition of our continuing to act as rational moral beings. Thus it is not an irrational leap in the sense of Pascal or Kierkegaard but a rationally justified hope that is required if we are not to abandon rationality. In Kant's own terms, "We have to assume [God's] existence in order merely to furnish practical reality to a purpose which pure reason . . . enjoins us a priori to bring about with all our powers."[27] This type of proof yields not theoretical knowledge but "a conviction adequate from a purely practical point of view."[28] God, as a *res fidei*, has objective reality for us only "in a practical reference."[29] The postulate argument "proves the Being of God as a thing of faith for the practical pure reason."[30]

Though Peukert cannot appeal to the Kantian notion of pure practical reason, his argument is structurally analogous to the postulate argument. Practical reason, conceived now as communicative rationality, has an inherent universal telos, for it refers moral-practical questions to agreement within a potentially unlimited community of discourse. In this sense, it remains a command of reason to pursue the goals of universal freedom, justice, and happiness. But history has not cooperated in this pursuit; it has been as Hegel put it, a slaughter bench. Consequently, no matter what happens in the future, the highest good of universal peace is unattainable, for the countless victims of history can never participate in it. They are dead and gone. Their suffering is irredeemable. Thus the command of practical reason to seek perfect justice must be, to use Kant's terms, "fantastic," directed to "imaginary ends," or, in Peukert's phrase, "a nightmare." Communicative action in universal solidarity with the innocent victims of history makes sense only if this end is attainable, and it is attainable only on the assumption of a Lord of History who will somehow redeem past suffering. Peukert puts it this way: political theology articulates "the experience of a definite reality corresponding to a certain way of acting," a reality that is "asserted," "assumed," "anticipated" in this way of acting.[31] On this reading, the Judeo-Christian tradition is concerned precisely with the reality "experienced" and "disclosed" in such "limit situa-tions" of communicative action and with modes of communi-cation possible in response to them.[32] Through faith, communicative action anticipates the salvation of annihilated innocents. Faith thus opens up a "possibility of existence"—the possibility of reciprocity and solidarity with the innocent other, of the redemption of his or her suffering—which is definitely closed without it. In the absence of this hope, anamnestic sol-idarity gives way to amnesiac self-interest. To act in solidarity with history's victims is to "affirm a reality that prevents them from being merely superseded facts of the past."[33] It is "to assert a reality that saves these others from annihilation."[34] This "experience" and "disclosure" of a "saving reality," which is "presupposed" by communicative action in universal solidarity, is the point of access to possible discourse about God. It is the starting point for a political theology.

The analogies to Kant are clear: God's reality is said to be a presupposition of sensibly pursuing the dictates of practical reason. To affirm it is not an irrational leap of faith but a rationally justified assumption required for the very possibility of continuing to act rationally. As an argument, however, this is less than airtight. The antinomy of communicative reason might elicit a number of different "subjective practical" out-looks compatible, or at least not per se incompatible, with communicative action in universal solidarity, from Horkhei-mer's pessimism, through Stoic resignation or existential com-mitment, to Benjamin's empathetic solidarity or the compassionate solidarity that Habermas models after it.[35] It is difficult to see how these attitudes could be ruled out on inter-subjectively valid grounds. Of course, Peukert might argue that it is only with the background of hope supplied by religious faith that the idea of perfect justice makes any sense at all, that the other attitudes are so many different ways of keeping a stiff upper lip in the face of the monstrous realities of injustice. But that might be the best we can do, or at least the best that some can do, while others might embrace the religious option on the strength of just such practical considerations. The point is that the justification of faith in question does not have the force of a proof either in objective terms or in terms of a *universal* subjective need. We are no longer dealing with the absolute dictates of a pure reason. The practice of striving for peace and justice might reasonably be defended on other, non-religious grounds.

Peukert implicitly acknowledges this when, as we saw, he recurs in the end to an interpretation of the Judeo-Christian tradition as "concerned with the reality experienced in the fundamental limit experiences of communicative action."[36] Religious *experience* and religious *tradition* remain key ingredients in his account of faith, which is thus not presented as susceptible of purely argumentative reconstruction. One lesson that might be drawn from this for the question of "normative foundations" is that we should not expect rational consensus on comprehensive conceptions of the meaning and value of life. Though it is incompatible with many such conceptions, communicative ethics, owing to its highly formal nature, could be compatible with a number of others. They would, of course, have to "overlap" in enjoining their adherents to resist injustice in the present and work to reduce it in the future, and to do so in compassionate solidarity with the victims of the past.

Notes

The following abbreviations sometimes appear in these notes or in the text:

B: H. Marcuse, "Beiträge zu einer Phänomenologie des historischen Materialismus," *Schriften*, vol. 1 (Frankfurt, 1978), pp. 347–384.

K: H. Marcuse, "Über konkrete Philosophie," *Schriften*, vol. 1 (Frankfurt, 1978), pp. 385–406.

LC: J. Habermas, *Legitimation Crisis* (Boston, 1975).

PMN: R. Rorty, *Philosophy and the Mirror of Nature* (Princeton, 1979).

TCA, 1 and 2: J. Habermas, *The Theory of Communicative Action*, vols. 1 and 2 (Boston, 1984, 1987).

TGST: J. Habermas and N. Luhmann, *Theorie der Gesellschaft order Sozialtechnologie* (Frankfurt, 1971).

Introduction

1. I attempt to sketch an alternative program in *Critical Theory*, coauthored with David Hoy, forthcoming from Basil Blackwell.
2. See Harold Garfinkel, *Studies in Ethnomethodology* (Englewood Cliffs, N.J., 1967).
3. Jürgen Habermas, *Nachmetaphysiches Denken* (Frankfurt, 1988), p. 55.
4. Michel Foucault, "Space, Knowledge, and Power," an interview with Paul Rabinow, in Rabinow, ed., *The Foucault Reader* (New York, 1984), pp. 239–256, here p. 249.
5. Michel Foucault, "What Is Enlightenment?" in *The Foucault Reader*, pp. 23–50, here pp. 45–46.

Chapter 1

1. From Rorty's introductions to R. Rorty, ed., *The Linguistic Turn* (Chicago, 1967) and R. Rorty, *Consequences of Pragmatism* (Minneapolis, 1982).
2. For an overview of this metaphilosophical situation, see K. Baynes, J. Bohman, and T. McCarthy, eds., *After Philosophy* (Cambridge, Mass., 1987).
3. See Richard Bernstein, *Beyond Objectivism and Relativism* (Philadelphia, 1983).
4. R. Rorty, *Philosophy and the Mirror of Nature* (Princeton, 1979), hereafter cited as *PMN*.

5. *PMN*, p. 390.

6. *PMN*, p. 340, n. 20.

7. *PMN*, p. 385.

8. *PMN*, p. 174.

9. See *PMN*, pp. 175 ff. and 357 ff.

10. *PMN*, p. 178. In "Solidarity or Objectivity," in J. Rajchman and C. West, eds., *Post-analytic Philosophy* (New York, 1985), pp. 3–19, Rorty characterizes his position as a frank "ethnocentrism," which he defines as "the view that there is nothing to be said about either truth or rationality apart from descriptions of the familiar procedures of justification which a given society—*ours*—uses in one or another area of inquiry" (p. 6, his emphasis).

11. *PMN*, p. 309.

12. "Solidarity or Objectivity," p. 6.

13. R. Rorty, "Pragmatics, Davidson and Truth," in E. Lepore, ed., *Truth and Interpretation: Perspectives on the philosophy of Donald Davidson* (New York, 1986), pp. 333–355, here pp. 334–335.

14. *PMN*, pp. 281–282.

15. *PMN*, p. 385.

16. *PMN*, p. 386.

17. See Hans-Georg Gadamer, *Truth and Method* (New York, 1975), esp. pp. 235 ff., and Habermas's review thereof in F. Dallmayr and T. McCarthy, eds., *Understanding and Social Inquiry* (Notre Dame, 1977), pp. 335–363.

18. "Habermas and Lyotard on Postmodernity," in Richard Bernstein, ed., *Habermas and Modernity* (Cambridge, Mass., 1985), pp. 161–175, here p. 172.

19. "Habermas and Lyotard on Postmodernity," pp. 174–175.

20. R. Rorty, "Taking Philosophy Seriously," *New Republic,* April 11, 1988, pp. 31–34, here p. 34.

21. "Philosophy as a Kind of Writing: An Essay on Derrida," in Rorty, *Consequences of Pragmatism* (Minneapolis, 1982), pp. 90–109, esp. pp. 99 ff.

22. "Nineteenth-Century Idealism and Twentieth-Century Textualism," in *Consequences of Pragmatism*, pp. 139–159, here p. 148.

23. Introduction to *Consequences of Pragmatism*, pp. xiii–xlvii, here pp. xxxvii ff.

24. "The Priority of Democracy to Philosophy," in M. Peterson and R. Vaughan, eds., *The Virginia Statute for Religious Freedom* (Cambridge, 1988), pp. 257–282, here p. 257.

25. "The Priority of Democracy to Philosophy," p. 264.

26. "The Priority of Democracy to Philosophy," p. 262.

27. "The Priority of Democracy to Philosophy," p. 259.

28. "Postmodernist Bourgeois Liberalism," *Journal of Philosophy* 80 (1983): 583–589, here pp. 583–584.

29. "Postmodernist Bourgeois Liberalism," p. 584.

30. R. Rorty, "From Logic to Language to Play," *Proceedings and Addresses of the American Philosophical Association* 59 (1986): 747–753, here pp. 752–753.

31. Nancy Fraser make this point in "Solidarity or Singularity? Richard Rorty between Romanticism and Technocracy," in Fraser, *Unruly Practices* (Minneapolis, 1989), pp. 93–110.

32. See J. Habermas, "What Is Universal Pragmatics?" in Habermas, *Communication and the Evolution of Society* (Boston, 1979), pp. 1–68; "Philosophy as Stand-In and Interpreter," in *After Philosophy,* pp. 296–315; *The Theory of Communicative Action,* vol. 1 (Boston, 1984), chapters 1, 3; and *Nachmetaphysiches Denken* (Frankfurt, 1988).

33. Compare Saul Kripke's stress on conformity and agreement in his *Wittgenstein on Rules and Private Language* (Cambridge, Mass., 1982), pp. 96 f., where he offers an account of rule following, and hence of meaning and rationality, in terms of a speaker's responses "agreeing with those of the community," of his or her behavior "exhibiting sufficient conformity" to the shared practices of the community.

34. I shall be relying principally upon Garfinkel's earlier studies, collected in *Studies in Ethnomethodology* (Englewood Cliffs, N.J., 1967), republished by Polity Press (Cam-

bridge, 1984). My interpretation is indebted to John Heritage, *Garfinkel and Ethno-methodology* (Cambridge, 1984).

35. H. Garfinkel, "Studies in the Routine Grounds of Everyday Activities," in *Studies in Ethnomethodology*, pp. 35–75, here p. 68.

36. H. Garfinkel, "What Is Ethnomethodology?" in *Studies in Ethnomethodology*, pp. 1–34.

37. See J. Heritage, *Garfinkel and Ethnomethodology*, pp. 75 ff., 115 ff.

38. Melvin Pollner, "Mundane Reasoning," *Philosophy of the Social Sciences* 4 (1974): 35–54. See also his *Mundane Reason* (Cambridge, 1987).

39. To acknowledge a constructivist dimension in our relation to the objective world is not *eo ipso* to endorse a sociocultural idealism.

40. Hilary Putnam draws this analogy in "Why Reason Can't Be Naturalized," in *After Philosophy*, pp. 222–244, here pp. 230 ff.

Postscript to Chapter 1

1. R. Rorty, "Truth and Freedom: A Reply to Thomas McCarthy," *Critical Inquiry* 16 (1990): 633–643, here p. 634. He is replying specifically to arguments advanced in "Private Irony and Public Decency: Richard Rorty's New Pragmatism," *Critical Inquiry* 16 (1990): 355–370.

2. "Truth and Freedom," p. 635.

3. R. Rorty, *Contingency, Irony, and Solidarity* (Cambridge, 1989). References to this volume, which appeared after the preceding essay was completed, will be indicated by parenthetical page numbers in the text.

4. It would also be possible and even easier to criticize Rorty's romantic individualism from a neo-Aristotelian standpoint by stressing the role that such factors as shared practices and beliefs, values and norms, memberships and experiences play *in* the process of identity formation. But I will stress the universalist component here—*not* in place of, but in addition to, such factors.

5. The fact that each person has to answer the questions, Who am I? Who do I want to be? for him- or herself does not entail that there are no common features to identity formation—not unless Freud and Piaget, Vygotsky and Mead, Kohlberg and Erikson, and many others were wholly mistaken in what they wrote. Rorty does consider Freud's contribution, but in a very idiosyncratic fashion: "His *only* utility lies in his ability to turn us from the universal to the concrete" (p. 34, his emphasis).

6. As I shall be concentrating on the notion of theory in what follows, I should note that I am not using the term "basic structures" in opposition to "malleable social structures" or "pressure points for structural change," as Rorty supposes ("Truth and Freedom," p. 643)—that would make the critical project pointless. The issue here is simply, Can we understand the world's ills in terms of greedy and shortsighted capitalists, cynical and ruthless oligarchs, and other such characters, or must we also understand the relatively stable patternings of social relations that these characters enact and reproduce and the systems of interdependencies in which their actions are located—in short, the causes, conditions, and consequences of their actions, which are often unrecognized and/or beyond their power to change? A good test case might be trying to understand how the liberal public sphere became the public-relations and public-entertainment monstrosity it is. See J. Habermas, *The Structural Transformation of the Public Sphere* (Cambridge, Mass., 1989).

7. "Truth and Freedom," p. 642.

8. "I think that contemporary liberal society already contains the institutions for its own improvement. . . . Indeed, my hunch is that Western social and political thought has had the last *conceptual* revolution it needs" (p. 63). Rorty takes himself to be in agreement with Habermas on political matters, but a main concern of *The Theory of Communicative Action* is to understand how capitalism has undercut democracy.

9. John Dewy, *Liberalism and Social Action,* reprinted in John J. McDermott, ed., *The Philosophy of John Dewey* (New York, 1973), vol. 2, pp. 647–648; cited after Richard Bernstein, "One Step Forward, Two Steps Backward: Richard Rorty on Liberal Democracy and Philosophy," *Political Theory* 15 (November 1987): 540.

Chapter 2

1. See Horkheimer's inaugural lecture (1931) as director of the Institut für Sozialforschung, "The State of Contemporary Social Philosophy and the Tasks of an Institute for Social Research," in S. Bronner and D. Kellner, eds., *Critical Theory and Society* (New York, 1989), pp. 25–36, and his contributions to the *Zeitschrift für Sozialforschung* from the early 1930s, some of which have been collected in Horkheimer, *Critical Theory* (New York, 1972) and Horkheimer, *Selected Essays* (MIT Press, forthcoming). Habermas's renewal of this program is elaborated in *The Theory of Communicative Action,* vols. 1 and 2 (Boston, 1984, 1987). The comparison that follows would look quite different if its reference point were the version of critical theory developed by Horkheimer and Adorno in the 1940s, particularly in their *Dialectic of Enlightenment* (New York, 1972), which is very close in spirit to the genealogy of power/knowledge that Foucault practiced in the 1970s. That period of Foucault's work, by far the most influential in the English-speaking world, is the other point of reference for the comparison in this section. The ethic of the self, which he developed in the 1980s, will be discussed in section 3. I will not be dealing with the first phase(s) of his thought, which came to a close around 1970–1971 with the appearance of "The Discourse on Language" (printed as an appendix to *The Archeology of Knowledge,* New York, 1972, pp. 215–237), and "Nietzsche, Genealogy, History" (in *Language, Countermemory, Practice,* Ithaca, 1977, pp. 139–164).
2. The early Horkheimer also appealed to a speculative philosophy of history.
3. The differences are as great among the various members of the Frankfurt School at the various stages of their careers.
4. M. Foucault, "Questions of Method," in K. Baynes, J. Bohman, and T. McCarthy, eds., *After Philosophy* (Cambridge, Mass., 1987), pp. 100–117, here p. 112.
5. M. Foucault, "Truth and Power," in Foucault, *Power/Knowledge* (New York, 1980), pp. 109–133, here p. 131.
6. The application of sociological and ethnographic approaches to the natural sciences has led to similar conclusions.
7. "Truth and Power," p. 131.
8. M. Foucault, *Discipline and Punish* (New York, 1979), pp. 27–28.
9. See J. Habermas, *Knowledge and Human Interests* (Boston, 1971). For his elaboration of the ideas that follow, see *The Theory of Communicative Action,* vol. 2.
10. He seems later to have adopted a more positive attitude toward hermeneutics when that was called for by his desire to appropriate—rather than merely to objectivate—Greek and Roman texts on the care of the self. In a note on page 7 of *The History of Sexuality,* vol. 2, *The Use of Pleasure* (New York, 1985), he characterizes his approach in classically hermeneutic terms: "to examine both the difference that keeps us at a remove from a way of thinking in which we recognize the origin of our own, and the proximity that remains in spite of that distance which we never cease to explore."
11. M. Foucault, "Truth and Power," p. 119.
12. *Discipline and Punish,* p. 114.
13. "Truth and Power," p. 131.
14. See Harold Garfinkel, *Studies in Ethnomethodology* (Cambridge, 1984).
15. N. Fraser, "Foucault on Modern Power: Empirical Insights and Normative Confusions," in Fraser, *Unruly Practices* (Minneapolis, 1989), pp. 17–34, here p. 32.
16. "Truth and Power," p. 116.

17. The quote is from "Truth and Power," p. 114.
18. "Two Lectures," in *Power/Knowledge*, pp. 78–108, here p. 98.
19. "Two Lectures," p. 98.
20. See "Truth and Power," p. 117.
21. "Two Lectures," p. 97.
22. See Erving Goffman, *Asylums* (New York, 1961).
23. See John Heritage, *Garfinkel and Ethnomethodology* (Cambridge, 1984), pp. 103–134.
24. See, for instance, *The History of Sexuality*, vol. 1 (New York, 1978), pp. 95–96.
25. See *The History of Sexuality*, vol. 1, p. 157.
26. For a discussion of this problem, see David Michael Levin, *The Listening Self* (London and New York, 1989), pp. 90 ff.
27. Charles Taylor, "Foucault on Freedom and Truth," in David Hoy, ed., *Foucault: A Critical Reader* (Oxford, New York, 1986), pp. 69–102, here pp. 91–93.
28. A revised version of part of the lecture was published as "The Art of Telling the Truth," in Michel Foucault, *Politics, Philosophy, Culture* (New York, 1988), pp. 86–95, here p. 95. Foucault sometimes writes as if the analytic of truth in general—that is, the traditional concerns with knowledge, truth, reality, human nature, and the like—should be abandoned as a lost, but still dangerous, cause. At other times he represents it as a still viable research orientation, which, however, he chooses not to pursue. See, for example, "The Political Technology of Individuals," in L. H. Martin, H. Gutman, and P. H. Hutton, eds., *Technologies of the Self: A Seminar with Michel Foucault* (Amherst, 1988), pp. 145–162, here p. 145. In either case, the fact that he pursues his "ontology of the present and of ourselves" in separation from any (explicit) "analytic of truth" constitutes a major difference from Habermas, whose diagnosis of the present is linked to a continuation of the critical project Kant inaugurated with his three *Critiques*. I shall not be able to explore that difference here.
29. In emphasizing the changes in Foucault's self-understanding in the 1980s, I am taking issue with commentators who stress the continuity with earlier work, often by treating Foucault's later *redescriptions* of it as accurate accounts of what he was "really" up to at the time. The frequent (and varied) redescriptions he offers are, in my view, better read as *retrospectives* from newly achieved points of view. Foucault himself was often quite open about the changes. See, for instance, the three interviews conducted in January, May, and June of 1984: "The Ethic of Care for the Self as a Practice of Freedom," in *The Final Foucault*, James Bernauer and David Rasmussen, eds. (Cambridge, Mass., 1988), pp. 1–20; "The Concern for Truth," in *Politics, Philosophy, Culture*, pp. 255–267 (on p. 255 he says "I changed my mind" after the publication of volume 1 of *The History of Sexuality*); and "The Return of Morality," in *Philosophy, Politics, Culture*, pp. 242–254 (where he says essentially the same thing on pp. 252—253). Among his published writings, see, for instance, the introduction to vol. 2 of *The History of Sexuality*, especially "Modifications," pp. 3–13. I find this straightforward acknowledgement of a theoretical shift hermeneutically more satisfactory than any of the attempts to read his earlier work as if it had been written from the perspective of the 1980s. For an overview of the development of Foucault's thought and the distinctive features of the last phase, see Hans-Herberg Kögler, "Fröhliche Subjektivität: Historische Ethik und dreifache Ontologie beim späten Foucault," forthcoming in E. Erdmann, R. Forst, A. Honneth, eds., *Ethos der Moderne—Foucaults Kritik der Aufklärung* (Frankfurt, 1990). For a somewhat different view, see Arnold I. Davidson, "Archeology, Genealogy, Ethics," in *Foucault: A Critical Reader*, pp. 221–233.
30. Translated as "What Is Enlightenment?" in Lewis White Beck, ed., *Kant on History* (New York, 1963), pp. 3–11. Foucault's fullest treatment can be found in a posthumously published text with the same title in Paul Rabinow, ed., *The Foucault Reader* (New York, 1984), pp. 32–50. In the 1980s he repeatedly expressed his appreciation of Kant's essay. In addition to text just cited, see his afterword to Hubert Dreyfus and Paul Rabinow, *Michel Foucault: Beyond Structuralism and Hermeneutics* (Chicago, 1982), "The Subject and Power," pp. 145–162, here p. 145, and "Structuralism and Post-

structuralism: An Interview with Michel Foucault," *Telos* 55 (1983): 195–211, here pp. 199, 206.

31. "The Subject and Power," p. 216.

32. "Polemics, Politics, and Problematizations," in *The Foucault Reader*, pp. 381–390, here p. 388. Compare Foucault's remark in the introduction to volume 2 of the *History of Sexuality* that the object of those studies is "to learn to what extent the effort to think one's own history can free thought from what it silently thinks, and so enable it to think differently" (p. 9).

33. "The Ethic of Care for the Self as a Practice of Freedom," p. 4.

34. The concept of mature adulthood (Kant *Mündigkeit*) is discussed in "What Is Enlightenment?" pp. 34–35 and 39. Dreyfus and Rabinow deal with this topic in "What Is Maturity? Habermas and Foucault on 'What Is Enlightenment?'" in *Foucault: A Critical Reader*, pp. 109–121. But their representation of Habermas's position is misleading on key points, e.g., as regards his views on "*phronesis*, art, and rhetoric" (p. 111), on authenticity (p. 112), and on reaching agreement (pp. 119–120).

35. "What Is Enlightenment?" p. 42. See also "The Art of Telling the Truth," pp. 94–95.

36. "Space, Knowledge, and Power," in *The Foucault Reader*, pp. 239–256, here p. 249.

37. "What Is Enlightenment?" pp. 45–96. Foucault sometimes takes a line closer to Habermas, for instance when he explains that "singular forms of experience may perfectly well harbor universal structures," in the original preface to *The History of Sexuality*, volume 2, in *The Foucault Reader*, pp. 333–339, here p. 335. But characteristically, he immediately goes on to say that *his* type of historical analysis brings to light not universal structures but "transformable singularities" (p. 335). As we saw in section 2, it nevertheless relies on an interpretive and analytic framework comprising universalist assumptions about the structure of social action. As I shall elaborate below, the same holds for his later investigations as well, but the framework has been altered in important respects.

38. The quotes are from "What Is Enlightenment?" p. 48.

39. "What Is Enlightenment?" p. 43. Foucault explicitly gives preference to "specific" and "partial" transformations over "all projects that claim to be global or radical" and "any programs for a new man" (pp. 46–47). Compare Habermas's remarks in *Knowledge and Human Interests*, pp. 284–285. There are many similarities between the Foucault of "What Is Enlightenment?" and the earlier Habermas, who pursued "an empirical theory of history with a practical intent." See my account of this phase of Habermas's thought in *The Critical Theory of Jürgen Habermas* (Cambridge, Mass., 1978), chapters 1, 2, and 3.

40. "Truth and Subjectivity," manuscript, p. 7. Foucault is apparently referring to the scheme Habermas proposed in his inaugural lecture at Frankfurt University in 1965 (printed as the appendix to *Knowledge and Human Interests*, pp. 301–317) and subsequently altered. On Page 313 Habermas characterized his three dimensions of analysis as labor, language, and domination (*Herrschaft*).

41. *Technologies of the Self*, pp. 18–19. It is clear, however, that Foucault has not yet fully disengaged from the ontology of power, for all four types of technologies are said to be "associated with" domination, and he characterizes his new field of interest as "the technologies of individual domination." See note 64 below.

42. "The Subject and Power," pp. 217–218.

43. *The Use of Pleasure*, p. 4. A version of this already appears in Foucault's discussions with Dreyfus and Rabinow at Berkeley in April 1983: "On the Genealogy of Ethics: An Overview of Work in Progress," in *The Foucault Reader*, pp. 340–372, here pp. 351–352. It is elaborated in the original preface to volume 2, pp. 333–339, as a distinction between fields of study, sets of rules, and relations to self.

44. "The Subject and Power," pp. 219, 221.

45. "The Subject and Power," p. 221.

46. "The Subject and Power," p. 224.

47. "The Subject and Power," p. 222.

48. "The Ethic of Care for the Self as a Practice of Freedom," pp. 11–12. This interview, conducted in January 1984, was twice reworked and edited by Foucault before he authorized its publication. The formulations that appear are thus no mere accidents of the occasion. See *Freiheit und Selbsorge*, H. Becker et al., eds. (Frankfurt, 1985), pp. 7, 9.

49. "The Ethic of Care for the Self," p. 19. The categories of power, domination, and strategy are of course used earlier as well, but not with the same meanings. In volume 1 of *The History of Sexuality*, for instance, "states of power" are said to be generated by virtue of the *inequality* of force relations (p. 93), and power is said to be exercised in *nonegalitarian* relations (p. 94); "major dominations" arise as the hegemonic effects of wide-ranging cleavages that run through the social body as a whole (p. 94), while strategies are embodiments of force relations (p. 93, with example on pp. 104–5).

50. "The Ethic of Care for the Self," p. 18.

51. "The Ethic of Care for the Self," p. 20.

52. Foucault's three-part definition of "strategy" in "The Subject and Power," pp. 224–225, is conventional enough. It is said to designate means-ends rationality aimed at achieving some objective, playing a game with a view to gaining one's own advantage, and the means to victory over opponents in situations of confrontation.

53. See "What Is Universal Pragmatics?" in Habermas, *Communication and the Evolution of Society* (Boston, 1979), pp. 1–68, esp. pp. 59–65, and *The Theory of Communicative Action*, vol. 1, pp. 273–337.

54. See "The Subject and Power," p. 220.

55. "The Subject and Power," p. 218.

56. "The Ethic of Care for the Self as a Practice of Freedom," p. 18.

57. "The Ethic of Care for the Self," p. 18.

58. See Foucault's discussion of the "morality that concerns the search for truth" in "Polemics, Politics, and Problematizations," pp. 381–382, where he describes what are essentially symmetry conditions among dialogue partners. See also his account of the role that communication with others has played in the care of the self in *The History of Sexuality*, volume 3, pp. 51–54. The reciprocity of helping and being helped by others that he describes there hardly accords with his official view of social relations as strategic relations.

59. Foucault draws a distinction between the "strategic" and "technological" sides of "practical systems" in, for instance, "What Is Enlightenment?" p. 48.

60. The original preface to *The History of Sexuality*, pp. 337–339.

61. *The History of Sexuality*, vol. 1, p. 11.

62. "Omnes et Singulatim: Towards a Criticism of Political Reason," in *The Tanner Lectures on Human Values*, vol. 2, Sterling McMurrin, ed. (Salt Lake City, 1981), pp. 225–254, here p. 227.

63. "Omnes et Singulatim," p. 240.

64. For example, in his Howison Lectures delivered at Berkeley the next fall (1980), he describes his project as an investigation of the historical constitution of the subject that leads to the modern concept of the self ("Truth and Subjectivity," manuscript, lecture 1, p. 4), and goes on to say that he is focusing on "techniques of the self" by which "individuals effect a certain number of operations on their own bodies, on their souls, on their own thoughts, on their conduct." But though he clearly distinguishes such techniques from "techniques of domination," they have to be understood precisely in relation to them (p. 7). The "point of contact" between the two is government: "When I was studying asylums, prisons, and so on, I insisted too much on the techniques of domination. . . . But that is only one aspect of the art of governing people in our societies. . . . [Power] is due to the subtle integration of coercion technologies and self technologies. . . . Among [the latter], those oriented toward the discovery and formulation of the truth concerning oneself are extremely important." Accordingly, in the closing passage of his lectures he asks rhetorically whether the time has not come to get rid of these technologies and the sacrifices linked to them (lecture 2, p. 20). In the first part of "The Subject and Power" (pp. 208–216), which was delivered

as a lecture at the University of Southern California the following fall (1981), the way in which we turn ourselves into subjects is described as an element in the "government of individualization" (p. 212). At the same time, however, Foucault notes the increasing importance of struggles against "forms of subjection" exercised through "individualizing techniques" (p. 213), the shaping of individuals to ensure their integration into the modern state (p. 214). And he concludes with a line that could serve as the epigraph of his last studies: "The political, ethical, social, philosophical problem of our days is not to try to liberate the individual from the state and from the state's institutions, but to liberate us both from the state and from the type of individualization which is linked to the state. We have to promote new forms of subjectivity through the refusal of this kind of individuality which has been imposed on us for several centuries" (p. 216). In an outline of his 1980/1981 course at the Collège de France, "Subjectivité et vérité" which dealt with the materials of the final volumes of *The History of Sexuality*, Foucault locates the care of the self at the crossroads of the history of subjectivity and the analysis of forms of governmentality. Studying its history enables him "to take up again the question of 'governmentality' from a new point of view: the government of self by self in its articulation with relations to others" (M. Foucault, "Résumé des cours, 1970–82," Paris, 1989, pp. 134–136).

65. "On the Genealogy of Ethics," p. 340. The subordination of his interest in sexuality as such to a broader problematization of techniques of forming the self is clearly stated in those volumes. It is, he writes, with sexual behavior as a "domain of valuation and choice," with the ways in which "the individual is summoned to recognize himself as an ethical subject of sexual conduct" that the later studies are concerned (vol. 2, p. 32). Thus his analyses of "prescriptive discourses" about dietetics, household management, erotics, and so forth focus on the modes of subjectivation presupposed and nourished in the corresponding practices. Very briefly, the genealogy of desiring man as a self-disciplined subject is Foucault's key to the genealogy of the subject of ethical conduct (vol. 2, pp. 250–251), and this is itself an element in a more comprehensive "history of truth" (vol. 2, p. 6). Similarly, in analyzing *parrhēsia*, or truth-telling, in antiquity, Foucault conceives of the genealogy of the parrhesiastic subject, the truth teller, as part of the "genealogy of the critical attitude in Western philosophy" (*Discourse and Truth: The Problematization of Parrhēsia*, a transcription by Joseph Pearson of a seminar given at the University of California, Berkely, in the fall of 1983, p. 114). These connections suggest the continuing relevance of Foucault's work to what I referred to as the critique of impure reason.

66. "On the Genealogy of Ethics," p. 341.

67. "On the Genealogy of Ethics," p. 348.

68. "On the Genealogy of Ethics," p. 352.

69. "The Ethic of Care for the Self," pp. 2–3.

70. "The Ethic of Care for the Self," pp. 6–7. The connections between governmentality, care of the self, and strategic interaction are suggested on pp. 19–20 of the same interview: "In the idea of governmentality I am aiming at the totality of practices by which one can constitute, define, organize, instrumentalize the strategies which individuals in their liberty can have in regard to each other. It is free individuals who try to control, to determine, to delimit the liberty of others, and in order to do that, they dispose of certain instruments to govern others. That rests indeed on freedom, on the relationship of the self to self and the relationship to the other." On the relation between self-mastery and the mastery of others in antiquity, see *The History of Sexuality*, vol. 2, pp. 73 ff.

71. "An Aesthetics of Existence," in *Philosophy, Politics, Culture*, pp. 47–53, here p. 49. Foucault's later studies abound in comparisons between ethical practices in antiquity and in Christianity. See, for example, *The History of Sexuality*, vol. 2, pp. 92, 136–139, and vol. 3, pp. 68, 140 ff., 165, 235 ff. These comparisons, so patently unfavorable to Christianity, bespeak Foucault's own commitment to an ethopoetics of existence. In my view, an analysis of the evaluative presuppositions underlying Foucault's last works, which are ostensibly constructed in a nonevaluative, descriptive mode, would reveal

them to be more or less the ones he openly espoused in the lectures, interviews, and methodological asides of the last period. In neither phase should the absence of explicit value *judgments* in his sociohistorical studies obscure the presence of implicit value *orientations* underlying them. (Compare Weber's distinction between *Werturteile* and *Wertbeziehungen*.) But the large gap between the avowed and the actually operative frameworks of evaluation in the 1970s was considerably closed in the 1980s.

72. *The History of Sexuality*, vol. 2, pp. 25–26.
73. *The History of Sexuality*, vol. 2, p. 29.
74. *The History of Sexuality*, vol. 2, p. 30.
75. *The History of Sexuality*, vol. 2, p. 29.
76. "An Aesthetics of Existence," p. 49. See also "On the Genealogy of Ethics," p. 343, and "The Concern for Truth," pp. 262–263.
77. *The History of Sexuality*, vol. 2, p. 10.
78. "What Is Enlightenment?" p. 42.
79. Nor, for that matter, is it Socrates', Plato's, or Aristotle's. There is more than one way to take issue with Foucault's notion of an ethics of self-invention. I will be stressing Kant's connection of autonomy to a rational will, but problems could also be raised from the standpoint of the ethics of community, character, virtue, and the like.
80. "The Concern for Truth," p. 253.
81. *The History of Sexuality*, vol. 2, p. 21.
82. See his *Moral Consciousness and Communicative Action* (Cambridge, Mass., 1990) and *The Theory of Communicative Action*, vol. 2, pp. 92–111.
83. "On the Genealogy of Ethics," p. 44. The masculinist and dominative orientation of Greek ethics is stressed throughout volume 2 of *The History of Sexuality*. See, for example, pp. 69–77, 82–86, 146–151, and 215–225.
84. "Politics and Ethics: An Interview," in *The Foucault Reader*, pp. 373–380, here p. 379.
85. "On the Genealogy of Ethics," p. 348.
86. "On the Genealogy of Ethics," p. 350.
87. "On the Genealogy of Ethics," p. 350.
88. "Fröhliche Subjektivität," manuscript, p. 29.
89. *The Use of Pleasure*, p. 10. To be sure, the studies of self-formative processes in volumes 2 and 3 of *The History of Sexuality* do view classical practices of the self in their sociocultural contexts. But Foucault is himself opposed to the shaping of individuals to fit societal contexts, be it the Greek polis or the modern state. As he conceives it, the practice of the self is a practice of liberty precisely insofar as it frees formation of the self from such functional contexts. The question of whether this is compatible with any type of social order is left largely open, as is that of the new types of community to which it could give rise. These are, of course, very important questions for *social* movements struggling to change *socially* imposed identities and to have those changes *legally* and *institutionally* secured. I am indebted to Michael Kelly for a discussion of this point.

Postscript to Chapter 2

1. W. Connolly, *Politics and Ambiguity* (Madison, Wis., 1987). Page references to this volume appear in parentheses in the text.
2. See chapter 2, pages 53–55.
3. For an argument to this effect, see Jürgen Habermas, *The Philosophical Discourse of Modernity* (Cambridge, Mass., 1987), lectures 4, 9, and 10.

Chapter 3

1. Letter to Maidon, 30 November 1921, cited in H. Gumnior and R. Ringguth, *Max Horkheimer* (Reinbek bei Hamburg, 1973), p. 24. See also Rolf Wiggershaus, *Die Frankfurter Schule* (Munich, 1986), p. 60.
2. Letter to Maidon, 30 November 1921.
3. Horkheimer, "The State of Contemporary Social Philosophy and the Tasks of an Institute for Social Research," in S. Bronner and D. Kellner, eds., *Critical Theory and Society* (New York, 1989), pp. 25–36, here pp. 29–30.
4. Letter to Scholem, 25 April 1930, cited in Douglas Kellner, *Herbert Marcuse and the Crisis of Marxism*, vol. 1 (Berkeley, 1984), p. 35.
5. *Gesammelte Schriften*, vol. 1 (Frankfurt, 1973), pp. 325–344 and 345–365.
6. His inaugural lecture was delivered only a few months after the one by Horkheimer mentioned in note 3, that is, March and January 1931, respectively.
7. See the extensive study by Hermann Mörchen, *Adorno und Heidegger: Untersuchung einer Kommunikationsverweigerung* (Stuttgart, 1982). On page 13 he notes that Adorno and Heidegger met once, very briefly, after the latter had given a lecture at Frankfurt University in January 1929.
8. Habermas describes himself as having "lived in" Heidegger's thought from 1949 to 1953 (Peter Dews, ed., *Autonomy and Solidarity: Interviews with Jürgen Habermas*, London, 1986, p. 77) and as having been a "thoroughgoing Heideggerian" during this period (p. 194), and he acknowledges that Heidegger's influence upon his work persisted into the 1960s ("Work and Weltanschauung: The Heidegger Controversy from a German Perspective," *Critical Inquiry* 15 (1989): 431–456, here p. 435, n. 12.)
9. In "Work and Weltanschauung" he describes this experience as follows: "I was so impressed with *Being and Time* that reading these lectures, which were fascist right down to their stylistic details, actually shocked me.... What shocked me most was that Heidegger had published in 1953, without explanation or comment, what I had to assume was an unchanged lecture from 1935. Even the forward made no reference to what had happened in between" (p. 451). The shock prompted the then 24-year-old student to write an influential and controversial article for the *Frankfurter allgemeine Zeitung* (25 July 1953), which concluded with the words, "The question behind this essay is the following: Can the planned murder of millions of human beings, about which we all know now, be made comprehensible in terms of the history of Being, as a fateful errancy? ... Isn't it the principal task of reflection to throw light on the past deeds responsible for it and to keep alive the knowledge of it? ... Instead, Heidegger publishes his now 18-year-old words about the greatness and inner truth of National Socialism." ("Mit Heidegger gegen Heidegger Denken: Zur Veröffentlichung von Vorlesungen aus dem Jahre 1935," reprinted in Habermas, *Philosophisch-Politische Profile*, Frankfurt, 1981, pp. 65–72, here p. 72).
10. It is clearly visible in Habermas's dissertation, "Das Absolute und die Geschichte: Von der Zwiespältigkeit in Schellings Denken" (Bonn, 1954) and in the essays in cultural criticism that he published throughout the 1950s. It can even be seen in certain aspects of *Knowledge and Human Interest* (1968).
11. In addition to the essays mentioned in notes 8 and 9, see "Martin Heidegger: The Great Influence," in Habermas, *Philosophical-Political Profiles* (Cambridge, Mass., 1983), pp. 53–60, and *The Philosophical Discourse of Modernity* (Cambridge, Mass., 1987), chap. 6, pp. 131–160.
12. Habermas uses the phrase "from Heidegger to Horkheimer" in comparing his philosophical development with Marcuse's in J. Habermas et al., *Gespräche mit Herbert Marcuse* (Frankfurt, 1978), p. 9. After 1953, as he was weaning himself from Heidegger and trying to reconcile his political and philosophical views, he came across Marcuse's early essays: "There you could see the exact breaking-point between an orthodox Heideggerian and a Marxist.... [Marcuse] rejects not just the ontological difference, but the difference between history and historicity" (*Autonomy and Solidarity*, p. 194).

13. Heideggerian modes of thought are still at work in, for example, *Reason and Revolution* (1941), *Eros and Civilization* (1955), and *One-Dimensional Man* (1964).
14. The sketch that follows is taken from D. Kellner, *Herbert Marcuse*, chap. 1.
15. "Heidegger's Politics," an interview conducted by Frederick Olafson, in R. Pippen et al., *Marcuse: Critical Theory and the Promise of Utopia* (South Hadley, Mass., 1988), pp. 95–104, here p. 96.
16. "Heidegger's Politics," p. 96.
17. *Schriften*, vol. 1 (Frankfurt, 1978), pp. 347–384 and 385–406. These will be cited in the text as B and K, respectively. The numbers in parentheses refer to the pagination of *Schriften*, vol. 1.
18. "Heidegger's Politics," p. 96.
19. "Heidegger's Politics," p. 97.
20. "Neue Quellen zur Grundlegung des historischen Materialismus," in *Schriften*, vol. 1, pp. 509–555.
21. Though a complete edition of *The German Ideology* was published only in 1932, the sections on historical materialism were available in 1928.
22. *Schriften*, vol. 1, pp. 407–422, here p. 418.
23. *Schriften*, vol. 1, p. 421.
24. *Schriften*, vol. 1., pp. 469–487, here p. 474.
25. Frankfurt, 1932. English translation by Seyla Benhabib, *Hegel's Ontology and the Theory of Historicity* (Cambridge, Mass., 1987). I am following the usual convention of referring to this work as Marcuse's *Habilitationsschrift*, though it was never actually submitted for that purpose.
26. "Neue Quellen," p. 519.
27. Marcuse later explained his decision not to proceed with the habilitation as follows: "It was completely clear by the end of 1932 that I would never be able to habilitate under the Nazi regime" ("Gespräche mit Herbert Marcuse," p. 12). There are other reports, some of them apparently stemming from Marcuse, that Heidegger himself was the problem (see Kellner, *Herbert Marcuse*, p. 406, n. 1; for an account of the two different versions, see Benhabib's introduction to *Hegel's Ontology*, pp. ix–xi). The issue could perhaps be cleared up by examining Husserl's letter to Kurt Riezler, the curator of Frankfurt University, asking him to intervene with Horkheimer on Marcuse's behalf. (Husserl had served on Marcuse's dissertation-examining committee in 1922, and they were in regular contact during Marcuse's time in Freiburg.) Rolf Wiggershaus, who has had access to the Marcuse archives in Frankfurt, reports in *Die Frankfurter Schule* that Husserl's letter names Heidegger as having blocked Marcuse's habilitation (p. 122). Marcuse has said, however, that he had no hint of Heidegger's Nazi sympathies before leaving Freiburg in December of 1932 ("Heidegger's Politics," p. 99). It is difficult to imagine that he could have been totally unaware of Heidegger's political leanings. As Hugo Ott points out in *Martin Heidegger—Unterwegs zu einer Biographie* (Frankfurt, 1988), there was talk in Freiburg about Heidegger's consorting with National Socialists (especially the National Socialist cadres of the Deutsche Studentenschaft) already in the summer of 1932 (pp. 28, 135) (by which time Heidegger had already closed off a letter to Carl Schmitt with "Heil Hitler!" See Habermas, "Work and Weltanschauung," p. 443, n. 34). Ott also remarks on the long-standing, open support of the National Socialists by Heidegger's wife. All things considered, the judgment of Henry Pachter, also a student in Freiburg at the time, that Marcuse could not have been wholly unaware of Heidegger's sympathies is hard to resist. (See Kellner, *Herbert Marcuse*, pp. 406–407, n. 3.) On the other hand, Heidegger apparently concealed his true feelings about such matters. For instance, as early as 1929 he followed up a formal statement of support for a fellowship for Eduard Baumgarten with a separate letter to the responsible official in which he wrote, "I can say here more clearly what I could only hint at indirectly in my formal statement: what is at stake here . . . is the choice between once again providing German intellectual life [*Geistesleben*] with genuinely settled [or indigenous: *bodenständige*] workers and educators or finally delivering it up to the growing Jewification [*Verjudung*] in the broader and

narrower senses" (letter of 2 October 1929, printed in *Die Zeit,* 22 December 1989; cited here after *Information Philosophie,* August 1990, 59–60). Marcuse may well have been a victim of this discrepancy between Heidegger's overt and covert behavior.
28. *Hegel's Ontology,* p. 5.
29. So are the divergences from Heidegger. Adorno caught this ambivalence in his early review of *Hegel's Ontology* in the *Zeitschrift für Sozialforschung* 1 (1932): 409–410. "At this point Marcuse seems clearly to diverge from the public views of Heidegger, which he otherwise follows as strictly as befits a disciple; he tends from 'the meaning of Being' toward the disclosure of entities, from fundamental ontology toward the philosophy of history, from historicity toward history." See also the discussions of *Hegel's Ontology* by Benhabib, Translator's Introduction, pp. ix–xl, and Robert Pippin, "Marcuse on Hegel and Historicity," in *Marcuse: Critical Theory and the Promise of Utopia,* pp. 68–94.
30. "Das Problem der geschichtlichen Wirklichkeit," pp. 477, 479.
31. In this connection it is worth nothing that in his 1931 review of Korsch, Marcuse cited Georg Misch's *Lebensphilosophie und Phänomenologie* (Bonn, 1930) and thus was familiar with the latter's critique of Heidegger's ontologistic reading of Dilthey.
32. "Neue Quellen," p. 519.
33. "Neue Quellen," p. 535.
34. *Schriften,* vol. 1, pp. 556–594.
35. *Schriften,* vol. 1, p. 559.
36. *Schriften,* vol. 1, p. 560.
37. *Schriften,* vol. 1, p. 580.
38. *Unterhaltungsblatt der Voßischen Zeitung* (14 December 1933). I shall be citing it after Kellner, *Hebert Marcuse,* and drawing upon his interpretation. There is also a discussion of this review in H. Brunkhorst and G. Koch, *Herbert Marcuse zur Einführung* (Hamburg, 1987), pp. 27–30.
39. See Kellner, *Herbert Marcuse,* p. 101.
40. See Kellner, *Herbert Marcuse,* p. 101–102.
41. Volume 3 (1934): 161–195. English translation, "The Struggle against Liberalism in the Totalitarian View of the State," in Marcuse, *Negations* (Boston, 1968), pp. 3–42.
42. Marcuse cites the letters of 3 and 10 November 1933, quoting from the former Heidegger's exhortation, "Let not doctrines and 'Ideas' be the rule of your being. Today and in the future only the *Führer* himself is German reality and its law" (p. 41).
43. "The Struggle against Liberalism," p. 32.
44. "The Struggle against Liberalism," p. 32.
45. "The Struggle against Liberalism," pp. 14–15. Kellner draws attention to this in *Herbert Marcuse,* pp. 102–103.
46. Generally, Habermas's critique of Heidegger elaborates upon the points earlier made by Marcuse and extends them to the development of Heidegger's thought after 1933. At the same time he raises a number of criticisms not formulated by Marcuse and partly in opposition to his views as well. These revolve around what he regards as inadequacies in Heidegger's conceptions of intersubjectivity and communication, propositional truth and scientific-technological development, normative validity and moral-political development. Moreover, with the advantage of hindsight, Habermas can interpret Heidegger's thought during the 1920s in the context of the cultural climate of the times, especially the cultural elitism, pessism, and antimodernism of the "German Mandarins," and he can read the shifts in Heidegger's thought after 1929 against the background of changing personal and political circumstances. This cultural-political reading of Heidegger's development explains Habermas's evident dismay at the decontextualized Heidegger that has reigned abroad: "The latest return of a felicitously de-Nazified Heidegger is, of course, based on the ahistorical reception of Heidegger in France and America—where he stepped on stage after the War, like a phoenix from the ashes, as the author of the 'Letter on Humanism'" (*Autonomy and Solidarity,* p. 159).

Chapter 4

1. "Deconstruction and the Other," an interview with Richard Kearney, in Richard Kearney, *Dialogues with Contemporary Continental Thinkers* (Manchester, 1984), pp. 107–126, here pp. 119–120.
2. Jacques Derrida, *Positions* (Chicago, 1981), p. 93.
3. "The Ends of Man," in Jacques Derrida, *Margins of Philosophy* (Chicago, 1982), pp. 109–136, here pp. 133–135. See also the opening "Exergue" in Jacques Derrida, *Of Grammatology* (Baltimore, 1976), pp. 3–5, where he writes of the "closure" of a "historico-mataphysical epoch" and characterizes grammatology as "a way of thinking that is faithful and attentive to the ineluctable world of the future which proclaims itself at present," a future that "can only be anticipated in the form of an absolute danger," as it "breaks absolutely with constituted normality." This was published in 1967. Sometime later in a paper read in 1980, "Of an Apocalyptic Tone Recently Adopted in Philosophy," *Semeia* 23 (1982): 63–97, Derrida claimed that his adoption of an apocalyptic tone had always been qualified, distanced, ironic (p. 90).
4. "Semiology and Grammatology," an interview with Julia Kristeva, in *Positions*, pp. 15–36, here p. 24.
5. "Semiology and Grammatology," p. 24.
6. "Positions," an interview with Jean-Louis Houdebine and Guy Scarpetta, in *Positions*, pp. 37–96, here p. 69.
7. See "Of an Apocalyptic Tone," esp. p. 94.
8. Derrida uses the German term for enlightenment in a number of places; see for example "Of an Apocalyptic Tone," p. 87; "The Principle of Reason: The University in the Eyes of Its Pupils," *Diacritics* 19 (1983): 3–20, here pp. 5, 19; and "Afterword: Toward an Ethic of Discussion," in Jacques Derrida, *Limited Inc.*, (Evanston, Ill., 1988) pp. 111–160, here p. 141.
9. "The Principle of Reason," pp. 9–10.
10. *Limited Inc.*, pp. 117, 119.
11. In *The Tain of the Mirror* (Cambridge, Mass., 1986), Rodolphe Gasché presents Derrida's project as an inquiry into the conditions of possibility and impossibility of philosophical discourse. On this account, the motifs of Derrida's "more philosophically discursive texts" also inform his "more literarily playful texts," which make essentially the same points in "a nondiscursive manner" (p. 4). In *Contingency, Irony, and Solidarity* (Cambridge, 1989), Richard Rorty contests this interpretation, arguing instead for a distinction between an earlier and later Derrida (pp. 122–137). Focusing chiefly on *The Post Card*, with supporting references to *Glas*, he takes Derrida to have finally gone beyond, the dream of philosophy, not by deploying new methods or techniques, but by experimenting with new styles. According to Rorty, in Derrida's later work the writing becomes "more eccentric, personal, and original" (p. 123). It relies on private "fantasies," "idiosyncrasies," and "associations" rather than on public "generalities" and "arguments." Because some of Derrida's "most vivid fantasies concern past philosophers," however, "only people who habitually read philosophy could possibly enjoy it" (p. 136). Christopher Norris sides, more or less, with Gasché, distinguishing two categories (rather than periods) of Derrida's writing in which the same points are made in very different ways ("Deconstruction, Postmodernism, and Philosophy: Habermas on Derrida," *Praxis International* 8 (1989): 426–446). My own view is closer to that of Gasché and Norris. The two-periods approach has a hard time accounting for some of the latest material, for instance, the fifty-page afterword to *Limited Inc.*, in which Derrida is on his best post-Kantian behavior. It has an even harder time explaining Derrida's continued insistence on the political relevance of his work. One has difficulty imagining the small band of philosophically schooled and literarily sensitive readers who can appreciate Derrida's "private fantasies" as the vanguard of the revolution, or even as the midwives of the "ineluctable world of the future."
12. *Positions*, p. 29.

13. *Positions,* p. 26.

14. *Positions,* p. 32. On the same page, he writes, "metaphysics has always consisted in attempting to uproot the presence of meaning, in whatever guise, from *différance;* and every time that a region or layer of a pure meaning or a pure signified is allegedly rigorously delineated or isolated this gesture is repeated."

15. *Of Grammatology,* p. 10. On the deconstructionist approach to philosophy, see Gasché, *The Tain of the Mirror,* pp. 124 ff.

16. "The Ends of Man," p. 135. For a more detailed account of the double gesture, see Gasché, *The Tain of the Mirror,* pp. 163 ff.

17. "The Ends of Man," p. 135. Compare "Structure, Sign, and Play in the Discourse of the Human Sciences," in Jacques Derrida, *Writing and Difference* (Chicago, 1978), pp. 280–281: "We can pronounce not a single deconstructive proposition which has not already had to slip into the form, the logic, and the implicit postulations of precisely what it seeks to contest."

18. "The Ends of Man," p. 135.

19. *Positions,* p. 19.

20. *Positions,* p. 42.

21. Richard Rorty has argued in "Deconstruction and Circumvention" (*Critical Inquiry* 11 (1984): 2–23) that it cannot succeed in escaping the orbit of Western philosophy, for, notwithstanding the differences in terminology and style, it appears to be just what philosophers have been up to all along, if not always so self-consciously. See pp. 12 ff. In *The Tain of the Mirror,* Rodolphe Gasché argues the opposite case, namely that "by taking the classical exigencies of philosophy to their logical end, . . . Derrida brings philosophy to a certain close" (pp. 250–251). He does this by showing that philosophy is necessarily "inscribed" in an "Other" that it cannot dominate and that this "limits its ultimate pretension to self-foundation" (p. 251). In my view, demonstrating that the conditions of possibility of philosophical discourse are at the same time the conditions of the impossibility of its achieving its aims could succeed in bringing philosophy to a certain close *only as* a foundationalist enterprise. The key difference from Kant's analogous undertaking vis-à-vis metaphysics would be in the nature of the conditions to which Derrida points: an irreducible multiplicity of "heterological infrastructures" that necessarily exceed and escape any reflective appropriation. This last feature points up, of course, the paradoxical nature of the deconstructive enterprise. It could at most succeed as a kind of "negative metaphysics." But just as negative theology remains theology, negative metaphysics remains (at the level of) metaphysics. Whether this is a good way to approach social, cultural, and political criticism will depend on whether metaphysics is as all pervasive as Derrida thinks it is.

22. "Deconstruction and Circumvention." See the response by Henry Staten, "Rorty's Circumvention of Derrida," in *Critical Inquiry* 12 (1986): 453–461. Derrida's qualifications still give philosophy a privileged place as "the most powerful *discursive* formation of our 'culture'" (*Positions,* p. 102, n. 21).

23. *Of Grammatology,* p. 3.

24. *Of Grammatology,* p. 3.

25. "The Ends of Man," p. 111.

26. "Implications," an interview with Henri Ronse, in *Positions,* pp. 1–14, here pp. 6–7 (my emphases).

27. *Positions,* p. 19. Derrida apparently holds that there are certain "effects of *différance*" built into the use of language that persistently and inescapably produce the kinds of illusions that lead to logocentrism. For instance, the conception of language as "expressive representation, a translation on the outside of what was constituted inside"—a conception basic to Western logocentrism—is, he tells us, "not an accidental prejudice, but rather a kind of structural lure, what Kant would have called a transcendental illusion. The latter is modified according to the language, the era, the culture." Western metaphysics is a "powerful systematization of this illusion" (*Positions,* p. 33). Elsewhere he seems to suggest that the fulfillment or "plenitude" toward which

intentionality inevitably tends (*Limited Inc.*, p. 129), truth (*Positions*, p. 105), the classical logic of binary opposition (*Limited Inc.*, p. 117), and the idealization intrinsic to conceptualization (*Limited Inc.*, p. 117) are "transcendental illusions" of this sort. Thus he seems to hold, like Kant, that the "ideas of reason" built into thought (language) inevitably give rise to illusions that we can with difficulty detect but never dispel. It is those illusions that, enhanced and systematized, comprise Western metaphysics: "Logocentric philosophy is a specifically Western response to a much larger necessity which also occurs in the Far East and other cultures" ("Deconstruction and the Other," p. 115). As these are some of the same "idealizing presuppositions of communication" that Habermas makes central to his "postmetaphysical" conception of rationality (Jürgen Habermas, *Nachmetaphysiches Denken*, Frankfurt, 1988), the Derrida-Habermas debate could, I think, be fruitfully continued around the question, Are the idealizations built into language more adequately conceived as pragmatic presuppositions of communicative interaction or as a kind of structural lure that has ceaselessly to be resisted? Or as both?

28. "The Ends of Man," p. 135.

29. *Positions*, p. 51.

30. He did, however, give it political expression during the period of his participation in National Socialism. For a recent discussion, see the symposium "Heidegger and Nazism" in *Critical Inquiry* 15 (1989): 407–490.

31. Max Horkheimer and Theodor Adorno, *Dialectic of Enlightenment* (New York, 1972).

32 See the brief comparisons in Peter Dews, *Logics of Disintegration* (London, 1987) and Jürgen Habermas, *The Philosophical Discourse of Modernity* (Cambridge, Mass., 1987) and the extended discussion in Christoph Menke-Eggers *Die Souveränität der Kunst* (Frankfurt, 1988).

33. Allan Megill, in *Prophets of Extremeity* (Berkeley, 1985), reads him in this way; see esp. pp. 303–320.

34. Of course, in his case the experiences were of French Fascism under the Vichy Government: "I came to France when I was nineteen. Before then, I had never been much past El-Biar [a suburb of Algiers]. The war came to Algeria in 1940, and with it, already then, the first concealed rumblings of the Algerian War. As a child, I had the instinctive feeling that the end of the world was at hand, a feeling which at the same time was most natural, and, in any case, the only one I ever knew. Even for a child incapable of analyzing things, it was clear that all this would end in fire and blood. . . . Then, in 1940, the singular experience of the Algerian Jews, incomparable to that of European Jews, the persecutions were nevertheless unleashed in the absence of any German occupier. . . . It is an experience which leaves nothing intact, something you can never again cease to feel. . . . Then the Allies land, and . . . racial laws were maintained for a period of almost six months, under a 'free' French government. . . . From that moment—how can I say it—I felt as displaced in a Jewish community, closed unto itself, as I would in the other. . . . From all of which comes a feeling on non-belonging that I have doubtless transposed" ("An Interview with Derrida," in David Wood and Robert Bernasconi, eds., *Derrida and Différance*, Evanston, Ill., 1988, pp. 71–82, here pp. 74–75). Elsewhere Derrida mentions the ensuing horror of France's wars in Algeria and Indochina (see "The Principle of Reason," p. 13). There is nothing like the "belatedness" of German history to explain how the "most civilized" of Western nations put its Enlightenment heritage into action.

35. "Deconstruction and the Other," pp. 115–116. Cf. note 27, above.

36. "The Principle of Reason," p. 8. The page numbers in parentheses in the following theses refer to this piece.

37. "Deconstruction and the Other," p. 114.

38. "Deconstruction and the Other," p. 115.

39. *Limited Inc.*, p. 139.

40. Jacques Derrida, "Racism's Last Word," in *Critical Inquiry* 12 (1985): 290–299, here p. 298.

41. *Limited Inc.*, p. 116, and "The Politics of Friendship," passim. The language of call and response appears repeatedly in Derrida's writings. In the afterword to *Limited Inc.* he plays this as a variation on a Kantian theme: the "injunction that prescribes deconstruction," he writes, "arouse[s] in me a respect which, whatever the cost, I neither can nor will compromise" (p. 153). But this is Kant at the limits of his thought, where he comes closest to Kierkegaard, whom Derrida mentions in a similar context in "The Principle of Reason," p. 20. The allusion to Kierkegaard seems to me better to capture what is involved here, though Derrida's "decision" is apparently located "in the order of ethico-political responsibility" (*Limited Inc.*, p. 116) rather than in that of religious faith.

42. "Deconstruction and the Other," p. 117. On pages 116–117 Derrida mentions several sources of the fissures in Western culture that serve as points of incision for deconstruction: the impact of non-European cultures on the West and the always incomplete attempts to absorb them; the heterogeneous elements of Judaism and Christianity that were never completely assimilated or eradicated; traces of alterity within Greek culture that philosophy could not completely domesticate.

43. *Limited Inc.*, p. 136.

44. "Deconstruction and the Other," p. 120.

45. Nancy Fraser, "The French Derrideans: Politicizing Deconstruction or Deconstructing Politics," *New German Critique* 33 (1984): 127–154.

46. For instance, Derrida reminds critics that deconstruction is not simply demolition but always operates within the context of established conceptualities. However, when the "double gesture" was introduced, the "positive" relation to received concepts and schemes was explained as a move to ensure that deconstruction has a critical purchase on what is to be deconstructed—it lodges itself within the old conceptuality so as all the more effectively to dismantle it, thus avoiding a simple "change of terrain" that would reinstate the old beneath the new. Another type of response has been to represent deconstruction as an attempt to understand how an "ensemble" is constituted (see, for instance, Derrida's "Letter to a Japanese Friend," in *Derrida and Différance*, pp. 1–5, here p. 3). This knowledge might then be used to restore or reconstruct the ensemble as well as to destabilize or dismantle it. In the abstract, there may be something to this. But if we look at what Derrida actually does with deconstruction, the reconstructive moment is not in evidence. A third sort of response is, as we have seen, to represent deconstruction as "motivated by some sort of affirmation," as a "positive response to an alterity which calls it" ("Deconstruction and the Other," p. 118). What is at issue is not whether deconstruction is a positive response, but whether that response is positive, that is, the nature of the activity engaged in as a result of the "decision" to respond affirmatively. Judged by actual practice, the call is apparently one to incessant subversion of established conceptual regimes. Finally, there are frequent mentions of deconstruction as a kind of memory that preserves tradition. (See, for instance, *Limited Inc.*, p. 141 and "The Principle of Reason," pp. 16, 20.) But in practice, it seems, the chief way in which deconstruction "keeps alive the memory of a tradition" is by deconstructing its texts, and that merely brings our question full circle. The contrast with hermeneutics is instructive in this connection. (See D. Michelfelder and R. Palmer, eds., *Dialogue and Deconstruction: The Gadamer-Derrida Encounter*, Albany, 1989.)

47. *Limited Inc.*, p. 141.

48. See the interpretation of Richard Bernstein, "Serious Play: The Ethical-Political Horizon of Jacques Derrida," *Journal of Speculative Philosophy* 1, no. 2 (1987): 93–115.

49. In Jacques Derrida and Mustapha Tlili, eds., *For Nelson Mandela* (New York, 1987), pp. 13–42.

50. "The Laws of Reflection," p. 38.

51. "The Laws of Reflection," pp. 38–39.

52. "The Laws of Reflection," p. 41. A similar combination of using existing schemes while simultaneously devaluing them and gesturing toward something wholly other, which is as yet ineffable, marks Derrida's discussion of women's studies in "Women in

the Beehive," in Alice Jardine and Paul Smith, eds., *Men in Feminism* (New York, 1987), pp. 189–203. There he acknowledges the "positive research" of feminist scholars, while noting their failure adequately to "put back into question the structural principles" of "university law" and "of social law in general" (p. 191). The more that feminist research "proves its positivity," the more it risks "repressing the fundamental question we must pose" and becoming "just another cell in the university beehive" (p. 191). The same can be said of the struggle for equal rights for women: it remains "caught in the logic of phallogocentrism" and thus rebuilds "the empire of the law" (p. 193). The analytic and strategic advantages of depreciating "calculable" results by comparison to the "unprogrammable" project of deconstructing structural principles and philosophical frameworks are never identified apart from one curious reference to joint appointments (p. 193).

53. Their critique, "No Names Apart: The Separation of Word and History in Derrida's 'Le dernier mot du racisme,'" appeared in *Critical Inquiry* 13 (1986): 140–154. Derrida's response, "But Beyond . . . ," appeared in the same issue, pp. 155–170. See also the analysis of this exchange by Alexander Argyros, "Prescriptive Deconstruction," in *Critical Texts* 4 (1989): 1–16.

54. Afterword to *Limited Inc.*, pp. 150–151. The numbers in parentheses in the next few paragraphs refer to that afterword.

55. See the discussion of Foucault above, pp. 53–55.

56. In *Logics of Disintegration* Peter Dews has argued that this line of thought, rigorously pursued, leads to a kind of Schellingian absolute (pp. 19–31). Whether one then characterizes the "non-originary origin" of identity and difference in terms of absolute identity, as Schelling did, or absolute difference, as Derrida does, becomes a matter of rhetorical strategy.

57. This is one of Habermas's points in *The Philosophical Discourse of Modernity*, pp. 204–210, where he distinguishes the "poetic, world-disclosing" function of language from its "innerworldly, problem-solving" functions. Derrida seems to accept this point in the afterword to *Limited Inc.* (pp. 132–138), but he simply takes all such social constructions for granted and zeroes in on deficiencies, delusions, and dangers. He does not, and in the deconstructive mode cannot, tell us what we should look for in reconstructing them, nor how to orient ourselves in judging sociopolitical arrangements as better or worse. Critical interrogation of limits is surely essential in the ethicopolitical sphere, and it is certainly open to Derrida to choose to do only or chiefly this. As I shall argue below, the problem arises when he claims that this is the only philosophically legitimate intellectual activity in this sphere, since substantive empirical and normative inquiries are all blinded by the metaphysics of presence.

58. These are Derrida's terms in *Of Grammatology*, p. 5, and "Deconstruction and the Other," p. 123.

59. See, for example, his discussion of Nietzsche in *The Ear of the Other*, Christie V. McDonald, ed. (New York, 1985), esp. pp. 23 ff.

60. *The Philosophical Discourse of Modernity*, p. 408, n. 28. On this point, see also Richard Rorty, "Deconstruction and Circumvention," passim.

61. *Of Grammatology*, p. 27.

62. *Logics of Disintegration*, pp. 5 ff., 15 ff., and 36 ff.

63. *Logics of Disintegration*, p. 19.

64. *Logics of Disintegration*, pp. 37–38.

65. Most recently in *Limited Inc.*; p. 118. See also *Positions*, p. 102, n. 21, where the alternative to the philosophical orientation of deconstruction, is characterized as "empiricist improvisation."

66. "The French Derrideans," p. 149.

67. I am referring here to Derrida's oral presentation at the 1988 Eastern Division Meeting of the American Philosophical Association, where he discussed at some length Schmitt's *Concept of the Political* (New Brunswick, 1976). Even then he selected only the quasi-ontological themes from among the diverse topics that Schmitt dealt with in that work.

68. See Habermas's contribution to the symposium "Heidegger and Nazism," cited in note 30, above, "Work and Weltanschauung," pp. 431–456.
69. "The Politics of Friendship," p. 638.
70. "The Politics of Friendship," p. 638.
71. In his oral presentation.
72. "The French Derrideans," p. 130.
73. "The Politics of Friendship," p. 641.
74. *Limited Inc.*, pp. 136–137.
75. I am not, of course, arguing that one should not study classical texts. The issue is whether deconstructing texts *suffices* as an approach to political theory.
76. In his oral presentation. The remarks on democracy referred to in what follows also come from the version delivered at the American Philosophical Association meeting.
77. See "Of an Apocalyptic Tone," p. 94: "Now here, precisely, is announced—as promise or threat—an apocalypse without apocalypse, an apocalypse without vision, without truth, without revelation, . . . an apocalypse beyond good and evil. . . . Our apocalypse now: that there is no longer any place for the apocalypse as the collection of evil and good"; and "Deconstruction and the Other," p. 119: "Unfortunately I do not feel inspired by any sort of hope which would permit me to presume that my work of deconstruction has a prophetic function. But I concede that the style of my questions . . . might produce certain prophetic resonances. It is possible to see deconstruction as being produced in a space where the prophets are not far away."
78. As well as from the assumption of a broad normative consensus with his readers, which, because it is presumably shared, need not be spelled out or defended.
79. For some details of this argument, see the postscript that follows.
80. See "The Politics of Friendship," pp. 633–636. The relation to democracy was drawn in the oral presentation.
81. "The Politics of Friendship," p. 635–636.
82. This was in the oral version, as was the question posed in the next sentence.
83. If no answer can be found, Derrida's "negative ontotheology" remains a "political theology manquée," as Nancy Fraser put it in a conversation. See the last essay in this volume for a discussion of political-theological attempts to ground critical social theory.

Postscript to Chapter 4

1. Page references to the published version of this paper, which appeared in the *Journal of Philosophy* 85 (1988): 632–645, will be given in parentheses in the text.
2. In "Force of Law: The 'Mystical Foundation of Authority,'" a text prepared for the conference Deconstruction and the Law held at the Cardoza Law School in 1989, Derrida adverts to the "*type* of horizon" represented by Kant's regulative ideas but notes that there are "numerous competing versions," including the "messianic promises" of certain religions and the "eschato-teleologies" of certain philosophies of history (manuscript, p. 32).
3. Thus a principal concern of "Force of Law" is to distinguish law from a justice that "not only exceeds or contradicts *droit* but also, perhaps, has no relation to law, or maintains such a strange relation to it that it may just as well command the *droit* that excludes it" (p. 4). One cannot speak directly about this justice, thematize or objectivize it, without immediately betraying it (p. 11). Unlike law, it is not accounted for in the application of a good rule to a correctly subsumed case (p. 20). For this justice is "infinite, incalculable, rebellious to rule and foreign to symmetry, heterogeneous and heterotrophic" (p. 27). In these respects it is closer to God than to law. (pp. 68–69). Derrida is aware that treating justice as something "unpresentable [that] exceeds the determinable" (p. 35) is risky, for "it can always be reappropriated by the most perverse calculation" (p. 36). And so he enjoins us to "negotiate" its relations with law, ethics,

politics, and so on (p. 36). But he gives no clear indication of how this is to be done; indeed, he deines that anyone could. All of this, it seems to me, leaves us with the ineffable and its sometimes good, sometimes "preverse" appropriations, without any "effable" principles to determine which are which.

Chapter 5

1. J. Habermas, *On the Logic of the Social Sciences* (Cambridge, Mass., 1988), pp. 143–170; H.-G. Gadamer, "On the Scope and Function of Hermeneutical Reflection," in *Gadamer, Philosophical Heremeneutics* (Berkeley, 1976), pp. 18–43; J. Habermas, "The Heremeneutic Claim to University," in Josef Bleicher, ed., *Contemporary Heremeneutics* (London, 1980), pp. 181–211; H.-G. Gadamer, "Replik," in K.-O. Apel et al., *Heremeneutik and Ideologiekritik* (Frankfurt, 1971), pp. 283–317. For a good overview, see Georgia Warnke, *Gadamer: Hermeneutics, Tradition, and Reason* (Stanford, 1987), pp. 107–138.
2. See T. McCarthy, *The Critical Theory of Jürgen Habermas* (Cambridge, Mass., 1978), pp. 261 ff., and "On the Changing Relation of Theory to Practice in the Work of Jürgen Habermas," in *PSA 1978*, proceedings of the 1978 Biennial Meeting of the Philosophy of Science Association, vol. 2., P. Asquith and I. Hacking, eds. (East Lansing, Mich., 1979), pp. 397–423.
3. H.-G. Gadamer, *Truth and Method* (New York, 1975), pp. 263–264.
4. J. Habermas, *On the Logic of the Social Sciences.*
5. For some of the details, see T. McCarthy, *The Critical Theory of Jürgen Habermas*, chapters 3 and 4.
6. Habermas considers this formulation in his contribution to Willi Oelmüller, eds., *Transzendentalphilosophische Normenbegründungen* (Paderborn, 1978), p. 114.
7. J. Habermas, "What Is Universal Pragmatics?" in Habermas, *Communication and the Evolution of Society* (Boston, 1979), pp. 1–68, here p. 2.
8. "What Is Universal Pragmatics?" pp. 8 ff., 21 ff. See also J. Habermas, "Philosophy as Stand-In and Interpreter," and "Reconstruction and Interpretation in the Social Sciences," both in Habermas, *Moral Consciousness and Communicative Action* (Cambridge, Mass., 1990), pp. 1–20 and 21–42.
9. What Is Universal Pragmatics?" p. 3.
10. I raised this objection in a contribution to *Transzendentalphilosophische Normenbegründungen*, pp. 134–136. Habermas responded along the lines indicated in the text, in the same work, pp. 136–139 and pp. 155–156. He later elaborated on this response in *The Theory of Communicative Action*, vol. 1 (Boston, 1984), pp. 286–295, where the crux of his argument was that success in achieving perlocutionary aims depends upon success in achieving illocutionary aims. But Habermas used the terms "illocutionary" and "perlocutionary" in a somewhat idiosyncratic manner there, and that opened his argument to objections that he might otherwise have avoided. (See, for example, Allan W. Wood, "Habermas's Defense of Rationalism," *New German Critique* 35 (1985): 145–164.) He subsequently reformulated the argument in his "Entgegnung," in A. Honneth and H. Joas, eds., *Kommunikatives Handeln* (Frankfurt, 1986), pp. 362–366, where he shows that the achievement of *strategically intended, undeclared perlocutionary aims* is parasitic on achieving illocutionary aims. In this restatement I find the argument convincing.
11. *Transzendentalphilosophische Normenbegründungen*, p. 156.
12. *Transzendentalphilosophische Normenbegründungen*, p. 138. The burden of proof for this claim is assumed in *The Theory of Communicative Action*, vols. 1 and 2 (Boston, 1984, 1987), especially in chapter 6, where Habermas argues that cultural reproduction, social integration, and socialization transpire in and through the medium of communicative action, and in chapter 8, where he argues that these functions of lifeworld reproduction cannot be subverted by systemic steering media (such as money and

power) without pathological consequences. These two volumes will henceforth be cited as *TCA*, 1, and *TCA*, 2.

13. *Transzendentalphilosophische Normenbegründungen*, p. 224. The same point can be made through an analysis of various pathologies and their origins in pathogenic structures of communication in the family. See J. Habermas, "Stichworte zur Theorie der Sozialisation," in his *Kultur und Kritik* (Frankfurt, 1973) pp. 138–194, and "Überlegungen zur Kommunikationspathologie," in his *Vorstudien and Ergänzungen zur Theorie des kommunikativen Handelns* (Frankfurt, 1984), pp. 226–270.

14. *Transzendentalphilosophische Normenbegründungen*, p. 128. Compare *TCA*, 1, p. 137.

15. *Transzendentalphilosophische Normenbegründungen*, p. 146.

16. *Transzendentalphilosophische Normenbegründungen*, p. 128.

17. *TCA*, 1, pp. 43–66.

18. *TCA*, 1, p. 137. The final sentence alludes to his differences with Karl-Otto Apel.

19. *TCA*, 1, p. 139.

20. See especially *Communication and the Evolution of Society*, *TCA*, 1 and 2, and *Moral Consciousness and Communicative Action*.

21. For relevant bibliography, see Patricia Teague Ashton, "Cross-Cultural Piagetian Research: An Experimental Perspective," *Harvard Educational Review* 45 (1975): 475–506; *Piagetian Psychology: Cross-Cultural Contributions*, ed. P. R. Dasen (New York, 1977); and Dasen's introduction, pp. 1–25.

22. Susan Buck-Morss, "Socio-economic Bias in Piaget's Theory and Its Implications for Cross-Cultural Studies," *Human Development* 18 (1975): 40–41, cited by Dasen in *Piagetian Psychology*, p. 6.

23. Dasen, *Piagetian Psychology*, p. 8.

24. See Ashton, "Cross-Cultural Piagetian Research."

25. Dasen, *Piagetian Psychology*, p. 11.

26. Dasen, *Piagetian Psychology*, p. 7.

27. John C. Gibbs, "Kohlberg's Stages of Moral Judgment: A Constructive Critique," *Harvard Educational Review* 47 (1977): 55.

28. Gibbs, "Kohlberg's Stages of Moral Judgment," p. 55.

29. Thus in "The Claim to Moral Adequacy of a Highest Stage of Moral Judgment" (*Journal of Philosophy*, 70 (1973): 630–646; reprinted in *Essays in Moral Development*, vol. 2, San Francisco, 1984, pp. 145–175; citations are to the latter edition), Kohlberg writes, "The developing human being and the moral philosopher are engaged in fundamentally the same moral task. . . . The task is arriving at moral judgments in reflective equilibrium . . . between espoused general moral principles and particular judgments about situations. . . . The process continues to lead to revision, sometimes of our principles, sometimes of our intuition as to what is right in a concrete situation" (p. 149). On this view, stages represent theories or principles through which concrete experiences are interpreted (assimilated) and that are revised to accommodate these experiences. They are "equilibrium points in the successive revisions of principles and concrete experiences in relation to one another" (p. 149). Thus in posing hypothetical moral dilemmas to subjects, the moral psychologist elicits both their concrete normative judgments, moral intuitions, and the justifications they offer for them, metaethical and normative moral theories (p. 172). The individual's moral theory is viewed as "a conscious reflection upon his actual normative judgments" (p. 172). And this implies a relation between the moral philosopher and the moral agent that is increasingly symmetrical: "The familiar concerns of moral philosophy correspond to the 'natural' concerns or modes of reflection at our highest stages" (p. 174). Moral philosophy or "formal moral theory" emerges from this "post-customary level of 'reflective' moral discourse," in which subjects attempt to justify and systematize their concrete judgments (p. 174). This view of moral philosophy as systematizing modes of reflective thought that are part and parcel of higher-stage morality clearly relativizes the asymmetry between prereflective intuition and reflective reconstruction. Habermas accepts this point in his "Reply to My Critics," in J. Thompson and D. Held, eds., *Habermas: Critical Debates* (Cambridge, Mass., 1982), pp. 258–261.

30. Kohlberg recognizes this in a certain way: "The isomorphism of psychological and normative theory generates the claim that a psychologically more advanced stage of moral judgment is more morally adequate by moral-philosophic criteria. The isomorphism assumption is a two-way street. While moral philosophical criteria of adequacy of moral judgment help define a standard of psychological adequacy or advance, the psychological advance feeds back and clarifies these criteria. . . . Our psychological theory claims that individuals prefer the highest stage of reasoning they comprehend, a claim supported by research. This claim of our psychological theory derives from a philosophical claim that a later stage is 'objectively' preferable or more adequate by certian *moral* criteria. This philosophical claim, however, would for us be thrown into question if the facts of moral advance were inconsistent with its psychological implications" ("The Claim to Moral Adequacy," p. 148). The "moral criteria" in question are taken largely from "the formalist tradition in philosophic ethics from Kant to Rawls" (p. 148). That is, the focus is narrowed to questions of "duties and rights" to the exclusion of questions of "ultimate aims or ends" and of "personal worth or virtue" ("From Is to Ought: How to Commit the Naturalistic Fallacy and Get Away with It in the Study of Moral Development," in *Cognitive Development and Epistemology*, ed. T. Mischel, New York, 1971, p. 214), and morality is regarded as having to do with "conflicts between competing claims" (p. 192), the moral aim being "to make decisions which anyone could agree with in resolving social conflicts" (p. 218) or, at another level, to discover a "universal prescriptive principle" (p. 221). Moral "theorists," whether lay members or philosophers, would, of course, want to debate much of this. In his "Reply to My Critics" (pp. 258–261 and in *Moral Consciousness and Communicative Action*, pp. 172–175), Habermas accepts this point and no longer speaks of "natural stages of development" at the postconventional level of morality. "Stages of reflection" can be distinguished at this level, but they are open to being philosophically contested.
31. *Communication and the Evolution of Society*, p. 74.
32. *Communication and the Evolution of Society*, p. 107. This is consistent with Habermas's earlier critique, following Hegel, of the monadological presuppositions of Kant's autonomous self (see "Labor and Interaction: Remarks on Hegel's Jena *Philosophy of Mind*," in Habermas, *Theory and Practice*, Boston, 1973, pp. 142–169). For a later elaboration of this relational view of the self, see Habermas, *Nachmetaphysiches Denken* (Frankfurt, 1988), pp. 187–241.
33. *Communication and the Evolution of Society*, pp. 93–94. This conception of a "seventh stage" going beyond formalist moral consciousness and reintegrating the "field dependency" of earlier stages in a higher synthesis offers a perspective for correcting the imbalance that results from focusing on autonomy at the expense of attachment. See Carol Gilligan, *In a Different Voice* (Cambridge, Mass., 1982). Habermas discusses Gilligan's work in *Moral Consciousness and Communicative Action*, pp. 175–184, where he no longer works with a seventh stage but with a richer conception of stage 6: There is no need for a "postconventional contextualist stage," he argues, if principled morality is adequately conceived and properly distinguished from and related to ethical life, more particularly, if problems of justification, application, and motivation are properly differentiated and reintegrated.
34. *Knowledge and Human Interests* (Boston, 1971), p. 35.
35. *Knowledge and Human Interests*, p. 26. My discussion appeared in *The Critical Theory of Jürgen Habermas*, pp. 110–136. Habermas's response to that discussion as well as to an earlier version of the argument advanced here can be found in "A Reply to My Critics," pp. 241–250.
36. *Knowledge and Human Interests*, p. 34.
37. *Knowledge and Human Interests*, p. 41.
38. *Theory and Practice*, pp. 21–22.
39. "A Reply to My Critics," pp. 243–244. This acknowledgement of nonobjectivating relations with nature may be sufficient grounds for relativizing the subject/object bifurcation in practice. But in view of the expanding universe of contemporary eco-

logical discourse, it will be worth our while to pursue the question of alternative *theoretical* approaches to nature a bit further.

40. "A Reply to My Critics," p. 245.

41. In "Questions and Counterquestions," in R. Bernstein, ed., *Habermas and Modernity* (Cambridge, Mass., 1985), pp. 192–216, Habermas grants this point but reaffirms his own "scepticism in the face of so many failed attempts . . . to retain Kant's insights and at the same time to return to the 'home' from which those same insights have driven us" (p. 211). He is responding there to an earlier statement of the present argument in my "Reflections on Rationalization in *The Theory of Communicative Action,*" in *Habermas and Modernity,* pp. 177–191, esp. pp. 189–190.

42. For these reasons it would be clearly unacceptable to "deep ecologists." But their endeavors seem rather to confirm Habermas's wariness about falling back "behind the levels of learning achieved in the modern age into a reenchanted world." See the critical overview by Tim Luke, "The Dreams of Deep Ecology," *Telos* 76 (1988): 65–92.

43. "A Reply to My Critics," p. 249.

44. The same could be said of his claim that ethical relations to nature could not be rationalized "at the same level that Kant attained in his moralization of social relations" ("A Reply to My Critics," p. 249).

45. It does not seem that a philosophy of nature is required to ground an ethics of compassion for beings capable of suffering. As Habermas suggests in "A Reply to My Critics," such an ethics might be introduced as a "limit concept" of communicative ethics. It would reflectively work up those prima facie moral experiences and intuitions that figure in our dealings with such beings, for instance, "the impulse to provide assistance to wounded and debased creates and to have solidarity with them, the compassion for their torments" (p. 245). Whereas morality in the strict sense, on this account, extends only as far as our dealings with subjects capable of speech and action, an ethics of compassion extends "beyond the domain of interpersonal relations to our relationships with creatures that cannot fulfill the conditions of responsible action," creatures that are affected by our behavior without being able to participate in discussions of its rightness (p. 247). Habermas notes that such an expanded solidarity reaches only to the limits of empathy and in any case must come to a halt with plant life if human survival is to take precedence. Nor does a philosophy of nature appear to be required to ground an ethics of "reform environmentalism." The standpoint of human well-being, of who we are and want to be, of what kind of world we want to live in, of our responsibility to other human beings and to future generations, seems to be adequate for that purpose. Thus it is the sorts of social-ecological ethics and politics deeper than animal rights and reform environmentalism, but not as deep as deep ecology, that might require a basis in a nonobjectivating philosophy of nature that did not regress behind historically achieved differentiations.

46. In "Contra Relativism: A Thought Experiment," in M. Krausz, ed. *Relativism: Interpretation and Confrontation* (Notre Dame, 1989), pp. 256–271, I defend the possibility of learning at the sociocultural level not by directly invoking a developmental schema but by working through the idea of dialogic encounter between different modes of thought. This approach remains at the level of situated reasoning while transforming the limits of specific situations.

47. Habermas objects only to attempts to reestablish the unity of reason in theory, not in practice. As he put it in "Questions and Counterquestions," p. 210, "For Marx, philosophy realized is philosophy *aufgehoben.* The theory of communicative action gives this idea another reading: the unity of reason cannot be reestablished on the level of cultural tradition in the form of a substantive worldview, but only this side of expert cultures, in a non-reified, communicative practice of everyday life." He also allows for a certain interpenetration of theoretically differentiated domains, for example, of moral and aesthetic criticism into the discourse of the human sciences, of cognitive and expressive concerns into moral discourse, and of moments of realism and engagement into post-avant-garde art. See *TCA,* 2, p. 398.

48. *Theory and Practice,* p. 40.

Chapter 6

1. J. Habermas, "Technology and Science as 'Ideology,'" in *Toward a Rational Society* (Boston, 1970), pp. 81–122, here p., 106.
2. J. Habermas, N. Luhmann, *Theorie der Gesellschaft oder Sozialtechnologie* (Frankfurt, 1971), hereafter cited as *TGST. Legitimation Crisis* (Boston, 1975), pp. 117 ff, hereafter cited as *LC*. Habermas's Hegel Prize lecture was "Können komplexe Gesellschaften eine vernünftige Identität ausbilden?" in J. Habermas, D. Henrich, *Zwei Reden* (Frankfurt, 1974), pp. 23–84, partially translated into English as "On Social Identity," *Telos* 19 (1974): 91–103.
3. *The Theory of Communicative Action*, volume 1, *Reason and the Rationalization of Society* (Boston, 1984), volume 2, *System and Lifeworld* (Boston, 1987). Page numbers in parentheses in the text will refer to volume 2. In footnotes, volume 1 will be cited as *TCA*, 1, and volume 2 as *TCA*, 2.
4. *The Differentiation of Society* (New York, 1982), p. 78.
5. *Zwei Reden*, p. 60.
6. *LC*, p. 3.
7. *TGST*, pp. 149 ff.
8. *TGST*, p. 151.
9. *TGST*, p. 164.
10. *TGST*, pp. 165–166.
11. W. Buckley, "Society as a Complex Adaptive System," in W. Buckley, ed., *Modern Systems Research for the Behavioral Scientist* (Chicago, 1968), p. 497. Buckely, like Habermas, seeks to combine the two levels of analysis.
12. Buckley, "Society as a Complex Adaptive System," p. 504.
13. Buckley, "Society as a Complex Adaptive System," pp. 504–505. The study he is referring to, by Anselm Strauss and others, appeared in E. Freidson, ed., *The Hospital in Modern Society* (New York, 1963). One might also think here of Foucault's studies of the asylum, the clinic, and the prison, of Goffman's study of asylums, of the numerous studies by ethnomethodologists of practical reasoning in organizational settings of all sorts, and so on.
14. Egon Bittner, "The Concept of Organization," *Social Research* 32 (1965): 239–255; reprinted in R. Turner, eds., *Ethnomethodology* (Hammandsworth, England, 1974), pp. 69–81, here pp. 76–78.
15. T. Parsons, "On the Concept of Political Power," in *Sociological Theory and Modern Society* (New York, 1967), pp. 297–354, here p. 308.
16. T. Parsons, "'Voting' and the Equilibrium of the American Political System," in *Sociological Theory and Modern Society*, pp. 223–263, here pp. 227 ff.
17. See *The Differentiation of Society*, pp. 150 ff.
18. *The Differentiation of Society*, p. 153.
19. *The Differentiation of Society*, p. 154.
20. *LC*, pp. 134 ff.
21. *LC*, pp. 33 ff.
22. The two traditions have been brought together by Claus Offe, with whom Habermas shares many basic ideas on the nature and functioning of the modern state. See, for instance, Offe's *Contradictions of the Welfare State* (Cambridge, Mass., 1984).
23. In his response to the following objections ("Entgegnung," in *Kommunikatives Handeln*, A. Honneth and H. Joas, eds., Frankfurt, 1986, pp. 377–396), Habermas emphasizes that *all* social phenomena can be viewed from *both* lifeworld and system perspectives. But as a result of the "uncoupling" of the system and the lifeworld in modern societies, in such a way that system-environment dynamics enter *into* society itself via differentiated subsystems that relate to other domains *as* environments, there are differences in depth of perception. In particular, processes of material reproduction become so complex and opaque that they can less and less be grasped and explained from the "foreshortened" perspective of participants (ibid., 381). The econ-

omy and the state are now "primarily" integrated systematically, that is, via a reciprocal stabilization of aggregate action consequences that is normally counterintuitive in relation to the orientations actors bring to interaction in these domains. "While modern societies can generally be studied under both aspects, economic and political interdependencies can be adequately grasped at this stage of system differentiation only if described as media-steered subsystems. As can be shown from the history of social theory, they can no longer be sufficiently explained from the lifeworld perspective." (ibid., 387). If the analyses of *The Theory of Communicative Action* were consistently carried through in this more-or-less (in contrast to an either-or) vein, I would have to revise some of the arguments that follow, but Habermas too, I think, would have to revise his analysis of the political system.

24. In respose to objections by E. Skjei and others, Habermas has revised his distinction between simple and normatively authorized imperatives. (See his "Reply to Skjei," *Inquiry* 28 (1985): 111 ff.) But the revisions strengthen rather than weaken my point here.

25. Habermas classifies the latter as "empirical" rather than "rational" motivations. But they are no less a matter of orientations and not of results.

26. Thus Thomas Luckmann's remark, cited by Habermas on page 311 of *TCA*, 2, to the effect that the objective meaning of action in specialized institutional domains typically does not coincide with its subjective meaning for the individual actor, could apply as well to actions whose point was known only to superiors.

27. As the flow of studies on the social psychology, human relations, politics, etc. of large organizations testifies. There is no obvious reason for drawing a sharp line between the "communicative engendering of power" and its "acquisition and maintenance," on the one hand, and the "rule or the exercise of power," on the other, so that the first two are to be studied by means of action theory and the last by systems theory, as Habermas does in "Hannah Arendt: On the Concept of Power" in *Philosophical-Political Profiles* (Cambridge, Mass., 1983), pp. 180–181.

28. *TGST*, p. 161.

29. *TGST*, p. 231.

30. *TGST*, p. 144–145.

31. *LC*, pp. 123–124.

32. See C. B. Macpherson, *The Life and Times of Liberal Democracy* (Oxford, 1977).

33. *LC*, pp. 130 ff.

34. *LC*, p. 138.

35. See *TGST*, p. 274; *LC*, p. 139.

36. J. Habermas, *Communication and the Evolution of Society* (Boston, 1978), p. 174. In seems clear that the same holds true for social organization.

37. *LC*, p. 130.

38. *TGST*, pp. 144–145.

39. *On the Logic of the Social Sciences* (Cambridge, Mass., 1989), p. 188. In his "Entgegnung" (p. 379) Habermas cites the work of Claus Offe and others as having in the meantime demonstrated the empirical fruitfulness of the systems approach to analyzing crises in the economic and political systems.

40. Thus in his introduction to organization theory, *Organizations: Structure and Process* (Englewood Cliffs, 1977), Richard Hall notes, "Few researchers have the tools or the ability to take into account all the various components that must be included in even a relatively simple open systems model." (p. 59). A problem he mentions shortly thereafter suggests, however, that this is more than just a question of tools and ability. He notes that the behavior of organizations usually change when they are threatened: "The power of the external pressures and threats is the key variable" (p. 63). "Unfortunately," he adds, "there are no available systematic measures of the power of such threats" (p. 63), nor, one might add, are there likely to be.

41. In their summary of the different perspectives on organization theory, *Complex Organizations: A Sociological Perspective* (New York, 1973), J. E. Haas and T. E. Drabek write of the open systems approach, "Terms like 'boundary,' 'adaptation,' 'feedback,'

and the like are useful as organizing concepts, but difficult to use operationally. Predictive statements are hard to make. . . . Empirical studies that would sharpen the concepts and test some of the hypothesized relationships are almost totally absent" (pp. 92–93). On viewing organizations as natural (adaptive) systems, they quote George E, Homans as saying that we have a "language without any sentences." And they add, "The 'words' in that language remain very vague—perhaps impossible to make operational" (p. 53).

42. Haas and Drabek, *Complex Organizations*, pp. 52–53. Though Habermas wants to combine the inside and outside perspectives *in general*, he seems to consign formal organizations to a systems analysis in which neither formal structure nor informal relationships play much of a role.

43. D. Silverman, *The Theory of Organizations* (London, 1970), p. 68. He cites R. Mayntz, "The Study of Organizations," *Current Sociology*, 13 (1964), in support of this view.

44. *The Rules of Sociological Method* (Chicago, 1938), p. 90.

45. St. Mennell, *Sociological Theory: Uses and Unities* (New York, 1974), p. 89.

46. See *Zwei Reden*, pp. 66 ff. In *TCA*, 2, the approach appears, for instance, in his discussion of new social movements, pp. 395–396.

47. "The New Obscurity: The Crisis of the Welfare State and the Exhaustion of Utopian Energies," in Habermas, *The New Conservatism* (Cambridge, Mass., 1989), pp. 48–70, here pp. 64, 67. See also J. Habermas, "Volkssouveränität als Verfahren," *Merkur* 1989, no 6: 465–467, and J. Habermas, *The Philosophical Discourse of Modernity* (Cambridge, Mass., 1987), pp. 336–367. Compare the essay by Claus Offe, "Competitive Party Democracy and the Keynesian Welfare State," *Contradictions of the Welfare State*, pp. 179–206, esp. pp. 188 ff.

48. I am focusing on the political system. Related considerations might be developed with respect to the economy. In this connection some very interesting "action research" with worker participation has been carried out by the LOM Program of the Swedish Center for Working Life in Stockholm under the direction of Björn Gustavsen.

49. *Knowledge and Human Interests* (Boston, 1971), pp. 254 ff.; *On the Logic of the Social Sciences*, pp. 182 ff.

50. *On the Logic of the Social Sciences*, p. 87.

51. *On the Logic of the Social Sciences*, pp. 187–189. As Habermas points out in his "Entgegnung" (p. 393), taking the analogies with individual enlightenment, emancipation, self-consciousness, and self-determination too literally leads to treating complex societies as centered macrosubjects, which he now wants explicitly to avoid. But one could conceive of democratization processes in a less holistic way, as contextually differentiated, decentered, and pluralistic. Then, of course, coordination at the level of society as a whole could not depend on democratic decision making alone. See the interesting remarks on this point in Habermas, *The Philosophical Discourse of Modernity* (Cambridge, Mass., 1987), pp. 357–367.

Chapter 7

1. In addition to *The Structural Transformation of the Public Sphere*, see the studies in moral theory collected in *Moral Consciousness and Communicative Action* (Cambridge, Mass., 1990) and the two lectures "Law and Morality," in *The Tanner Lectures on Human Values*, vol. 8 (Salt Lake City and Cambridge, 1988), pp. 217–299. See also *Legitimation Crisis* (Boston, 1975), and "Legitimation Problems in the Modern State," in Habermas, *Communication and the Evolution of Society* (Boston, 1979), pp. 178–205.

2. For recent discussions of these questions, see Stephen K. White, *The Recent Work of Jürgen Habermas* (Cambridge, 1988), Seyla Benhabib and Fred Dallmayr, eds., *The Communicative Ethics Controversy* (Cambridge, Mass., 1990), and Kenneth Baynes, *From Social Contract Theory to Normative Social Criticism* (Albany, 1991). See also the special

issues of *Philosophical Forum* 21 (1989/1990), nos. 1–2, and *Philosophy and Social Criticism* 14 (1989), nos. 3–4.

3. *The Theory of Communicative Action,* vol. 1 (Boston, 1984), p. 92.

4. *Moral Consciousness and Communicative Action,* p. 177. "Ideas of the good life are not notions that simply occur to individuals as abstract imperatives; they shape the identities of groups and individuals in such a way that they form an integral part of culture and personality."

5. *The Theory of Communicative Action,* vol. 1, p. 19.

6. *The Theory of Communicative Action,* vol. 1, p. 20. "Values are candidates for interpretations under which a circle of those affected can, if the occasion arises, describe and normatively regulate a common interest."

7. See "Wahrheitstheorien," in Habermas, *Vorstudien und Ergänzungen zur Theorie des kommunikativen Handelns* (Frankfurt, 1984), pp. 127–183, here pp. 166–174.

8. *The Theory of Communicative Action,* vol. 1, p. 42.

9. "Individual Will-Formation in Terms of What Is Expedient, What Is Good, and What Is Just," paper read at Northwestern University, fall 1988, pp. 15, 17. See also *Moral Consciousness and Communicative Action,* pp. 177–178: "A person who questions the form of life in which his identity has been shaped questions his very existence. The distancing produced by life crises of that kind is of another sort than the distance of a norm-testing participant in discourse from the facticity of existing institutions."

10. See *The Theory of Communicative Action,* vol. 1, pp. 20–21, 40–42, and the table of types of argumentation on p. 23.

11. *The Theory of Communicative Action,* p. 21. Compare the interesting discussion by James Bohman, "Communication, Ideology, and Democratic Theory," *American Political Science Review* 84 (1990): 93–109.

12. *The Theory of Communicative Action,* p. 20. Following Albrecht Wellmer, Habermas has recently expanded his conception of the "illuminating power" of aesthetic experience. In addition to affecting our evaluative language, he now holds, it can also affect "our cognitive interpretations and normative expectations, and transform the totality in which these moments are related" ("Questions and Counterquestions," in R. B. Bernstein, ed., *Habermas and Modernity,* Cambridge, Mass., 1985, pp. 192–216, here p. 202). See also Albrecht Wellmer, "Truth, Semblence, Reconciliation: Adorno's Aesthetic Realization of Modernity," in Wellmer, *The Persistence of Modernity,* forthcoming, MIT Press.

13. "Wahrheitstheorien," p. 149. See also *Moral Consciousness and Communicative Action,* pp. 60–62.

14. Habermas ties the cogency or "consensus-producing power" of arguments to their capacity to provide "adequate motivation" for accepting a warrant as "plausible," in "Wahrheitstheorien," pp. 164–165. It seems obvious that this type of motivating force will not be the same in all contexts.

15. See *Moral Consciousness and Communicative Action,* pp. 67–68.

16. "A Philosophico-political Profile," in Peter Dews, ed., *Habermas: Autonomy and Solidarity* (London, 1986), pp. 149–189, here p. 174.

17. See *Moral Consciousness and Communicative Action,* pp. 68–76.

18. *Moral Consciousness and Communicative Action,* p. 72.

19. *The Theory of Communicative Action,* vol. 2 (Boston, 1987), p. 94. Habermas's terminology tends to cover over the distinction in point. He uses "general interest," "generalizable interest," "common interest," "shared interest," and "equally good for all" as synonymous. But a fair general regulation need not be equally good for all or in the interest of all as regard its consequences for first-order needs.

20. I am focusing on differences in evaluative perspective, but an argument could be made with regard to differences in interpretative perspective generally. (The two are, in fact, connected.) Focusing on the hermeneutic dimension of interpretive social science and narrative history would make clear that not even the "facts of the matter" are beyond dispute in moral-political debates. In sociohistorical inquiry there is no agreed upon general interpretive framework that functions as, say, general theory

does in physics. Hence, not only the assessment of consequences but their very description, not to mention their probability, will frequently be at issue.

21. *The Theory of Communicative Action*, vol. 2, pp. 95–96. For a discussion of this "transformative moment of practical discourse," see Seyla Benhabib, *Critique, Norm, and Utopia* (New York, 1986), pp. 313–316.

22. Compare Albrecht Wellmer, *Ethik und Dialog* (Frankfurt, 1986), pp. 81–102; English translation forthcoming in *The Persistence of Modernity*.

23. See especially "Volkssouveränität als Verfahren," *Merkur* 6 (1989): 465–477, and "On the Relationship of Politics, Law, and Morality," paper read at Northwestern University, fall 1988. An expanded version of the first essay appeared in *Die Ideen von 1789 in der deutschen Rezeption*, ed. by Forum für Philosophie, Bad Homburg (Frankfurt, 1989), pp. 7–36.

24. "On the Relationship of Politics, Law, and Morality," p. 11.

25. See *The Theory of Communicative Action*, vol. 2, esp. chap. 8; "The New Obscurity: The Crisis of the Welfare State and the Exhaustion of Utopian Energies," in Habermas, *The New Conservatism* (Cambridge, Mass., 1989), pp. 48–70; and "Volkssouveränität als Verfahren."

26. See my discussion of this shift in chapter 6.

27. "Volkssouveränität als Verfahren," p. 474.

28. Michael Walzer discusses the ways in which democratic theory and practice must adapt to processes of social differentiation in "Liberalism and the Art of Separation," *Political Theory* 12 (1984): 315–330. In *Spheres of Justice* (New York, 1985) he analyzes the differentiation of social goods, with different internal logics, that is part of such processes. For a discussion of the "politics of need interpretations" stressing their essential contestability and their connection to questions of social identity, see Nancy Fraser, *Unruly Practices* (Minneapolis, 1989), esp. chaps. 7 and 8.

29. For instance, when competing conceptions of the common good are at issue, arguments may serve to get others to see the authenticity or inauthenticity of core values and hence to give them the appropriate weight in shaping a political accord. In *this* respect, the constitutive suppositions of discussions of the common good may resemble those with which participants engage in what Habermas calls "critique and criticism": they need not assume that there is only one correct view. Compare Joshua Cohen's model of public deliberation on the common good in "Deliberation and Democratic Legitimacy," in A. Hamlin and P. Pettit, eds., *The Good Polity* (London, 1989), pp. 17–34. Cohen emphasizes the need to offer "reasons pursuasive to others" in making claims on social resources.

30. In his published works Habermas has not given this distinction the significance it deserves in *political* theory, as he has been chiefly concerned to elucidate and justify the *moral* point of view. In "On the Relationship between Politics, Law, and Morality," however, he adopts a tripartite scheme that distinguishes the "aggregate will" resulting from bargaining processes, the "common will" shaped in hermeneutic self-clarification, and the "general will" formed in universalizing moral discourse (p. 16). All three are treated as forms of "rational will formation" relying on argumentation of different types. But he is not always consistent in applying this distinction. For instance, in another unpublished manuscript entitled "Erläuterungen zur Diskursethik," he writes that morality, in contrast to ethics, has to do not with questions of the good life but with questions concerning "what norms we want to live by together and how conflicts can be resolved in the common interest" (p. 7). But normative questions and questions of the general interest arise already at the level of forming a common political will in a particular society. The distinction he needs here is not between values and norms but between binding social norms that are also moral norms and those that are not. Habermas uses the same model of discursively achieved consensus for both, but in one case the circle of potential participants includes the members of a political community and in the other all human beings. It should be noted that in his view there can be no a priori determination of which issues are moral and which ethical. That too is a matter for discussion.

31. John Rawls, "The Idea of an Overlapping Consensus," *Oxford Journal of Legal Studies* 7 (1987): 1–25.

32. Habermas allows that philosophically based moral theories do not exhaust the "semantic potential" even of postmetaphysical religious discourse (see his *Nachmetaphysiches Denken*, Frankfurt, 1988, p. 60) and that as the latter is rooted in particular traditions, practices, and experiences, it comes in a variety of types ("Transzendenz von Innen, Transzendenz ins Diesseits: Eine Replik," ms., pp. 8 ff.). Precisely because of its highly formal nature, discourse ethics is compatible with different substantive conceptions of the meaning and value of life. Inasmuch as these differences figure in assessments of the general acceptability of anticipated consequences, they will play a role in deliberation about justice.

33. As the circle of potential participants in moral discourse trenscends all political boundaries, moral consensus will always be counterfactual, and hence contestable, in ways that political consensus need not be.

34. Rawls takes a similar track in "The Idea of an Overlapping Consensus." Of course, Habermas would view the basis of such consensus differently than Rawls. He discusses this issue under the rubric of "legality and legitimacy" in *Legitimation Crisis*, pp. 97–102, *The Theory of Communicative Action*, vol. 1, pp. 264–267, and "Wie ist Legitimität durch Legalität möglich?" *Kritische Justiz* 20 (1987):1–16. His basic thesis is that formally correct procedures can legitimate decisions only if they are part of a legal-political system that is itself recognized as legitimate on grounds that all can rationally accept. (See note 35.)

35. As I indicated at the outset, I am not dealing here with the justification that Habermas offers for the basic rights and principles that define the public sphere. In contrast to Rawls's hermeneutic appeal to ideas implicit in our public political culture, Habermas argues that the basic structures of justice are themselves justified only if they are ones that free and equal persons could agree to in practical discourse. On this difference, see Kenneth Baynes, "The Liberal/Communitarian Controversy and Communicative Ethics," *Philosophy and Social Criticism* 14 (1989), nos. 3–4: 293–313. He explains how, on Habermas's view, civil and political rights, and some social rights as well, can be justified as necessary preconditions for free and equal participation in democratic will formation; as such, they could be *reflectively* agreed to in the very discourses they are meant to secure. I am indebted to Baynes for a discussion of the points in section 4 of this essay.

Chapter 8

1. H. Peukert, *Science, Action, and Fundamental Theology* (Cambridge, Mass., 1984).

2. I. Kant, *Critique of Pure Reason*, trans. N. Kemp Smith (New York, 1961), p. 650.

3. I. Kant, *Critique of Practical Reason*, trans. L. W. Beck (Indianapolis, 1956), p. 147.

4. Allen Wood, *Kant's Moral Religion* (Ithaca, 1961), p. 17.

5. I shall not be directly concerned with the argument for immortality, which has a rather different structure.

6. *Critique of Practical Reason*, pp. 114–115.

7. *Critique of Practical Reason*, p. 118.

8. *Critique of Practical Reason*, p. 130.

9. Cited in *Critique of Practical Reason*, p. 149, n. 6.

10. I shall be dealing here with the work of such German theologians as Johann Baptist Metz, Jürgen Moltmann, and Helmut Peukert. See, for instance, Metz; *Faith in History and Society* (New York, 1980); Moltmann, *Theology of Hope* (New York, 1967); and Peukert, *Science, Action, and Fundamental Theology*.

11. *Theology of Hope*, pp. 290–291. See also "The Cross and Civil Religion," in J. Moltmann et al., *Religion and Political Society* (New York, 1974, pp. 9–47, esp. pp. 41 ff.

12. This is particularly stressed by Latin American liberation theologians. See Matthew Lamb, *Solidarity with Victims* (New York, 1982).

13. *Science, Action, and Fundamental Ontology*, pp. 206 ff. Peukert Builds on earlier treatments by R. Tiedemann, "Historische-Materialismus oder politischer Messianismus?" in P. Bulthaup, ed., *Materialien zu Benjamins Thesen "Über den Begriff der Geschichte"* (Frankfurt, 1975), pp. 77–121, and Christian Lenhardt, "Anamnestic Solidarity: The Proletariat and Its *Manes*," *Telos* 25 (1975): 133–153.

14. M. Horkheimer, letter to Benjamin, 16 March 1937; cited in Tiedemann, "Historischer Materialismus oder politischer Messianismus?" p. 87.

15. M. Horkheimer *Kritische Theorie*, vol. 1 (Frankfurt, 1968), p. 198.

16. *Kritische Theorie*, vol. 1, p. 372.

17. W. Benjamin, *Passagen*, cited in Tiedemann, "Historischer Materialismus oder politischer Messiansmus?" p. 88.

18. The "Theses" are included in W. Benjamin, *Illuminations*, ed. H. Arendt (New York, 1969), pp. 253–264. The phrase quoted appears in his *Origin of German Tragic Drama* (London, 1977), p. 166.

19. M. Horkheimer *Kritische Theorie*, vol. 1, p. 372.

20. See J. Habermas, *The Theory of Communicative Action*, vol. 1, (Boston, 1984). For an overview of the theological reception of Habermas's work, see Edmund Arens, ed., *Habermas und die Theoloie* (Düsseldorf, 1989).

21. On what follows, see T. McCarthy, *The Critical Theory of Jürgen Habermas* (Cambridge, Mass., 1978), pp. 310–333, esp. pp. 325 ff.

22. *Science, Action, and Fundamental Theology*, pp. 209–210.

23. I. Kant, *Critique of Judgment*, trans. J. Bernard (New York, 1951), sections 86–91, pp. 292 ff. On p. 303 Kant says of the righteous man, "Deceit, violence and envy will always surround him . . . and the righteous men with whom he meets will, notwithstanding all their worthiness of happiness, be yet subjected by nature, which regards not this, to all the evils of want, disease and untimely death . . . until one wide grave engulfs them together (honest or not, it makes no difference) and throws them back . . . into the abyss of the purposeless chaos of matter from which they were drawn."

24. *Critique of Judgment*, p. 301, n. 15 (added in the second edition).

25. *Critique of Judgment*, p. 304.

26. *Kant's Moral Religion*, p. 154.

27. *Critique of Judgment*, p. 308.

28. *Critique of Judgment*, p. 314.

29. *Critique of Judgment*, p. 322.

30. *Critique of Judgment*, p. 327.

31. *Science, Action, and Fundamental Theology*, pp. 212 ff.

32. *Science Action, and Fundamental Theology*, p. 315.

33. *Science Action, and Fundamental Theology*, p. 234.

34. *Science, Action, and Fundamental Theology*, p. 235.

35. J. Habermas, "A Reply to My Critics," in J. Thompson and D. Held, eds. *Habermas: Critical Debates* (Cambridge, Mass., 1982), pp. 219–283. On pages 246–247 he writes, "There remains a stain on the idea of a justice that is bought with the irrevocable injustice perpetrated on earlier generations. This stain cannot be washed away; at most it can be forgotten. But this forgetting would have to leave behind traces of the repressed. . . . Those born later can compensate for the contradiction contained in the idea [of complete justice] only by supplementing the abstract thought of universality with the anamnestic power of a remembering that goes beyond the concepts of morality itself. This remembering is actualized in compassionate solidarity with the despair of the tormented who have suffered what cannot be made good again."

36. *Science Action, and Fundamental Theology*, p. 215.

Index

Index

DATE DUE

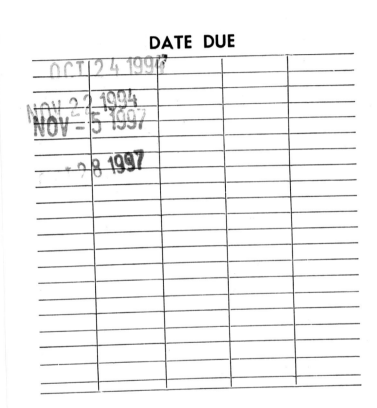